Disaster in the

Disaster in the Mountains

Gerry Brown • Randall S. Peterson

Disaster in the Boardroom

Six Dysfunctions Everyone Should Understand

palgrave
macmillan

Gerry Brown
READING, UK

Randall S. Peterson
1-26
London Business School
London, UK

ISBN 978-3-030-91660-2   ISBN 978-3-030-91658-9   (eBook)
https://doi.org/10.1007/978-3-030-91658-9

Cover illustration: eStudioCalamar

This Palgrave Macmillan imprint is published by the registered company Springer Nature Switzerland AG.
The registered company address is: Gewerbestrasse 11, 6330 Cham, Switzerland

'To my sisters and brothers for their encouragement throughout my life.'
Gerry Brown
'To my mother the person who taught me to value ideas and use critical thinking skills.'
Randall Peterson

Acknowledgements

Our thanks go to many contributors who have all made significant efforts in getting this book published.

To Carrie Fletcher for researching and writing so many case studies.

To Morgen Witzel for his total commitment to help our ideas become the reality of a manuscript.

To Marilyn Livingstone for creating the index.

To Graham Russel for some final edits.

To Jeff Scott of Platypus, a very professional publicist.

To Gerry's son Mario and granddaughter Aurora for assisting in designing the book cover.

To Gerry's daughter Cayetana and Stray Cat for organizing the book launch.

To Simon Osborne, Nuala Walsh, Vyla Rollins and Michael Payne for their critical appraisal of the manuscript.

To Michael Clegg-Butt for supporting Randall through late-night and weekend editing.

To all of those who have endorsed the book.

Praise for *Disaster in the Boardroom*

"This powerful book fuses story-telling with rigorous research to present a highly readable, compelling analysis of corporate boards' influence—and failures. The juicy examples and case studies, ranging across time and around the globe, paint a picture of what goes wrong, why the different types of board dysfunction arise, and why we should all care. This important book should (!) appeal to a wide variety of readers well beyond the boards themselves—taxpayers, managers, lawyers, investors and ordinary citizens whom all have a stake in how boards perform. Perhaps, most importantly, Brown and Peterson bring together their unique strengths and experiences to outline practical strategies and tactics to strengthen board effectiveness. *Disaster in the Boardroom* is fascinating, well-researched, and a more important read than ever."

—Heidi K. Gardner, Distinguished Fellow, *Harvard Law School* & author of *Smart Collaboration*

"Boards continue to let us down. Brown and Peterson carefully and comprehensively tell us why but also what can be done about it. They diagnose and document an array of scandals and board pathologies—ranging from the subordinated board to the bureaucratic board—to learn valuable lessons as well as present a compelling case for a concerted emphasis on board culture, complete with many highly tangible recommendations. Anyone reading *Disaster in the Boardroom: Six Dysfunctions Everyone Should Understand*—whether you're a director, company stakeholder or casual reader—will greatly benefit from this engaging, thoughtful and timely book."

—Donald C Hambrick, *Evan Pugh University Professor & Smeal Chaired Professor of Management at Penn State University*

"In *Disaster in the Boardroom* Peterson and Brown go beyond standard narratives on board performance to offer evidence-based insights on the drivers of behaviour on boards, and of the individuals who serve on them. Using real-life case studies, they provide illuminating examples of how such dynamics manifest, the impact that they can have, and offer practical suggestions on how to increase board effectiveness. This book is a must-read for board members, Chairs, charity trustees, board evaluators, aspiring board members and all stakeholders who engage with boards."

—Vyla Rollins, Executive Director, *London Business School, Leadership Institute*

"*Disaster in the Boardroom* is an exceptionally well written, authoritative and impressively accessible book which addresses key questions in corporate governance. How can we make boards more accountable to their stakeholders? How can we avoid disasters which happen under the watch of the board? How do we train board members to be more vigilant? Gerry Brown and Randall Peterson do a wonderful job in specifying the six dysfunctions of a board as well as identify over seventy board failures in this evidence based and highly insightful book. *Disaster in the Boardroom* is a must read for all board chairs, non-executive directors, financial journalists, policy makers and students of governance."

—Patrick C. Flood, *Professor of Organisational Behaviour, Dublin City University Business School*

"*Disaster in the Boardroom* makes an impassioned plea for people to consider the extensive ramifications of corporate failures from shareholders, to the human cost and impact on the broader society. Importantly authors Peterson and Brown provide concrete tools towards building a successful board. They combine academic rigour with practitioner insight as well as provide coherent theoretical foundations, empirical evidence, and compelling case studies. Eminently readable, *Disaster in the Boardroom* is a must for any student of business, aspiring executives along with board directors seeking to build better boards. This book should, obviously, be compulsory reading for all board directors too."

—Christine de Largy, *Impact Performance and ex-Chair of Board Services, Harvey Nash*

"Gerry Brown and Randall S. Peterson take us on a well-argued, fair-minded and very readable journey of corporate corruption, greed, crass mistakes and mis-judgments in *Disaster in the Boardroom: Six Dysfunctions Everyone Should Understand*. Corporate Governance is failing too often. Usually via fraud, bribery, industrial accidents and deaths, sexual harassment, tax evasion and gross mis-selling amongst other boardroom blunders.

Though scandal causes and consequences vary, the thread common to the South Sea Bubble, Lehman Brothers, BP's Deepwater Horizon, Facebook, Uber or Miramax's Harvey Weinstein is the need for much better corporate governance. The authors not only eloquently describe and investigate these scandals but are just as analytical, considered and detailed in their proposals to rectify them. One of the solutions to these various corporate governance problems are better trained, more diverse, powerful and plentiful Independent Directors.

Disaster in the Boardroom is essential reading not only for new directors but also for existing directors, many of whom—on this evidence—need to substantially raise their game."

—Barry Bateman, *Former CEO and Vice-Chair of Fidelity International*

"Finally there is a business book on the market that is a practical, thought-provoking and useful read for existing and aspiring board directors and executives. Better still, *Disaster in the Boardroom* identifies six types of board failing that should become the essential metrics by which anyone who wishes to accurately judge any business anywhere in the world needs to understand and use. There is little doubt that every business needs to be assessed to see if they exhibit or fall into one of the six types of failing board the authors Brown and Peterson so persuasively identify."

—John Allan, *Chairman Tesco and former President of the CBI*

"There have been many corporate scandals and collapses over the last few decades. *Disaster in the Boardroom: Six Dysfunctions Everyone Should Understand* not only summarises them in an interesting manner but also places them into an historical context and demonstrates that very little has changed! Despite the apparent advance of technology and governance principles, there remains an almost unlimited capacity for boards to get things wrong. Of course, the common thread across the historical scope of this book is human beings—whose behaviour the authors analyse and explain in a compelling manner. With case-studies on Facebook, Google and Uber amongst others, authors Brown and Peterson also provide possible solutions and best practices. *Disaster in the Boardroom* is a really good read! It takes in the drama of real business situations and places them within a useful and insightful framework of explanation. It's a real pager turner—a rare achievement in a non-fiction volume!"

—Dr Roger Barker, *Director of Policy and Corporate Governance,*
Institute of Directors

"*Disaster in the Boardroom* highlights why and how things have gone wrong in boardrooms across the corporate world. The authors provide thoughtful analyses and many great insights into how to ensure boards develop and provide the right balance of support, challenge and oversight. *Disaster in the Boardroom* shines a light on the many ways boards can use the lessons of the past and present, to predict and avoid executive suite scandals and corporate governance mis-steps in the future."

—Dame Inga Beale, *Portfolio Director*

"*Disaster in the Boardroom* is a fascinating must read about boards, their long history, responsibilities, critical skills and high profile inadequacies. Through careful presentation and stimulating examples, this superlative book shows how necessary it is to be constantly diligent so as to maintain institutional integrity, cultural excellence and long term competitive edge. Authors Brown and Peterson's research finds six carefully constructed dangers that we should all think about, discuss and apply.

Balanced navigation across independence, management and technology in today's fast changing world will demand more skills, wisdom and courage from boards. A thorough reading of *Disaster in the Boardroom* bridges gaps for those with experience and also provides an important framework for executive managers, aspiring board members, professionals, other advisors and students alike to understand more fully the critical role of oversight and governance. I recommend this book wholeheartedly."

—Sir *Dennis* Gillings, *CBE, FMedSci, Chairman and CEO,*
GF Management

Contents

List of Figures

Part I

1

Where Was the Board?

Where was the board? This is the cry that emerges among investors and in the financial press each time a company disastrously collapses or becomes enmeshed in a scandal. The board of directors are, in principle, the guardians of the company, the people who ensure it is well-managed, financially secure and operates in the best interests of its shareholders and, increasingly, other stakeholders. Yet, time after time, when companies come crashing to the ground, it emerges that the board has failed in its fiduciary duty to the organization to ensure it is managed responsibly and sustainably, and to all stakeholders including shareholders to ensure their interests are not harmed.

Sometimes this is out of ignorance. In the aftermath of disaster, when the press and the regulators begin picking over the wreckage and analysing the black boxes, it emerges that the board literally had no idea what was going on inside the company for which it was supposedly responsible. Even when worrying signals were detected, the board failed to join the dots and develop a complete picture of what was happening. 'Asleep at the wheel' is the phrase one regulator used to describe a singularly inept board, and it is hard to dispute this. In other cases, members of the board were knowingly complicit in what was happening, turning a blind eye to financial irregularities, sexual harassment and assault, unsafe working conditions and a host of other abuses. Ignorant or criminal, that is often the choice, and it is hard to know which is worse.

The really damning indictment of our systems of corporate governance around the world is that there is nothing new about this. Scandals, collapses and bankruptcies have been going on for centuries. Over the course of time, we have learned a great deal about how and why they happen, yet they still

© The Author(s), under exclusive license to Springer Nature Switzerland AG 2022
G. Brown, R. S. Peterson, *Disaster in the Boardroom*,
https://doi.org/10.1007/978-3-030-91658-9_1

happen with shocking regularity. In the same way that we know much more about how and why wars start—and yet more people died in wars in the twentieth century than in any preceding century—our knowledge of how and why business disasters happen does not seem to be doing us any good. Indeed, some people simply shrug and accept these things as transaction costs, an unavoidable part of the system that nonetheless has produced incredible wealth around the globe. As Norman Dixon says in his book *On the Psychology of Military Incompetence*, 'like the common cold, flat feet or the British climate, [failure] is accepted as a part of life.'[1]

But it should not be this way. We should not, as Dixon says, grow blasé about the scandals that rock economies and societies and cause enormous amounts of personal suffering and hardship all around the world. We should not tolerate abuses of power by toxic executive teams, CEOs and chairs, nor should we tolerate the failures of those who are ineffective. We should be holding those responsible for corporate failures to account and making changes to prevent these boardroom disasters from happening in the future. Now more than ever in the aftermath of the global pandemic that has put hundreds of millions out of work, destroyed thousands of companies and brought entire economies to their knees, we *need to* have proper governance. Boards must improve and take responsibility. If they fail to do so, our chances of economic recovery and continuing to economic prosperity will become vanishingly small.

In this book, we will look not so much at the disasters themselves but as to *why* they happen. Why do they fail to act as the independent guardians they should be? And more importantly, what can be done about this? How can we strengthen boards, improve their culture and competence and give directors and others the power to take action and prevent disasters from happening? We will attempt to answer those questions, in the hope of providing a better, stronger and more responsible foundation on which to build a system of corporate governance. Whatever happens in the future, we need to do better and not accept these disasters as the cost of wealth creation.

In researching this book, we investigated scores of business scandals, some in the distant past, others so recent as to be fresh in the memory. Appendix 1 gives summaries of around seventy cases. It is by no means a complete list, but readers who wish to learn more about the breadth of business scandals and the forms they take will find this an important resource. For the moment, let us remind ourselves of the long history of scandals and their consequences, and how dysfunctional boards allow these events to happen.

Moments in a History of Scandals and Disasters

1720. During a summer of feverish speculation, shares in the South Sea Company rose steadily, from their initial level of £100 a share to just over £1000 a share in August. The Company, which had been established to convert government debt into equity—holders of government debt could exchange it for shares in the Company—had deliberately encouraged speculation on the back of wild promises of future income. The Company had been granted a monopoly on the slave trade to South America and the 'South Seas,' and although it never made much money from this barbaric trade (which was controlled by Spain and Portugal at the time), it promised investors huge returns.

The speculation around the South Sea Company became contagious. Dozens of other ventures, ranging from the dubious to the downright fraudulent, clamoured for shareholders' money. People sank their life savings into these companies, deluded by the promise of getting rich quickly. Projects ranged from investing in manufacturing and fisheries to importing walnut trees from Virginia and establishing trade on the Orinoco River. One promoter even advertised 'a company for carrying on an undertaking of great advantage, but nobody to know what it is.' He collected more than £2000 in investments, a huge sum for the time, and then disappeared without a trace, taking the money with him.[2]

The inevitable happened. Smart investors in the South Sea Company saw through the false promises and began to withdraw their money. The bubble burst; by September the share price had collapsed to its original level. Thousands of investors who had bought shares on credit went bankrupt. Finally, the government took action; the directors of the company were dismissed and stripped of most of their wealth and the Chancellor of the Exchequer, who had abetted the Company at every turn, was sent to the Tower of London. Unfortunately, all of this came too late for the ruined investors who then had to rebuild their lives.[3]

The South Sea Bubble was by no means unique at the time. Just a few months later another bubble burst in France when the Mississippi Company, which had also artificially inflated its share price, collapsed and nearly sent the entire nation of France into bankruptcy. A century earlier, 'tulip mania' in the Netherlands had seen a market develop in which the price of a single tulip could sell for ten times the average annual wage; the collapse of this bubble also ruined thousands of lives and impoverished the nation. The passage of the Bubble Act by the British parliament offered some protection to investors until its repeal in 1825. History then repeated itself; from the mid-1830s onwards, increasing numbers of railway companies put themselves forward, inviting investors to speculate. For example, in 1846, at the height of 'railway mania,' over 270 new companies were founded. Almost a third of these companies never laid a single mile of track; their sole purpose was to acquire the money of the greedy and the gullible.[4]

Land Grab

1794. Some of the schemes proposed during the South Sea Bubble had involved investments in land, and land speculation continued to be an arena for shady dealings for many years to come. In 1789 a secretive group of investors known as the Combined Society used influence and bribery to persuade the governor and legislature of the American state of Georgia to annex around twenty million acres of land between the Mississippi and Yazoo rivers, and then sell this land to the investors for the very cheap price of $207,000, or a little over a penny an acre. The scheme was carried through and the land was sold to a series of shell companies including the Georgia Company, the Georgia-Mississippi Company and the Tennessee Company.

The problem was that the land was not the government's to sell. Part of the land was claimed by Spain as part of its overseas empire, and the remainder by two Native American peoples, the Choctaw and the Chickasaw. The investors knew this and bribed any legislator or government official who raised an objection to stay silent. They then sold the land at very large profits to people seeking new places to settle. When the Yazoo land scandal finally broke in 1794, there was popular outrage. A new governor, Jared Irwin, was elected in Georgia, and in early 1796 he nullified the legislation authorizing the land sale. The investors appealed to the US Supreme Court, which overturned Irwin's decision and allowed the sale to stand. The investors in the Combined Society kept their profits; Spain bargained its rights away and the Native American peoples were ultimately displaced from their homelands and sent into exile in Oklahoma.[5]

Railways and Ruin

1866. For decades, the British wholesale bank Overend & Gurney had been the world's leading discounter of bills of exchange. Known in the trade as the 'banker's banker,' the bank was a byword for sound financial management.

But after the death of its long-time leader Samuel Gurney in 1856, the directors threw out Gurney's Quaker values of thrift and careful management in favour of a series of investments in, among other things, railways. When the next economic downturn came along, the so-called Panic of 1866, Overend & Gurney was dangerously exposed. Its situation was not unlike that of Lehman Brothers in 2008, when reckless investments had drained away cash reserves and left debts the bank could not cover. When the Bank of England declined to give support, Overend & Gurney collapsed with debts of £11 million, equivalent to about £1 billion in today's money. The directors were prosecuted for fraud but escaped prison when the judge decided they had merely made a 'grave error.'[6]

Even as Overend & Gurney was collapsing into bankruptcy, on the other side of the Atlantic a new financial scandal was gathering steam. Executives at Union Pacific Railroad, then in the process of building the first transcontinental railway, set up a fraudulent subsidiary, Crédit Mobilier (no relation to the French bank of the same name), to manage the construction of the line. Crédit Mobilier billed the US government, which was underwriting the project, for $94 million, whereas in fact the true construction costs were around $50 million. The remaining $44 million was distributed among Union Pacific executives. Crédit Mobilier shares were also handed out as bribes to politicians in exchange for support for legislation favouring the railways. The board of directors of Union Pacific were either ignorant of the fraud or complicit in it. The scandal eventually came to light in 1872, forcing the resignation of several senior political figures, nearly bankrupting Union Pacific and causing a huge loss of public confidence in corporate institutions.[7]

Cash for Influence

1922. Continuing the long tradition of bribing politicians to gain preferential treatment, two oil companies, Mammoth Oil and the Pan American Petroleum and Transport Company, paid US Secretary of the Interior Albert Fall around $500,000 in gifts and interest-free loans. They wanted Fall to give them access to oil fields which had been designated as strategic oil reserves assigned to the US Navy. Fall persuaded President Warren Harding to transfer control of the reserves from the navy to his own department and then leased out the Teapot Dome oilfield in Wyoming and two other fields in California to the oil companies. The leases were granted secretly, on very favourable terms, and no other companies were allowed to bid. This was a violation of Federal law.

By skimming off oil reserves which the navy would need in time of war, the two companies stood to make vast profits. Unfortunately, Fall, who had not hitherto been a rich man, began spending his money lavishly and this attracted the notice of journalists. A Congressional inquiry was established and Fall was ultimately convicted and sent to prison, the first serving US cabinet minister to suffer this fate. The reputation of President Harding's administration was fatally compromised, and he died of a heart attack in 1923. The US Supreme Court ultimately revoked the leases and handed control of the oil reserves back to the navy. On this occasion the corruption had come to the surface, but cynical observers wondered how many other cases had gone unnoticed.[8]

The Rise of the False Prospectus

1929. The rise of modern capitalism brought about new and ever-more inventive forms of corruption and fraud. The issuing of a false prospectus, a deliberately misleading financial disclosure document that made the company's finances seem to be in better condition than they actually were, became a staple.

One of the most famous practitioners of the art was Clarence Hatry, a former insurance clerk turned profiteer during the First World War. Hatry was widely respected in financial circles in both London and New York, and at one point was a director of fifteen companies. He put together the Hatry Group of companies, including investment banks and finance houses in Europe, North America and East Asia, which by 1928 was valued at $24 million. Big names in business and society sat on his boards; the Marquess of Winchester was a close friend and director of several companies in the group.

But what Winchester does not seem to have known is that Hatry's fortune was a sham. The group had few assets and had amassed millions in debt. Hatry had kept the group afloat through a form of Ponzi scheme by issuing false prospectuses to attract investors, and when that failed, to issue false share certificates as well. He obtained a $1 million loan from New York banks based on forged bearer bonds. Even this was not enough, and when rumours of illiquidity began to circulate in 1929, Hatry begged the Bank of England to rescue him. The Bank refused, and Hatry's empire collapsed, a few days before the Wall Street crash which brought about a global economic recession.

Hatry was arrested for fraud and spent nine years in prison. The Marquess of Winchester was also taken to court, but was discharged after the judge described him as a fundamentally honest man who had been duped by Hatry. He nevertheless went bankrupt and spent most of his life living in exile.[9]

Possession of blue blood, a title and his high-level connections probably helped him avoid his responsibilities, but these did not prevent Lord Kylsant, director of the Royal Mail Steam Packet Company, from going to prison in 1931 when he too tried to prop up his failing company by issuing false accounts.

The idea of the false prospectus lives on today. In January 2020, Lord Berkeley's dissenting report on the HS2 rail project in the UK, a high-speed railway designed to link London and the north of England, accused directors of issuing a false prospectus in all but name. Berkeley, who had been deputy chair of a government review of HS2, accused the company in charge of the project of not only understating the cost of building the line but also the revenue that could be generated from operating it: 'even before taking into account the much higher scheme costs, the ratio of benefits to costs in the 2017 case is totally false, based as it is on more trains than any other high speed line can operate, on higher speeds, and on trains running full all day with high fare paying passengers than any other high speed line can operate.'[10] In fairness, the majority of members of the review panel disagreed with Berkeley.

Rise and Fall

1990. Polly Peck International had been one of the stars of British and European business. Originally founded as a textile business, it had been taken over by the entrepreneur Asil Nadir in 1980. As CEO and chief shareholder, Nadir masterminded Polly Peck's rapid growth through the 1980s, acquiring firms in sectors as varied as textiles, electronics and bottled water in Europe, Turkey and China. In fewer than ten years, the market capitalization of the group increased from £300,000 to over £1.7 billion.[11] The purchase of the American canned fruit brand Del Monte in 1989 pushed Polly Peck into the FTSE-100 and made it a favourite of investors, who regarded it as a model of a well-run company.

By the following year, though, rumours were beginning to surface about Polly Peck's finances. Nadir and his managers strongly denied these, but late in 1990 the company suddenly went into administration. A subsequent investigation found that while the company claimed assets of nearly £1 billion, it actually had debts of £522 million. The same investigation found 'an almost complete lack of internal controls at its London office.'[12] It emerged that Nadir had secretly transferred around £150 million to bank accounts controlled by himself and associates. The firm's auditors, Stoy Hayward, were fined heavily for failing to spot the problem, and Nadir himself was charged with seventy counts of theft and false accounting. He fled to Northern Cyprus, which has no extradition treaty with the UK, but eventually returned to London to stand trial. He was sentenced to ten years in prison.

Polly Peck was not the only star to fall in the late 1980s and early 1990s. The collapses of the Bank of Credit and Commerce International amid persistent rumours of money-laundering, and the disintegration of Robert Maxwell's publishing empire after the mysterious death of its founder also led to public outcry and a demand for reform. The collapse of Polly Peck in particular led to the establishment of the Cadbury Committee (formally, the Committee on the Financial Aspects of Corporate Governance) and, eventually, to a reform of company law and the establishment of the UK Corporate Governance Code. Other countries have followed suit. India, for example, established its first corporate governance code in 1998, and subsequently the Birla Committee recommended that at least half the members of all boards should be independent directors.[13] Japan introduced its corporate governance code in 2015, again influenced by the UK example.[14]

So, in an oblique sort of way, Asil Nadir may have done the cause of global corporate governance a real service; the sheer audacity of the fraud was a wake-up call for governments and regulators to do more. But did they do enough? Given the continuing stream of boardroom disasters, apparently not.

Shocked and Appalled

2020. Another week, another scandal: in early July 2020 it was fashion brand Boohoo's turn in the spotlight as allegations emerged that workers at some of Boohoo's UK suppliers were working in sweatshop conditions, earning less than half the legal minimum wage. Boohoo's board pronounced itself 'shocked and appalled' and established an independent inquiry into the allegations, but this was a case of locking the stable door after the horse had bolted. More than one observer commented that the independent inquiry should start by looking at the board itself. 'Did the board wilfully ignore the abuses under its nose?' asked *The Guardian*'s business correspondents.[15]

Once again, this was hardly an isolated case. In the same week that Boohoo was being castigated, Deutsche Bank was fined $150 million by New York state regulators for compliance failures relating to its dealings with the convicted sex trafficker Jeffrey Epstein. Two weeks later, Goldman Sachs paid the Malaysian government $3.9 billion to cover claims of corruption over its relationship with sovereign wealth fund 1Malaysia Development Berhad

(1MDB), attempting to draw a line under a scandal that had been dogging the bank for five years. British readers may also have noticed that around the same time, audit firm Grant Thornton was fined £3 million by the UK's Financial Reporting Council for audit failures relating to the failure of the drinks company Conviviality in 2018.[16] But Grant Thornton is hardly alone; for example, in 2020 Ernst & Young also came under fire for its role in the collapse of German financial services firm Wirecard. Discussing the failings of audit firms, the *Financial Times*'s assessment was blunt: 'Is it time to audit the auditors?'[17]

The Tip of the Iceberg

And these are just a few of the thousands of cases that have made headlines over the past three centuries, the tip of the iceberg. Beneath the iceberg's tip, below the waterline and hidden from the public gaze are a mass of struggling organizations whose boards are, deliberately or through ignorance, failing to govern in a fit and proper manner. In many cases, they have been failing to do so for a very long time, perhaps a carry-over from decades ago when boards had only a high-level overview of the business. Many of these under-performing organizations escape public scrutiny when the economy is prospering. Good times disguise a lot of sins. When crisis comes, however, they have nowhere to hide. As Warren Buffett's famous metaphor suggests, when the tide recedes you discover who has been swimming naked.

Sometimes corruption is involved; sometimes there is hubris or wilful blindness; sometimes there is a failure to ask the right questions, to listen to weak signals and pursue them; and sometimes there is simple ignorance of duties and responsibilities on the part of directors. The problem takes many forms and facets, but it comes back to one simple, irrefutable fact. Boards are failing to do their job of protecting stakeholders, including shareholders. It is an old problem, and it is not going away. The scandals and disasters continue; and, because corporations and other organizations are so much larger now, the damage inflicted when they fail is greater than ever. Sometimes, like Enron or Lehman Brothers, their collapse is an earthquake that sends shock waves around the world and causes billions of dollars of value destruction and damage.

It would be easy to dismiss these failures as isolated incidents, outliers that are not indicative of the real picture. Research suggests otherwise. In 2019, research conducted by Harvey Nash and the London Business School (LBS) Leadership Institute found that globally, 34 per cent of directors rate their own boards as not effective, 40 per cent report regularly backtracking on decisions made and 46 per cent believe there is a high level of friction in the boardroom. Other research, notably from Henley Business School looking at public sector and third-sector institutions, finds similar results.[18] The Harvey Nash/LBS research also suggests that the problem is widespread. Overall, it is estimated that around 40 per cent of corporate boards around the world are dysfunctional in some significant way.

All around the world, our system of corporate governance is failing us all too often. Scandals in financial services often make the greatest headlines, but this is not a problem that affects just one sector. As Appendix 1 shows, companies in every sector from high-tech to mining have been involved. So too have organizations in the public sector and third sector. Charities, hospitals, sports organizations, schools and universities and government bodies have been affected just as badly as businesses; sometimes worse.[19] Organizations are collapsing, money is disappearing into black holes, jobs are being lost, lives are being ruined and the environment is suffering perhaps irreversible harm. And, as the snapshots above show, this has been going on for at least *300 years*.

Thus far, the answer to the problem has usually been more regulation after each major disaster. Every major economic and financial disaster is typically followed by waves of new regulation designed to prevent such events from ever happening again, starting with the Bubble Act of 1720. For example, over the past few decades in the UK there have been a series of reports and inquiries, including the Cadbury Report on corporate governance in 1992 following the collapses of Maxwell Communications and the Bank of Credit and Commerce International. This was followed in succession by the Greenbury Report (1996), the Hampel Report (1998), the Higgs Report (2003), the Walker Report (2009) and the UK Code of Corporate Governance (2012)—the latter of which is regularly revised and updated.

In the USA the Glass-Steagall Act of 1933, which regulated the banking sector, and the establishment of the Securities and Exchange Commission (SEC) in 1934 marked the beginning of attempts to establish tighter governance controls, leading ultimately to the Sarbanes-Oxley Act (2002), which established the Public Company Accounting Oversight Board, and the Dodd-Frank Act (2010), which created a number of public bodies designed to regulate financial services in particular.

These efforts have not achieved what they were designed to accomplish. Some of the legislation has been badly designed; other laws were simply repealed by successive governments who wished to curry favour with business (e.g. in 2018 parts of the Dodd-Frank Act were repealed at the instigation of President Trump, while other parts were deemed unconstitutional by the US Supreme Court). Regulatory bodies and watchdogs have been tasked with controlling abuses and ensuring organizations—charities and public sector bodies as well as businesses—behave responsibly in nearly every country of the world. These too have made little impact on the tidal wave of failures and scandals. Even where these bodies do have teeth and are able to impose substantial penalties on organizations and their boards, their efforts are nearly always after the fact and thus too little and too late. By the time the regulators take action, the failure has already happened, and the damage is done. What the rules have consistently failed to do is ensure long-term, effective, sustainable corporate governance.

Laws and regulators are necessary but insufficient because they try to tackle all problems in the same way. That means that many common boardroom dysfunctions are being addressed from the wrong end. The power that can most effectively monitor and control an organization is the board of directors itself. Shareholders and investors have, in theory, the power to sanction or even remove directors, but as we will argue later in this book, in practice shareholders are often too far removed from the company. They cannot take action if they are unaware of problems in the first place. Front-line responsibility must rest with the board.

In addition to punishments and sanctions for wrongdoing, we also need strong and lasting reform from within. The culture of boards, right across the spectrum of private, public and third sectors, needs to change. Boards need to learn to act independently and safeguard the interests of stakeholders—all stakeholders, including but not limited to shareholders.

That last point needs to be emphasized. Regulation can only take us so far. True reform requires boards not to just remember their responsibilities to stakeholders but also to actively engage with them. Boards need to listen to their stakeholders, and not just investors. Employees, customers, governments and citizens of the communities in which companies operate are all affected by the company's work, and, especially, by its mistakes and failures. When a business collapses or suffers from a scandal or a disaster, it is not just shareholders that pay the price; we all do. For sound practical reasons as well as ethical and moral ones, boards need to engage with all their stakeholders, take those views on board and build these into their decision-making processes.

The Cost of Failure

When scandals and failures happen, the financial press tends to measure their impact in terms of what happens to the share price. Virtually every press article describing the situation at British fashion retailer Boohoo made mention of the collapse in the value of its shares, around 40 per cent, and the impact on shareholder wealth. In fact, the share price quickly recovered, and some institutional investors did very well for themselves by buying shares at bargain prices. But the real impact of these events goes far beyond shareholders. When corporations fail, the real cost is borne by all of us, as individual consumers and taxpayers, collectively as nations and increasingly across national borders. We pay the cost for these failures, and often we go on paying for a very long time, long after the event is forgotten.

Sometimes, corporate failures mean that people die. In India, more than 16,000 people died at Bhopal in 1984 after Union Carbide's plant near the city released toxic methyl isocyanate gas into the air; 40,000 more were left with long-term health problems. In 2018–2019, 346 people were killed in two separate incidents in Indonesia and Ethiopia when Boeing 737-MAX aircraft crashed due to malfunctioning flight control systems. According to the *Wall Street Journal*, Boeing had known about potential problems with the system for nearly a year prior to the first crash.[20] It later emerged that the Federal Aviation Administration (FAA) had allowed Boeing to 'self-govern' on issues relating to safety verification. In effect, Boeing was allowed to mark its own homework. And, as noted previously, the problem is not just confined to the private sector. Failures of governance at Mid-Staffordshire NHS Foundation Trust in the UK played a role in as many as 1200 unnecessary hospital deaths between 2005 and 2008.

When companies collapse, they stop paying taxes. That means there is less revenue for government to spend on vital services such as health, education, policing and defence, and this in turn undermines public health and wellbeing. Government then has three choices: to fund these services through borrowing, to raise taxes or to reduce the level of service provision. Whichever alternative it chooses, the rest of us pay in the end, now or in the future. This is the choice that governments faced in the aftermath of the COVID-19 pandemic. In the short term, most governments chose to borrow to support as many businesses as they could, but the global shortage of foresight means it was inevitable that many firms will fail. This in turn means a massive loss of tax revenue for governments around the world.

Supporting failing firms also costs everyone as taxpayers, as money is diverted from other vital services. It took nine years for the Lloyds banking group to pay back the £20 billion that the UK government handed out after the 2008 financial crisis—the £45 billion given to Royal Bank of Scotland has still not been fully returned. The US annual budget deficit rose by $1 trillion in 2008, largely as a result of the Emergency Economic Stabilization Act authorizing the bailout of the big American banks. Trillions of dollars were spent supporting badly prepared firms during the first wave of the pandemic.

Collapses also mean job losses, sometimes on a very large scale, as witnessed during the global crises of 2008 and 2020. According to the International Labour Organization, the 2008 crash increased global unemployment by as much as fifty million. Fewer people in work also means less tax money being paid into the national treasury and more flowing out of government in the form of welfare payments and income support. There is also a very powerful knock-on impact on the people who lose their jobs, who often suffer economic and psychological stress and harm. Studies have shown that people who have been made redundant once have higher chances of losing their jobs again. They and their families also have reduced life chances.

And finally, much though some sections of society love to castigate fat-cat shareholders, institutional investors are also important and when disaster strikes, they too suffer. Among the largest institutional investors are pension funds and insurance companies, both of which play an essential role in modern society. Collapses in share value do more than just cause these companies to lose money. In the aftermath of the Deepwater Horizon disaster in 2010 and the oil spill in the Gulf of Mexico, there were concerns that BP might not be able to bear the costs of cleaning up after the spill and paying the fines levied by the American government. Every major British pension fund and many foreign ones had investments in BP. Had the oil giant collapsed, the future of some of these pension funds—and the pensioners who relied on them for income—might have been in serious doubt.

The failure of governance, then, is not just an economic problem. It is a social and moral one as well. This is not merely a manner of money, but of human beings, their livelihoods, their families and their health and wellbeing.

The Pandemic Reality

The COVID-19 pandemic of 2020 exposed many weaknesses and failures of governance in a cruel and unforgiving manner. Around the world, tens of millions of jobs were lost and hardship and inequality increased as businesses and other institutions tried and failed to cope with the effects of the pandemic. The World Health Organization and the medical community more generally had been warning of the dangers of a pandemic for years—in the UK alone, major scientific reports in 2016 and 2018 had highlighted the risks and consequences—and previous epidemics such as SARS, MERS, Ebola and swine flu had shown on a local level the damage that disease could cause. In other words, we knew a pandemic was coming and the only open question was not if, but when. We also knew it would have a massive impact on business and society.

Even so, governments around the world were caught unprepared. Few businesses seemed ready either. A few larger corporations had pandemic plans ready to be put into place; some organizations had taken out specific pandemic insurance, rather than relying on broader business interruption insurance policies which were often vaguely worded. These were the exceptions. Most organizations had no business continuity plans in place; most had not even considered a pandemic as a risk worth evaluating.

In fairness, this probably will not happen again. The memory of what happened during the pandemic will inform boards' thinking and we can expect that business continuity plans, pandemic insurance and all the other measures that should have been put in place will now be there. Future damage should be mitigated. But we are entitled to ask questions—not just of our governments but of all organizations—why the warnings were ignored and why we were so unprepared. We can say two things for certain about the pandemic. The first is that the failure to prepare for it has been a colossal failure of risk management. The second is that the consequences of that failure in terms of economic damage and physical and mental health problems will be with us for many years to come.

Dysfunctional Boards

But how did we get here? Why have we tolerated this near-perpetual crisis in governance for so long? Is this just the natural cost of a system that delivers wealth over time? Why have we apparently learned nothing from previous corporate scandals and disasters?

There are two related problems. The first is widespread ignorance within society—including some sections of the media—about the role of boards and the impact they have on our everyday lives.[21] What do boards do? What do chairs do? Many people, including a startling number of board members themselves, do not know, and not enough effort has been made to bring this issue to the public's attention. To some, the role of the board is scrutiny and challenge, holding the executives to account and intervening when things go wrong. To others, the board's purpose is to support the executive, gathering resources and processing information to help the company make better decisions about strategy and risk. In fact, the role encompasses both of these things and much else besides. What often gets forgotten is that boards are the stewards of the organization, responsible for ensuring it is run wisely and well and, to repeat the point made earlier, that it functions in the best interests of its stakeholders.

The board holds the executive to account, but the board itself is also accountable to those stakeholders, and the fiduciary duty it has to stakeholders needs to be more widely understood and put into practice. But when boards become dysfunctional, they fail in that duty and stakeholder groups are neglected and forgotten.

The Impact of CEO Personality

One thing that boards do *not* do, of course, is run the company. Corporate governance codes and existing research on the subject are all quite clear on this point. Day-to-day operations are the responsibility of the executive team, and the line between operations and governance is a boundary best not crossed. This separation between management and governance inevitably means that much power lies in the hands of the CEO and the top management team, and this in turn means that much depends on the character of the CEO. As research shows, the CEO has a strong influence on the rest of the top team and how they do their work, and how well the top team discharge their duties in turn affects the performance of the company.[22] Put simply, a 'good' CEO will enable the top management team to be effective; a 'bad' one will create a climate and culture where the organization starts to go off the rails.

It is all the more important, therefore, that boards remember their duty of holding the CEO to account. Even more importantly, they need to act carefully when choosing a CEO in the first place. The cases we developed for this book are full of examples of charismatic CEOs who were corrupt, incompetent, or both. Fixing this problem is difficult; current legislation and regulations do not prohibit smooth-talking narcissists from applying for jobs or gullible boards from hiring them. It is clear that boards need to get better and more professional at hiring. As Robert Hogan and Robert Kaiser have argued, the mechanisms commonly used for choosing a CEO are not always the best, to say the least:

> Most formal selection tools are rarely used. Former subordinates—those who are best able to report on a person's talent for leadership—are almost never consulted. Often new executives are recruited from outside the organization, making it even more difficult to evaluate the candidate appropriately. The most common selection tool is an interview, and the dark side tendencies are designed

to create favourable immediate impressions; narcissists and psychopaths excel during interviews. ... many executives are hired for the very characteristics that ultimately lead them to fail.[23]

Much has been written about the psychological warping effect that the experience of power typically has, and we will not go into this in detail here. The important point is that the relationship between the board, especially the chair, and the CEO is fundamental to ensuring good governance; the board must be able to trust the CEO (and, of course, vice versa). Some of the scandals and collapses we describe in this book happened because a narcissistic and/or greedy and corrupt CEO misled the board and withheld information from directors. In other cases, they used their power to override the board's wishes or ignore the board altogether. And sometimes too, the corruption spreads to the board, who become complicit in the CEO's misdeeds. Hiring a CEO who is honest and trustworthy and who will work willingly with the board is one of the hardest tasks boards undertake. It is also one of the ones they get wrong all too often.

Board Culture

Dig more deeply on why boards hire dysfunctional CEOs and you'll find that the real underlying problem is the culture of boards themselves. The culture of the board has a powerful role to play in determining what happens, not just within the board itself but across the organization and its ecosystem. Losing control of board culture—or worse, failing to establish an effective board-room culture in the first place—is akin to opening Pandora's box. Once events begin to spiral out of control, it is very difficult to recover. Corporate disasters are not the problem in and of themselves; they are symptoms of a deeper cultural dysfunction that oftentimes has its roots at the board level, or at the very least are the responsibility of the board.

When we speak of 'board culture,' we are talking about three things. The first is the shared values, beliefs, mindsets and attitudes of board members, the way people interact, especially the independent directors and the chair. Gone are the days when independent directors attended board meetings once a quarter and enjoyed a free lunch. Today they are expected to play a vital role in corporate governance and are expected to commit to the organizations they govern, to be both impartial judges and strong supporters, coaches and referees. Things have improved over the past thirty years, but they have not improved enough. We shudder to think where we would be if boards had not improved over recent decades. However, given the steady stream of disasters we continue to see, we still have to question whether many independent directors have the mindset, experience, knowledge and skills to ask the important questions and help the organization make effective decisions.

The board is also the custodian of the wider organization's culture. It is the board that decides what the organizational culture should be, not the other way around. If a toxic organizational culture begins to seep into the board culture, then the organization as a whole is at greater risk because board priorities and practices will flow into the organization via the top management team.

The third element of board culture is the ability of the board collectively to assert its independence and avoid being dominated by overly powerful individual executives or shareholders. That means that as well as having the right people on the board, the board itself has to be structured in such a way that everyone has equal freedom to speak and express their views, and vested interests do not dominate the board. Independence, then, is something that needs to be in place at both a personal and a group level. The directors must lead by being independent and able to challenge the executive, and so too must the board as a whole.

When all these things come together, when the board has a strong culture of its own based on the values of independence and with a finger firmly on the pulse of the wider organizational culture, then companies can weather disasters, even ones that are not of their own making. In 1982, an unknown person or persons tampered with packets of the drug Tylenol and inserted fatal quantities of potassium cyanide. Seven people died. When the news broke, the drug's makers, Johnson & Johnson, reacted swiftly. All stocks of Tylenol were withdrawn from the market immediately, and the company provided information to the public about the steps it was taking to prevent future poisonings. It also cooperated with local authorities in an (ultimately unsuccessful) attempt to find the culprit. The *Washington Post* wrote approvingly that 'Johnson & Johnson has demonstrated how a major business ought to handle a disaster.'[24]

When the initial news broke, some observers predicted that the Tylenol brand would be destroyed, but in fact it recovered and remains one of America's most trusted brands for pain relief. Johnson & Johnson recovered from the crisis in large part because of its long-held culture and values going back to its foundation. Customers came first (interestingly, in the company's list of priorities, shareholders are only fourth in importance) and the company's leadership made customer safety a top priority.

A similar case is food processor Maple Leaf Foods, which in August 2008 became aware of an incident of listeriosis contamination at one of its meat-processing plants near Toronto. By the time the incident was contained, twenty-three people had died and many more were seriously ill. Maple Leaf Foods responded by closing all its plants for decontamination, not just the affected one, and like Johnson & Johnson, kept the public fully informed of the steps it was taking. Maple Leaf Foods also immediately accepted full responsibility for the event and did not use legal evasions, agreeing to settle out of court with the victims and their families. Such a crisis might have broken another company, but the prompt response and the trust it engendered in the public helped the firm back to profitability.[25]

Designed to Fail

Too often, though, board culture is complacent and unquestioning. Board evaluation is supposed to offer boards and directors a regular reality check, and good board evaluation offers boards and their members a chance to learn, develop and grow. In practice many evaluation exercises are ineffective, some boards seek an evaluator who will tell them they have done well, and other boards do not seek external evaluation at all. Even when evaluation is practised, it too often fails to provide practical outputs that will allow boards to easily spot problems and make improvements.

But is effective evaluation the cure? Or do the problems lie deeper, at the heart of boards themselves? In a provocatively titled article, 'Are Boards Designed to Fail?,' Steven Boivie and colleagues argue that there are three critical barriers preventing board from governing effectively:

- individual barriers, related to the competence of individuals and their ability to assess and process information;
- group barriers, which arise when board dynamics are weak and board members fail to work effectively together; and
- firm contextual barriers, factors within the firm which can impede good governance including such things as ownership structures and the character and behaviour of senior executives.[26]

These barriers are built into board structure and culture, and we can see them at work in many cases of board failure. Often more than one barrier is involved; and when all three are present, then we have the ingredients for a perfect storm of governance failure. We are less pessimistic. We do not believe that boards are destined to fail. Rather, we believe there are a small number of dysfunctions that typically affect boards, dysfunctions that are understandable and treatable. In particular we see boardroom disasters as being driven not so much by these critical barriers, but by boardroom culture. Disasters, as opposed to less than optimal decision-making, tend to come from not managing risk, which tends to be about culture.

We referred earlier to the figure of 40 per cent of boards being dysfunctional in some significant way. That dysfunctionality nearly always stems from distortions of board culture. A high-functioning board has a strong culture that removes the barriers, allowing it to think and act independently and to monitor and scrutinize the actions of the executive. As soon as that strong board culture is compromised, however, problems begin.

Types of Board Dysfunction

Our research has identified six different types of board dysfunction (see Fig. 1.1): *lack of independence from management, missing key voices, cultural amplification, diffusion of responsibility, rule-bound cultures* and *groupthink*. Each in turn manifests itself in a particular type of board behaviour:

1. Subordinated boards—lack of independence
2. Imbalanced boards—missing key voices
3. Distended boards—cultural amplification
4. Bystander boards—diffusion of responsibility
5. Bureaucratic boards—rule-bound cultures
6. Conforming boards—groupthink, focus on agreeing more than making good decisions

Six Causes of Board Dysfunction

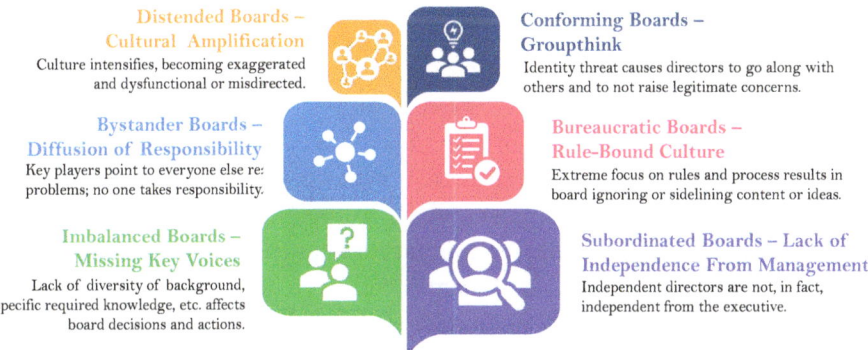

Distended Boards – Cultural Amplification
Culture intensifies, becoming exaggerated and dysfunctional or misdirected.

Conforming Boards – Groupthink
Identity threat causes directors to go along with others and to not raise legitimate concerns.

Bystander Boards – Diffusion of Responsibility
Key players point to everyone else re: problems; no one takes responsibility.

Bureaucratic Boards – Rule-Bound Culture
Extreme focus on rules and process results in board ignoring or sidelining content or ideas.

Imbalanced Boards – Missing Key Voices
Lack of diversity of background, specific required knowledge, etc. affects board decisions and actions.

Subordinated Boards – Lack of Independence From Management
Independent directors are not, in fact, independent from the executive.

Fig. 1.1 Six causes of board dysfunction

Of course, dysfunctional boards rarely exhibit just one of these behaviours. Two or more dysfunctions are often work at the same time, and some dysfunctions tend to breed others.

The Subordinated Board

The subordinated board is unable or unwilling to be *independent from management*. It is vital that the board is independent of the executive and is able to take an objective view and make enforceable decisions. The executive will generally have a bias in favour of actions the company has already taken, and this is particularly true during a crisis. This is perfectly natural; in most cases, they will have taken decisions for what they believed to be valid reasons, based on what they regard as reliable evidence. But there needs to be a system of checks and balances whereby these decisions are scrutinized and questioned as necessary. Most of all the board needs to keep its eye on the longer term and develop and support a sustainable strategy to help the organization meet its goals. A key cultural dysfunction occurs when the board cannot separate itself from the executive in order to critically examine what is before them.

The Imbalanced Board

The imbalanced board is *missing key voices*, often as a result of lack of engagement with a full range of stakeholders. Diversity of background, thought, experience and knowledge are vitally necessary at board level. If it is not present, decisions are made without the benefit of a full range of perspectives and experience. The less diverse the board is, the less likely it is to understand when key viewpoints are absent. Homogenous boards tend to make decisions that are not fully informed (i.e. by the missing voices).

The Distended Board

The distended board suffers from *amplification of culture*. In this situation, the existing culture intensifies so much that it becomes dysfunctional or misdirected. This is a particular problem where an organization has 'outgrown' its original culture, yet clings to a system that is no longer working. Start-ups, for example, often benefit from a dynamic and aggressive culture that focuses attention on getting through the problems of establishment and early growth, but studies of entrepreneurship have shown how this culture needs to change and mature with time. As many companies and organizations have discovered, the road to hell is paved with good intentions, and the hard-working get-the-job-done culture they thought they had at the beginning has turned into something dark and toxic with the passage of time.

The Bystander Board

The bystander board is characterized by *diffusion of responsibility*. Here, the cultural dysfunction takes the form of abdication of responsibility by some individuals, or even the board as a whole. Key players point at one another (or possibly a fall guy), and collective ownership of major problems is absent. Weak board relationships—for example, the presence of a large number of new board members who have not yet had time to get to know and trust each other—and/or a weak or inexperienced chair can be among the causes of the problem. Boards need to act collectively and communicate with a single voice. This does not preclude dispute and debate in private before a decision is made, far from it, but these discussions need to be brought to a resolution so that boards think and act with one voice.

The Bureaucratic Board

Bureaucratic boards suffer from an *overly controlled culture*. While processes and rules are critical to a board's ability to operate, the focus on these can sometimes be so strong that additional information which falls outside the usual channels or systems is collectively ignored or disregarded. This risk is especially present when a board is wedded to processes it knows and is comfortable with (and which have often been in place for a long time). There are two problems here. The first is confirmation bias; if the information placed before the board is in line with prior expectations, then no one is going to challenge or make waves, it confirms expectations. The second problem is the optimism bias; when information is received which contradicts received wisdom, boards find reasons to exclude it from decision-making. The problem is particularly acute when there is a lack of independent scrutiny from the board.

The Conforming Board

As noted above, boards need to take collective responsibility, but sometimes the desire for harmony and 'smooth' decision-making can lead to an overly strong bias in favour of consensus. Board members are less likely to raise controversial points or 'rock the boat' if their peers seem otherwise in agreement; no one wants to be the lone voice of dissent and question the process or any idea being debated. The dangers of *groupthink* are exacerbated still further where there is a strong and directive leader who shapes the thinking of the board in conformance with his or her will.

The Need for Independence

These board dysfunctions do not appear from nowhere. They evolve out of weak, poorly defined cultures where board members are not actively shaping the culture of their board and organization. Boards fail to pre-emptively plan and adapt to meet changing times and in the end, as the old metaphor has it, fight the next war with the same weapons as the last one. In the Middle Ages when the Black Death struck, priests took holy relics out of the churches and paraded them through the streets, hoping this would keep the plague at bay. It did not work. In March 2020 the Patriarch of the Russian Orthodox Church reportedly drove around the Moscow ring road in a car, holding up an ikon to ward off coronavirus, with similar results. Boards that fail to innovate and create new solutions for new problems are in danger of looking equally out of touch.

The real guardians of corporate governance are, or ought to be, the independent directors (sometimes known as non-executive directors, trustees or governors, depending on the type of organization). Their purpose on boards is to provide an independent perspective, scrutinizing executive actions and holding them to account. Independent directors are there to ask those hard questions that will expose the reality of what is actually going on and engage them to address it. The responsibility of independent directors led by the chair is to speak truth to power and act as an early warning system so that future problems can be identified and addressed before they happen. They are there to guard the guardians.

So what needs to be done? There is an urgent need to change and reform board culture. Actually, there is a role for each and every one of us; there needs to be more and better education for directors and chairs, and regulatory bodies need to have more teeth and take prompt and firmer steps to discipline weak boards, before they fail rather than after. But most of all, boards need to change themselves.

These are the issues that this book seeks to address. We have examined a wide range of corporate disasters and scandals, not to castigate individuals or to apportion blame, but simply to try to understand why they happen, why they continue to happen, and to offer some remedies to this at least three centuries-old problem. It is important to recognize that these events are not a random series of accidents or errors, things that could happen to anyone. Failures of corporate governance have underlying causes, deep-rooted dysfunctions that are rooted in board and corporate cultures. Our purpose here is to look at the roots of those cultures, how they influence the actions (or inactions) of the board and what can be done to enable change.

The world is getting increasingly complex and boards need to rise to this challenge. At the moment we face a series of interlocking crises: the aftermath of the pandemic, a fragile and deeply damaged economy, rising inequality and hardship, the climate emergency. In ten years' time, there will be more complex problems, not less. We need solutions to the problems these crises pose before the situation gets even tougher. Now more than ever, good governance is absolutely vital. But we are not getting it. Something is broken. We need, urgently, to fix it.

The Structure of This Book

The next three chapters amplify this need for change. In Chap. 2 we look at some examples of board failure and the role played by board dysfunctions. Chapter 3 describes in more detail the impacts of failure for all of us, and how the consequences can last for years, even generations. Chapter 4 covers more detail on the dysfunctional cultures that lead to these failures and describes their roots and origins.

In Part II, we offer detailed case studies that show how these cultures manifest themselves, including in some of the world's largest and more powerful companies. These cases show clearly how the board failed to act in the best interests of stakeholders, sometimes through inaction or lack of knowledge of what was going on, sometimes because their independence had been compromised and they had become aligned with the interests of the executive.

Finally, in Part III we will look at some suggested remedies. Many of these revolve around the proposed reform of board culture and aimed at ensuring board independence, better boardroom culture, and supporting directors and boards to be successful in their duties. Regulation of course has a role to play, and we will be making recommendations on this issue too, but to repeat the point made above, the body best placed to ensure effective governance is the board itself. The dangers of distorted board culture and need for reform is the central theme that runs throughout this book.

Notes

1. Lawrence LeShan and Henry Margenau, *Einstein's Space and Van Gogh's Sky*, New York: Macmillan, 1982; Norman Dixon, *On the Psychology of Military Incompetence*, London: Cape, 1976.
2. Charles Mackay, *Extraordinary Popular Delusions and the Madness of Crowds*, London: Bentley, 1852, pp. 55, 60–2.
3. Helen Paul, *The South Sea Bubble: An Economic History of its Origins and Consequences*, London: Routledge, 2013.
4. Mark Casson, *The World's First Railway System: Enterprise, Competition and Regulation on the Railway Network in Victorian Britain*, Oxford: Oxford University Press, 2009.
5. C. Peter Magrath, *Yazoo: Law and Politics in the New Republic*, New York: W.W. Norton, 1967.
6. Geoffrey Elliott, *The Mystery of Overend & Gurney: A Financial Scandal in Victorian London*, London: Methuen, 2007.
7. Richard White, *Railroaded: The Transcontinentals and the Making of Modern America*, New York: W.W. Norton, 2012.
8. J. Leonard Bates, *The Origins of Teapot Dome: Progressives, Parties and Petroleum, 1909–1921*, Urbana: University of Illinois Press, 1963.
9. Chris Swinson, *Share Trading, Fraud and the Crash of 1929: A Biography of Clarence Hatry*, London: Routledge, 2019.
10. https://www.transport-network.co.uk/HS2-based-on-false-prospectus-Berkeley-claims/16371.
11. https://www.accountancyage.com/2002/01/15/stoys-faces-fine-and-lessons-over-polly-peck/.
12. Ibid.
13. https://www2.deloitte.com/in/en/pages/risk/articles/governance-101.html.
14. https://www.worldfinance.com/strategy/japan-steps-up-corporate-governance-code.
15. Philip Inman and Richard Partington, 'Business View', *The Guardian* 9 July 2020.
16. *Financial Times*, 8 July 2020.
17. *Bloomberg*, 26 June 2020, https://www.bloomberg.com/news/articles/2020-06-26/wirecard-auditors-say-elaborate-fraud-led-to-missing-billions; *Financial Times*, https://on.ft.com/3ivJtRN.
18. Gerry Brown, Andrew Kakabadse and Filipe Morais, *The Independent Director in Society*, Basingstoke: Palgrave Macmillan, 2020.
19. Ibid.
20. *Wall Street Journal*, 5 May 2019, https://www.wsj.com/articles/boeing-knew-about-safety-alert-problem-for-a-year-before-telling-faa-airlines-11557087129.

21. Gerry Brown, *The Independent Director: The Non-Executive Director's Guide to Effective Board Presence*, Basingstoke: Palgrave Macmillan, 2015; Brown et al., 2020.
22. Randall S. Peterson, D. Brent Smith, Paul V. Martorana and Pamela D. Owens, 'The Impact of Chief Executive Officer Personality on Top Management Team Dynamics: One Mechanism by Which Leadership Affects Organizational Performance', *Journal of Applied Psychology* 88 (3), 2003; Robert Hogan and Robert B. Kaiser, 'What We Know About Leadership', *Review of General Psychology* 9 (2), 2005.
23. Hogan and Kaiser, p. 176.
24. https://www.washingtonpost.com/archive/business/1982/10/11/tylenols-maker-shows-how-to-respond-to-crisis/bc8df898-3fcf-443f-|bc2f-e6fbd639a5a3/.
25. https://www.ft.com/content/8c8d3668-adb5-11e2-82b8-00144feabdc0.
26. Steven Boivie, Michael K, Bednar, Ruth V. Aguilera and Joel L. Andrus, 'Are Boards Designed to Fail? The Implausibility of Effective Board Monitoring', *Academy of Management Annals*, February 2016.

2

The Faces of Disaster

In Chap. 1 we talked about the past 300 years, but the problem of failing organizations—and the lack of oversight over them—is as old as human history. The former *FT* journalist Patrick Cockburn, writing about the scandal that erupted in 2016 around the Panamanian law firm Mossack Fonseca, which had helped international clients hide billions of dollars in tax havens, wryly quoted Rudyard Kipling:

> Who shall doubt the secret hid
> Under Cheops' pyramid
> Was that the contractor did
> Cheops out of several millions?[1]

Kipling was closer to the truth than perhaps he knew; fraud was rife among officials in ancient Egypt, as it was during the Roman Empire. The history of banking collapses in the European Middle Ages is reminiscent of those of our own time, and a collection of stories from Ming-dynasty China known as *The Book of Swindles* also sounds depressingly familiar. Fraud, scandals and corruption have always been with us.

In modern times, too, this is not just a British or an American problem. Our research has found major corporate scandals over the past forty years involving companies domiciled in Japan, Sweden, Iran, Malaysia, China, Brazil, India, Nigeria, Angola, Australia and many others. This is also a problem that cuts across sector barriers. From financial services to resource extraction, high-technology to catering, Silicon Valley start-ups to firms with a century and more of history behind them, no sector or type of company is exempt. National and sector cultures are not responsible for scandals and failures, or at least not solely. Culture plays an influencing role, of course, but this is a problem that happens everywhere.

Corporate scandals and disasters take many forms, but the causes are depressingly similar and almost always come back to the vitally important issue of the competence of the board to govern. If the board does not act, or is unable to act, then the business is at the mercy of those who wish to manipulate it for professional or personal interests. The need for independent scrutiny and oversight are vital and cannot be stressed strongly enough. And equally, we need to remember that these are not problems that affect a few companies, in a few sectors, in a few countries. These problems happen in every sector, all around the world, and they have an impact on all of us.

Why do boards fail to act? In many specific instances we can never know for certain. Boardrooms are closed rooms with public unanimity required, and the proceedings of meetings are often jealously guarded secrets. Even if we did have access to board minutes, in many cases the real decisions are made through back channels and side conversations.[2] However, we can infer a great deal from the actions boards take, and even more from their inaction, as well as the observable behaviours of board members. These give us deeper insight into the workings of boards and helping us to understand why they become dysfunctional.

One observation that can be drawn from the cases of corporate scandals we have studied is that the problem doesn't usually start with the board, or at least, not with the board as a whole. Individual members, usually executive directors, may be initially culpable; the rest of the board is usually conspicuous by its ignorance, at least until the disaster explodes in their faces. The point that needs to be made, however, is that just because the board was ignorant of what happened, that does not mean its individual members are not personally, morally and financially responsible. Ignorance of the facts is not—or at least, should not be—a defence in law.

However, we should also be wary of crude generalizations about misconduct. Individual behaviour, as we noted in Chap. 1, has a very important role to play, and the relationships between boards and executives, whether good or bad, can affect outcomes quite strongly. Narcissistic or greedy individuals who rise to positions of power may often try to dominate their boards or else sideline them and take no notice of them. But corruption is not solely inherent in individuals. Research going back at least as far as the 1960s by psychologists such as Stanley Milgram has shown that situational pressure is a very important factor. Individuals may be 'bad apples,' but their wrongdoing may be as much a result of 'bad barrels' (the situation they find themselves in) or even 'bad cellars' (the culture in which they are working).

As an example, let us take the LIBOR scandal in 2012, where it emerged that traders from several banks had been effectively rigging the London Inter-Bank Offered Rate, the rate of interest at which major global banks lend to each other. The traders who took part in the rigging could be classified as bad apples; they had broken regulations deliberately in order to profit their institutions and themselves. However, many claimed they were under peer pressure to break the rules and that their bosses not only turned a blind eye but actively encouraged them, thus creating a bad barrel. Finally, there was the prevailing culture within the banking industry, which observers described as 'moral anomie' and 'lacking a moral compass.' This was the bad cellar, the system-wide failure to see law and regulation as moral boundaries.[3] The pressure of the situation and the wider culture may have driven some who would otherwise have been compliant to break regulations.

Appendix A gives a list of the scandals and disasters we have investigated, with short descriptions of a sample of these. In this chapter, we will try to understand the interaction between the board and the rest of the organization and how these combined factors, the behaviours of executives, the situation and the culture combined to create the conditions for failure. In these cases, a strong board with a high-functioning culture, like Johnson & Johnson, might have spotted the problems or at least developed a rapid and effective response when the crisis came. However, when these behaviours are combined with our six board dysfunctions, failure becomes not so much a matter of 'if' but 'when.'

Behaviours and Dysfunctions

The failures we investigated cover a fairly wide spectrum from outright criminal behaviour such as theft, fraud and bribery, through various shades of grey such as concealing data, fiddling the books, cutting regulatory corners and abuse of power, to the human failings of incompetence and blind ambition, and finally to cases such as excessive compensation for executives and tax evasion which, though not illegal, are morally dubious to say the least. Let us take a look at some of these behaviours and see how their interactions with dysfunctional boards led to catastrophe.

Robbing the Till

At one end of the spectrum is outright theft, where executives steal from the company and its customers to enrich themselves. There is not even a fig leaf of pretence that this is being done for the good of the company or anyone else. We looked at examples like the Ponzi scheme run by Bernie Madoff that bilked around $65 billion from customers of his investment company (substantial sums were later recovered) or security firm Tyco where the CEO and CFO worked together to defraud the company of around $150 million.[4] As noted in Chap. 1, investment bank Goldman Sachs was forced to repay nearly $3.9 billion to the Malaysian government after it emerged that two Goldman executives were siphoning money from the Malaysian sovereign wealth fund 1MDB.

As with other similar cases, the executives in question were working secretly, sometimes with a small cabal of allies to help them. Their actions were flagrantly illegal, and if caught they would go to prison (as they did in the Tyco and Madoff cases). It can therefore be argued that the boards of these companies had no way of knowing this was happening, and it is unfair to blame them for the scandal. However, a closer examination shows that the boards of these organizations are usually suffering from some form of dysfunction which means they did not ask the probing questions or demand further information that might have allowed issues to be seen. In the case of Madoff Investment Securities, a privately owned company, Madoff himself was chairman and CEO, his brother was managing director and chief compliance officer, and several of his children held key positions. In other words, the entire top structure of the organization was subordinated to Madoff.

The same was true at Tyco, where the charismatic CEO Dennis Kozlowski dominated the board to such an extent that the audit committee did not seem to notice the large sums which were disappearing from the accounts, or if committee members did notice, they took no action. Edward Breen, the incoming chairman of the board tasked with cleaning the mess after Koslowski was arrested, noted that 'The fall of Tyco was brought about by a lack of governance and accountability.' Subordinated and suffering from diffusion of responsibility, the Tyco board seems to have sat on its hands throughout the crisis. The board of Goldman Sachs also remained silent throughout the 1MDB scandal. Were they unaware of what was going on? Possibly, but it seems unlikely; this was not the first major scandal to affect Goldman Sachs in the decade leading to the scandal. This too looks like diffusion of responsibility; there is a problem, everyone is aware of it, but no one is going to volunteer to take the lead on confronting the abuses.

We contend that had these been high-functioning boards with truly independent directors, then either the problems would have been noticed, spotted and dealt with before they occurred, or at the very least the board would have constructed a much more robust response to the crisis. Greed is a real human issue, and people will always be tempted to put their hands in the till. To continue the metaphor from earlier, there will always be rotten apples. The board's task is to ensure that the culture of the company does not permit or encourage the rot to spread.

Other Forms of Fraud

The board did not identify and confront wrongdoing at Wells Fargo bank, where for at least fourteen years employees engaged in systematic fraud against customers. Fake accounts were opened in customers' names using forged signatures, false identification numbers were created, and money was transferred in and out of customers' accounts without their consent.[5] Although senior managers denied it, subsequent inquiries showed that Wells Fargo had a high-pressure culture in which employees were driven to meet financial targets and were punished if they did not. The culture of the bank clearly accelerated the problem. A similar culture existed at the investment bank Salomon Brothers in the 1980s, leading employees to forge applications for US Treasury Bonds.[6]

This was not a case of a few bad apples. In both cases, the culture of the organization led to intolerable pressure being put on employees so that to keep their jobs or earn promotion they had to bend the rules. That bending was not only tolerated but encouraged by people at the top of the business. Thousands of Wells Fargo employees were later dismissed for their conduct, and thousands of others disciplined, indicating how widespread malpractice was. And so to the perennial question: where was the board? We can detect elements of diffusion of responsibility here; financial performance was good, profits were flowing, so why question where those profits came from. In public, at least, if board members had doubts they kept them quiet.

There was also an element of subordination in both cases. At Salomon Brothers an aggressive and charismatic CEO held the company in thrall, and the head of retail at Wells Fargo was known as 'the most powerful woman in banking.' The board were unable or unwilling to confront and contain these money machines. We also detect an element of groupthink; the boards of both companies were composed largely of industry insiders and there was not enough diversity of thinking to enable constructive challenge. Finally, there may also have been an element of amplification of culture, as aggressive behaviour became not so much a means to an end as a way to justify what was happening.

Aggressive, larger-than-life figures tend to advance to positions of power in business when corporates reward individual performance without considering how it was achieved. Others see who gets ahead and copy that behaviour. If that behaviour is aggressive, for example, that encourages others to become even more aggressive to get ahead. The key lesson for boards is that once these figures do begin crossing ethical and legal lines, it can be very difficult to identify and contain. Even more importantly, they have the power to infect the culture of the organization—sometimes, even to influence the culture of the entire sector. Monitoring culture and holding the executive to account for the culture of the business are important. Directors need to have their finger on the pulse of the organization's culture to measure it regularly and to ensure that it is healthy and functioning well. Doing this requires independence of thought and action, but it also requires board members to be alert and take responsibility, not just wait for information to come to them but to actively seek information about the culture of the business and understand what is happening across the organization.

Bribery

While clearly outlawed in almost every legal jurisdiction on the planet, the payment of bribes to win business or get influence is a widespread practice. Privately, some executives will even defend bribery as a transaction cost, without which it would be impossible to do business.[7] We looked at several cases of large-scale bribery including mining company Rio Tinto, which reportedly paid $10.5 million to secure a valuable mining licence in Guinea,[8] catering firm Compass which bribed United Nations officials to win contracts to supply food to UN peacekeepers[9] and Samsung, which paid bribes to people close to the president of South Korea.[10] Both the president and the chair of Samsung later went to prison.

The board's relationship to each of these scandals is slightly different. At Samsung we can see evidence of subordination of the board. The chair of Samsung, Lee Jae-yong, was the grandson of the company's founder, and like his father and grandfather before them he exercised a great deal of power over the company. This included control of a slush fund which senior Samsung executives allegedly used to pay bribes, the existence of which was unknown to the board. At Compass the wider issue appears to have been diffusion of responsibility; the bribes were paid by a subsidiary company, and it is not clear that this subsidiary's actions were scrutinized in as much detail as they should have been. At Rio Tinto we can see evidence of amplification of culture. Although the board initially denied knowledge of the payments, the senior independent director was later charged with conspiracy to commit fraud.

Here again it is hard to dismiss those who pay bribes as just a few bad apples. Given how widespread the practice is, and given how many executives are prepared to defend that practice, the problem is much wider than individuals. We are dealing here with a mindset and culture that is proving stubbornly resistant to change. As with fraud, boards need be proactive and look for evidence, not just sit back and accept assurances from the executive team that everything is above board.

Fiddling the Books

Accounting fraud and concealing data is another widespread practice. Unlike bribery, very few people will volunteer to defend it; rather like breaking the speed limit, everyone knows it is wrong but surprising numbers of people are still prepared to do it. We looked at several examples of false accounting. Some were long-term affairs like the overstating of income and profits at Satyam Computer Services which lasted for several years,[11] or the deception at British construction firm Carillion where directors conspired to conceal mounting losses from the board[12]; some were one-offs, like the false overstatement of profits at supermarket chain Tesco.[13] We also looked at concealment of technical data, including auto components maker Takata, which concealed test data about the performance of its airbag inflators,[14] and Kobe Steel, which falsified data about the strength and durability of its products.[15]

Again, there are some variations. The executive chair of Satyam claimed sole responsibility for the accounting fraud, but does not appear to have acted with malicious intent. Faced with a run of poor results, he created a false picture in order to keep the board happy. The Tesco incident happened at a time when the company and its share price were under pressure; its American venture, Fresh & Easy, had been disposed of at a massive loss, and discount retailers were cutting into its home market. At Takata and at Kobe Steel, data were concealed because revealing the truth about the company's products would have undercut its competitive position and led to a loss of income and profits.

There is a strong possibility of subordination of the board at Satyam, whose founder and executive chair was a widely admired figure in Indian business and society. But at Satyam and every other case mentioned earlier we can also see diffusion of responsibility and groupthink. So long as the figures looked good the board was happy, and if anyone thought to question whether the figures were accurate, they either failed to press the matter strongly enough or kept their mouths shut.[16] There was also a strong lack of diversity on some of these boards, especially Satyam and Takata, meaning board independence was probably compromised.

The same problems can be seen in each case; the board was not active enough, did not challenge enough, and was content to listen to the executive team rather than going out and searching for the truth. At Carillion, group-think culture was so strong that even when an internal whistleblower reported the finance director and insisted the figures were wrong, no one listened.

The point about culture and situation needs to be repeated here too. Even at Satyam it can be argued that this is not simply a case of rotten apples. Instead, very severe pressure to perform by hitting financial targets drove people to cross the line. Boards need to be alert to this. In most cases, they will have responsibility for approving performance targets. Sometimes, though, they do not seem to be fully aware of what those targets mean for managers and employees, especially in terms of psychological pressure. Shareholders will often press boards to set unrealistically high targets, and that pressure has to be resisted. Otherwise, there is a very real risk of creating a culture where otherwise good people will break under the pressure and commit fraud.

Cutting Corners

The same applies to other forms of corner-cutting which happens when financial pressures are building. We looked at several cases where the aggressive drive for growth at all costs once again led employees and managers to cross the line. The 'always be hustlin' culture at Uber led to a variety of problems including bullying and sexual harassment, attempted cover-ups of data breaches and allegations against employees, and the infamous Greyball software tool used in an attempt to deceive local authorities investigating Uber's practices (see Chap. 5). We also looked at the scandal at Volkswagen where a 'defeat device' was used to give false data on diesel engine emissions,[17] and the mis-selling of payment protection insurance (PPI) by UK financial institutions.[18] The first two were examples of corner-cutting at a single company (though there have been rumours of defeat devices at other car makers as well), while the PPI scandal affected nearly every major retail financial institution in the UK.

Here again we can see pressure to perform pushing people to undertake unethical and sometimes illegal actions. At Uber and Volkswagen there was considerable amplification of culture, with a win-at-all-costs ethos prevailing and very much driven from the top, by CEO Travis Kalanick in the case of Uber and supervisory board chair Ferdinand Piëch at Volkswagen. In neither case was the board able to confront effectively, in part at Uber because Kalanick and his allies exercised strong control over board appointments and voting rights. In the PPI case the pressure came from an industry-wide ethos of putting profits above all else. Employees were encouraged to hit sales targets, and diffusion of responsibility and element of groupthink meant that boards did not inquire too closely about the methods they used.

We will talk about Uber in more detail later in the book, but one point is worth mentioning in passing. Even when boards *are* aware of abuses being committed on their watch, it can be very difficult for them to make their voices heard in any meaningful fashion. The structure of Uber's board was such that Kalanick could simply ignore any challenge coming from the independent directors. There is a lesson here not just for directors and chairs of boards but also for regulators. Boards need to be constructed in such a way that no single dominant individual can control and subordinate them. That is partly a matter of board culture, but legal and regulatory intervention can also prevent this problem from developing in the first place.

Abuses of Power

The Uber case also shows an abuse of power by those in control of the company, and we have seen other cases where dominant people used their position to abuse others. We looked at labour market abuses at companies such as Nike and Sports Direct, sexual abuse scandals at Google and Oxfam, and, in a variation on the theme, the abuse of consumer trust at Facebook, which authorized outside organizations to harvest data on customers without their consent.

It is tempting here to point fingers at individuals, like the senior managers at Google, who are alleged to have abused women employees of the company, or the Oxfam field managers, who abused women refugees in Haiti. At Facebook the finger is usually pointed at Mark Zuckerberg, the founder and most visible figure in the top management team. But in all these cases, other executives and managers knew about the problem. In some cases they tried to speak up but were unable to make themselves heard; in others, there was a conspiracy of silence.

We have noted how lack of diversity can be linked to a loss of independence, and we can see very strongly in these cases how missing key voices on the board led to the board not seeing and not hearing what was going on under their noses. In all these cases, rumours had been circulating long before the scandal broke. If the board—especially the independent directors—had listened to key stakeholders, they would have been able to see and analyse the problem and attempt to take corrective action. How successful they would have been is difficult to say, given the presence once again of charismatic, dominant figures on the boards of most these organizations (Oxfam is an exception here); reforms at Facebook, for example, have met with mixed success at best.

Subordination and lack of independence are also issues here, but the main problem remains those missing voices. Boards need to be able to listen to stakeholders, whether this means consultation with outside groups or bringing stakeholder representatives onto the board. Whatever method is chosen, boards must have alternative sources of information so they can triangulate information and establish what is going on in the company and in its environment, rather than relying on information spoonfed to them by the executive team.

Errors and Blunders

Not every business scandal is the result of a conspiracy. Businesses are composed of human beings, and human beings make mistakes and errors of judgement. Carelessness and lack of attention to detail can be just as disastrous as malicious intent. We have seen this in cases of environmental disasters like the *Deepwater Horizon* blowout and subsequent oil spill in the Gulf of Mexico, the toxic gas cloud from Union Carbide's plant at Bhopal or the Mariana dam disaster in Brazil where mining firm BHP Billiton was a partner.[19] On a different level, we looked at the audit work of the Big 4 international accounting firms where a succession of blunders by auditors meant that major client weaknesses were overlooked; in some cases, auditors signed off on the accounts of firms that were about to collapse, apparently not noticing that anything was wrong.

Once again the temptation is to lay blame on individuals, the auditors who failed to spot the problems, or the health and safety managers who failed to ensure that safety systems at Bhopal and Mariana were in working order. At BP the usual scapegoat is CEO Tony Hayward, who insisted on taking personal charge of capping the well and organizing the clean-up, and became the public face of BP's failings. But in each of these cases, the problem ran far deeper than individuals. Inadequate supervision at Union Carbide and Mariana had been going on for months, if not years. Although BP insisted it had a culture of safety, subsequent inquiries established that the company had been cutting corners on safety and that the culture was one of profit first. The accounting firms too have put profit first, ignoring the conflict of interest between independent audit and their rich profit-generating consultancy businesses, who often serve the same client.

Board dysfunction takes different forms, from the strait-jacketed overly controlled culture we saw at the Big 4 to a more general diffusion of responsibility at BP and BHP, and probably at Union Carbide as well. On the one hand there is a rigid adherence to rules which means no one is able to speak out; on the other hand, directors are coasting along, not really paying attention to problems bubbling up below the surface. Independent directors, where they exist at all—historically, accounting firms have tended to have few independent directors, if any—are not seeking the right information and asking the right questions, and so the problems go undetected until, like landmines, they blow up in the board's face.

Blind Ambition

Like aggression, ambition on the part of a CEO is a good thing provided it comes with limits. Part of a board's task is to contain in over-ambitious CEOs and ensure they are acting in the best interests of the company and its stakeholders and not merely serving their own ends.

At Royal Bank of Scotland (RBS) and at Lehman Brothers, they failed spectacularly. RBS under the direction of CEO Fred Goodwin embarked on a wildly ambitious and expensive programme of acquisitions, culminating in the takeover of ABN AMRO. Not only did Goodwin pay over the odds for the Dutch bank, he and his executive team had formulated no plan for absorbing it into the group and seemed to have very little idea of what they were buying. One school of thought believes that he was only interested in buying ABN AMRO to forestall a rival takeover bid from Barclays. Lehman Brothers also took on more and more risky ventures, ramping up debt until the bank finally collapsed. RBS was saved by the British government and taxpayers, but Lehman Brothers disappeared entirely.

In both cases, the board had the power to stop this ultimately destructive behaviour. As CEO, Goodwin was responsible to the board, and the board had the power to reject his proposed takeover bids. The power dynamic at

Lehman Brothers was different, as Richard Fuld served as both chairman and CEO, but nevertheless the board could have voted down his principles. Neither board did so.

The problem here is partly subordination; Goodwin and Fuld were both forceful characters who tended to dominate whatever room they were in, and the independent chair of RBS seemed to have no power to prevent Goodwin from getting his way. The board of Lehman were also very inexperienced; only two of the twelve directors had any prior banking experience. But the main problem we identified here was groupthink. On both boards, directors seemed more interested in establishing a consensus than in conducting wide-ranging debate. Dissenting voices, if any, were silenced.

There is a chicken-and-egg situation here. Which came first: the domineering CEO who led the company into disaster, or the culture that enabled that person to rise to power in the first place? The answer is probably that both evolved together. Richard Fuld was both a product of the win-at-all-costs culture that had been developing at Lehman Brothers since the 1970s and a major influence on that culture going forward. For boards, the tricky task is to scrutinize both the individual *and* the culture, and to hold the former to account for his influence over the latter. Even when the numbers look good— and for a long time at both RBS and Lehman Brothers they looked very good—insidious changes and erosions of culture may be going on. Boards need to be alert for the signs of this by actively monitoring organizational culture and be ready to take corrective action.

Just About Legal

Even when companies are operating on the right side of the law, their actions can still have moral consequences that damage their reputations. Glencore broke no laws when it spied on employees and environmental groups in Australia and generated fake news websites and reports denigrating clean energy, but that did not prevent Australia's prime minister from describing the company as a 'national disgrace.'[20] Amazon was within its rights to domicile in low-tax regimes in order to reduce its tax payments to risibly small levels, but this did not prevent the company from becoming a byword for tax avoidance.[21]

We also looked at the scandals around executive compensation, examining cases where remunerations committees awarded huge increases in pay, bonuses and pensions which bore absolutely no relation to corporate performance. Few had quite the audacity of New York Stock Exchange CEO and chair

Richard Grasso, who in 2003 was awarded a compensation package worth just under $140 million,[22] but we found plenty of other examples of inflated pay awards.

This can be a tricky subject, as chief executives will argue that they are worth the money they are paid and that in a competitive market situation they are entitled to ask for as much money as they can get. That may be so, but are boards justified in paying it? Board remunerations committees, which set pay and other compensation, are meant to ensure that the company is getting value for money, but in practice that consideration sometimes goes out the window.

We can see examples of subordination here, and also diffusion of responsibility, but there is also amplification of culture. Glencore had a reputation as an aggressive company that tended to bulldoze opposition, and Amazon's board may simply have been responding to a prevailing ethos that suggests companies should minimize their tax payments in order to return money to shareholders. Within reason that is true, but companies have obligations to other stakeholders as well, and even Milton Friedman, the champion of shareholders' rights, argued that companies should always pay their fair share of taxes. In terms of executive compensation, too, boards and remuneration committees may be responding to the culture in which they find themselves, in which high price supposedly connotes quality.

But does paying top dollar necessarily mean the company gets the best executives? It is a little like asking whether a $100 bottle of wine is ten times better than a $10 bottle; will a CEO who is paid $10 million increase corporate performance ten times more than one who is paid $1 million? The answer in both cases is no, or at least, highly unlikely. Copycat pay awards by boards need to stop, and remuneration committees need to reward executives for what they can realistically accomplish rather than getting into bidding wars.

One of the duties of the board is to guard the organization's reputation. Doing this requires establishing real independence and objectivity, and being vigilant and stopping any attempt by executives to do things that will damage that reputation. At Glencore and Amazon and many others, the board could have intervened to protect the company. Failure in both cases led to considerable reputational damage.

Consequences of Dysfunction

Board dysfunction is not a direct cause of executive malpractice, but if the board fails to exercise its powers fully, this creates empty spaces where malpractice can flourish. Nature abhors a vacuum, and if the board is perceived to be weak, strong forces will come to fill the gaps.

It is difficult to draw direct links between board dysfunctions and particular types of malpractice, but we can observe some very general patterns, as follows.

Subordinated boards are prisoners of their situation. They are unable or unwilling to push back against dominant executives and do not scrutinize or challenge their actions. This doesn't mean they cannot see what is going on; they just cannot do anything about it. They could perhaps undertake corrective action to relieve pressure on the organization and deal with wider cultural issues that are leading to corruption and malpractice, but their way is blocked by those dominant individuals. In practice, this domination takes two forms: *charismatic*, where the executive dominates through reputation, character and force of personality, and *structural*, where the executive dominates usually controlling a larger share of the vote. The former can sometimes be dealt with by bringing new blood onto the board, directors of a more independent character who are willing to challenge; in extreme cases, as at Tyco, the entire board may need to be replaced. The latter can be almost impossible to shift without legal or regulatory support.

Imbalanced boards which are missing key voices may be less vulnerable to the individual bad apples, but they struggle to make headway against deeper cultural issues. This is because, lacking diversity of points of view, they struggle to empathize with other stakeholders who may be adversely affected by the company's actions. They cannot fix problems, either because they don't know the problems exist or because they do not recognize the situation as problematic. Malpractice and bad behaviour, like paying bribes or sexual harassment, is normalized and seen as part of the culture. As we shall argue later in this book, imbalanced boards need to engage more closely with stakeholders and encourage dialogue so that all views are properly represented in board discussions.

Distended boards, suffering from amplification of culture, will find it hard to deal with bad apples because their own culture has been warped to the point where they cannot see the apple is bad in the first place. As with imbalanced boards, they will normalize bad behaviour and see it as acceptable, provided the bottom line is not affected. Going further, not only will distended boards fail to prevent the darker aspects of organizational culture from growing and gaining strength, but they can actively contribute to those cultures; again, attitudes to bribery are a case in point. These boards become part of the problem rather than part of the solution. The answer in some cases is a wholesale cleaning and reconstitution of the board, or at the very least bringing in a new chair and establishing clear expectations around a truly independent board culture.

Bystander boards, where diffusion of responsibility rules, offer even more space for malpractice to emerge. Whether the problem is bad apples, bad barrels or bad cellars doesn't really matter, because bystander boards do not take responsibility. They have the power to act; there are no strong constraints or barriers blocking their freedom of action. They do nothing because no one will take responsibility.

As discussed elsewhere in this book, the role of the chair is particularly important in ensuring board effectiveness. In the case of bystander boards, the chair must take primary responsibility for changing the culture and ensuring directors act independently. Board evaluation and development can perhaps be used to remind directors of their duties and galvanize them into action. However, the chair cannot do this on their own. All the board needs to put their hand up, recognize their failings and set to work changing the culture.

Bureaucratic boards with their overly controlled cultures are in a strait-jacket similar to subordinated boards, only this time the constraints are largely of their own making. To be fair, those constraints often have deep cultural roots, but there are no external barriers preventing boards from reforming and changing their culture if they want to. In some ways the overly controlled culture is similar to groupthink, where the pressures to conform are so intense that dissent, disagreement and discussion are all stifled. Bureaucratic boards are trapped and cannot spot cultural dysfunctions because they are part of the culture, trapped like flies in amber. Changing these board cultures is extremely difficult and, unless the broader cultural foundation changes, essentially impossible.

Conforming boards, where groupthink rules, are similarly caught in a mental trap. Because consensus and harmony are prioritized over all else, legitimate concerns about the actions of executives are never brought to the surface. Sometimes, rather like subordinated boards, directors can see the problem facing them, but constraints on discussion and dissent mean that no one can talk about these openly. As a result, conforming boards are equally bad at dealing with just about everything that comes their way, from the actions of a single rogue executive to situational pressures and wider cultural shifts. Changing these cultures again is extremely difficult, but sometimes the

introduction of a few outsiders with different points of view and more independent attitudes can break the mould; once a few people start speaking up,
others may follow their example.

As noted too, not every catastrophe or failure is the result of a single board
dysfunction. Some boards will suffer from two, three or more dysfunctions at
the same time. But whatever the nature of the dysfunctions, the impact in
human, social and environmental terms remains the same. It is time to look
in more detail at the damage that these board failures cause and why it is so
important to remedy these defects.

Notes

1. https://www.counterpunch.org/2016/04/11/the-corruption-revealed-in-the-panama-papers-opened-the-door-to-isis/.
2. Heidi K. Gardner and Randall S. Peterson, 'Back Channels in the Boardroom: How to Prevent Side Conversations from Blocking Progress', *Harvard Business Review*, September–October 2019.
3. https://www.ft.com/content/dc5f49c2-d67b-11e1-ba60-00144feabdc0; Mouhamed El Bachire Thiam, Jonathan Liu and John Aston, 'Ignoring Personal Moral Compass: Factors Shaping Bankers' Decisions', *Journal of Financial Regulation and Compliance* 27 (3), 2018; Irene van Staveren, 'The Misdirection of Bankers' Moral Compass in the Organizational Field of Banking', *Cambridge Journal of Economics* 44 (3), 2020.
4. http://edition.cnn.com/2002/BUSINESS/asia/09/12/us.tyco/.
5. The Price of Wells Fargo's Fake Account Scandal Grows by $3 Billion. *The New York Times* (21 February 2020).
6. https://www.nytimes.com/1994/08/19/business/ex-salomon-chief-s-costly-battle.html.
7. https://www.forbes.com/sites/alexandrawrage/2017/01/25/bribery-is-bad-for-business/?sh=5f6c8da74a42; https://hbswk.hbs.edu/item/should-i-pay-the-bribe.
8. https://www.dailytelegraph.com.au/business/rio-tinto-bribery-scandal-two-former-chief-executives-embroiled-in-email-trail/news-story/fe4216a2852d6a25fa150e6acbd257f4.
9. 'UN Oil for Food Scandal Spreads to Compass Arm.' *The Telegraph* (19 October 2005).
10. https://www.bloomberg.com/news/features/2017-07-27/summer-of-samsung-a-corruption-scandal-a-political-firestorm-and-a-record-profit.

11. https://timesofindia.indiatimes.com/business/india-business/Satyams-chairman-Ramalinga-Raju-resigns-admits-fraud/articleshow/3946088.cms; https://economictimes.indiatimes.com/articleshow/62452514.cms.
12. *Carillion: Second Joint Report from the Business, Energy and Industrial Strategy and Work and Pensions Committees of Session 2017–19*, London: House of Commons, 2018.
13. https://www.telegraph.co.uk/business/2019/01/23/former-tesco-executive-carl-rogberg-cleared-fraud-charges/; https://www.bmmagazine.co.uk/in-business/how-did-the-tesco-accounting-scandal-unfold/.
14. Takata Corporation Pleads Guilty, Sentenced to Pay $1 Billion in Criminal Penalties for Airbag Scheme. *U.S. Department of Justice* (27 February 2017).
15. Japan's Kobe Steel Indicted over Quality Scandal, *BBC.* (20 July 2018).
16. https://www.thehindu.com/todays-paper/tp-business/Riding-a-tiger-without-knowing-to-get-off-Raju/article16348024.ece; https://timesofindia.indiatimes.com/business/india-business/Satyams-chairman-Ramalinga-Raju-resigns-admits-fraud/articleshow/3946088.cms; https://economictimes.indiatimes.com/articleshow/62452514.cms.
17. https://www.forbes.com/sites/bertelschmitt/2016/09/25/winterkorn-behind-dieselgate-coverup-new-docs-suggest/#7cf6b1d1477d.
18. https://www.fca.org.uk/data/monthly-ppi-refunds-and-compensation#header.
19. https://www.bloomberg.com/news/articles/2015-11-05/samarco-says-dam-in-brazil-burst-teams-are-working-on-site.
20. https://www.mining-technology.com/features/mining-scandals-four-incidents-that-shook-the-industry/; https://www.cmcmarkets.com/en-gb/opto/can-glencores-glen-share-price-withstand-project-caesar-scandal; https://www.theguardian.com/business/2019/mar/07/revealed-glencore-bankrolled-covert-campaign-to-prop-up-coal.
21. https://www.bbc.co.uk/news/magazine-20560359.
22. https://www.nytimes.com/2008/07/02/business/02grasso.html.

3

Dealing with the Consequences

When disasters occur and companies engage in corrupt practices or fail entirely, the consequences are felt far wider than company boundaries. These are not victimless incidents. The externalities, the costs of failure, must be financed and most often it is the taxpayer and society at large that pick up the bill.

Are boards aware of this when they make decisions? Do they consider all the consequences, especially the unintended consequences, of their actions? We know that some do, but clearly too many do not appear to take this onboard. The sociologist Robert Merton listed the causes of unanticipated consequences:

- Ignorance of facts and the situation, making it impossible to anticipate every outcome.
- Analytical errors, including use of the same habits of analysis as have always been used in the past, but which may not necessarily be appropriate for new data.
- Short-term interests overriding long-term interests.
- Basic values which may require or prohibit certain actions on the grounds that these are not considered acceptable by the current culture.
- Self-defeating prophecies, whereby people seek to find solutions before an anticipated problem occurs, without realizing that the problem itself may not actually occur.[1]

As Steven Boivie and his colleagues point out, 'in order to effectively monitor management, directors need to be able to obtain, process and then share

© The Author(s), under exclusive license to Springer Nature Switzerland AG 2022
G. Brown, R. S. Peterson, *Disaster in the Boardroom*,
https://doi.org/10.1007/978-3-030-91658-9_3

information.'[2] Information processing in particular, they say, is an area where boards often fail, both at the individual and at the group level. Individual directors may be able to process information, but they are unable to share it effectively with the rest of the board. The argument is that these blockages are often designed into the structure of the boards, which have in-built barriers to good communication. Problems include information asymmetries, where information is not shared equally and some board members are left in the dark, and the infrequency of board meetings which means the board can have trouble cohering as a group. So-called side conversations, whereby board members exchange information outside of the context of formal meetings, can help solve the problem if handled sensitively. Sometimes, though, these side conversations turn into exclusive groups that talk among themselves and do not share with other directors. This is not necessarily a deliberate action; exclusion can be accidental, directors developing a habit of talking to the same people without even realizing it. Either way, sometimes these side conversations can actually make the problem worse.[3]

All this means that, for reasons that are partly structural and partly cultural (remembering, of course, that culture influences structure, and vice versa), boards sometimes make decisions with far-reaching consequences, without being remotely aware of what those consequences will be. Very few boards deliberately drive companies into the ground. Most are well-intentioned, trying to do their best in a difficult world.

But the road to hell is paved with good intentions, and the unintended consequences for which other people pay the price take a number of forms. We can categorize these roughly as the *human costs, social damage, economic damage, environmental damage*, and *financial and brand reputational damage* to the organization itself.

Human Costs

We have already discussed disasters such as the Bhopal gas leak, the Mariana dam collapse and the Boeing 737-MAX crashes in which hundreds of people died as a direct result of corporate failures. These are far from isolated incidents. To give just a few more examples:

- On 7 May 2020 a gas leak from a storage facility, a plant owned by South Korean company LG Chemical near Visakhapatnam in Andhra Pradesh, killed 11 people and injured more than 1000. Subsequent investigations showed that other facilities at the same plant were also showing signs of leakage and the plant was shut down. Although LG Chemical moved swiftly to clean up the leak and support people affected by the leak, the company is under investigation by the Indian government.[4]

- On 24 April 2013 the Rana Plaza, an eight-storey building occupied by workers involved in garment manufacturing, collapsed in the Savar district of Dhaka, killing 1134 people and injuring 2500. Cracks in floors and walls had been previously reported to the owners, who ignored them. Workers in the building made garments for many high-profile Western brands including some luxury brands. None of these companies was apparently aware of conditions in the Rana Plaza, despite commitments on the part of most of them to ethical supply chain management. Walmart had allegedly attempted to block earlier attempts to improve pay and working conditions for Bangladeshi garment makers.[5]

- According to the US Surgeon-General's office, between 1991 and 2017 the number of prescriptions for painkilling drugs handed out in America rose by more than 400 per cent. Most of these drugs were based on opioids, leading to an 'epidemic of addiction.' The Surgeon-General also estimated that in 2017 alone, 42,000 Americans died of drug overdoses, the great majority of whom were addicted to prescription drugs. Although the medical establishment must take a share of the blame, aggressive marketing of opioid drugs by pharmaceutical companies has played an important role in the expansion of the epidemic.

- On 14 April 1912, the liner *Titanic* sank in the North Atlantic with a loss of more than 1500 lives. After the sinking it emerged that the ship carried only enough lifeboats to accommodate less than half of her passengers and crew. This was an act of deliberate policy by White Star's directors, who assumed that (a) the ship was unsinkable thanks to its supposedly watertight compartments and therefore lifeboats were unnecessary and (b) even if the worst did happen, the *Titanic* was operating in busy sea lanes and other ships would be able to take off her passengers and crew. In his book *A Night to Remember*, the American writer Walter Lord also suggested that cost factors were an issue. No one on the board thought to question what would happen if the ship sank and other vessels were not able to come to the rescue.

Even when no one dies, the effect on human lives can be dramatic. In 2008, management at the Fukushima Daiichi nuclear power plant in Japan received an in-house report suggesting that the plant needed better protection from inundation by seawater and should build a protective wall capable of stopping tsunami waves of up to ten metres. Headquarters deemed this unrealistic and ignored the report, considering the current height of the defences to be adequate.[6] The earthquake of 11 March 2011 produced tsunami waves that overwhelmed the defences and flooding the plant, causing a nuclear disaster and leading to the evacuation of more than 150,000 people over and above those already displaced by the tsunami. The extent of the long-term health problems for those who survived is still unknown.

These are the dramatic, headline-making events. Much more widespread, and much less discussed, is the impact on people who lose their jobs as a result of corporate failures. The collapse of energy trading company Enron cost thousands of jobs and also brought down the accounting firm Arthur Andersen which employed 85,000 people worldwide (although many of these were able to find work with other firms like Ernst & Young and Deloitte, which took over former Andersen practices). The failures of the Weinstein Company and Lehman Brothers also had a human cost, as people's livelihoods were interrupted or even destroyed.

The losses go beyond the immediate failure, too. When a company becomes insolvent, there is an impact on suppliers, distributors and others in the value chain who depended on contracts with their company for their own business. Unemployed workers are no longer spending money in local catering and retail outlets, so those businesses suffer as well. The failure of a large company can often have a domino effect, sending many other smaller companies into bankruptcy as well, and this in turn leads to more job losses.

A study in the *Annual Review of Sociology* in 2015 found that losing a job can have a very powerful impact on socio-economic circumstances and life outcomes. For example, people who have been made redundant once are statistically more likely to be made redundant again. Other consequences include long-term earnings losses, lower quality of future jobs, a decline in psychological and physical well-being, social withdrawal, family disruption including failures of relationships such as marriages, and finally, lower levels of attainment and well-being for the children of those who have lost their jobs. It is not just the unemployed workers who pay the psychological and emotional price but their families as well, and that damage can last for generations.[7]

Pension funds also suffer. When companies begin to struggle, the tendency to fail to maintain contributions to the pension pot, or even to raid it for ready cash, becomes irresistible. Enron had also been mismanaging its pension fund, and more than 20,000 people lost their pensions. Some had been paying into those pensions for thirty or forty years and then faced destitution in their old age. Carillion, which failed in 2019, had a pension fund deficit of £587 million, and the collapse of British Home Stores in 2016 threatened the pensions of thousands of employees and former employees. The situation at BHS was partly resolved when former owner Philip Green was persuaded to contribute £343 million towards the shortfall.[8] But according to one estimate, UK corporate pension funds had a combined deficit of £119 billion at the end of 2018.[9]

Social Damage

Corruption and scandals in business also damage the reputation of entire sectors, sometimes business as a whole—this is different from the reputational damage to individual brands, which we shall come to in a moment. The Glencore scandal and the Mariana dam collapse led to a loss of faith in the integrity of the mining industry. Incidents such as the Rana Plaza collapse coupled with greater scrutiny of how the fashion industry makes its money— take for example the highly successful documentary film 'Fashion's Dirty Secrets' by journalist Stacey Dooley—have led to increasing scepticism and loss of trust in fashion brands, which are increasingly being challenged by the rise of 'ethical fashion.'[10]

Social damage tarnishes good companies with the same brush as the bad and makes it harder for them to recruit good people into the sector and to gain consumer trust. Following the 2008 banking crash, surveys in North America and the UK suggested a high level of loss of trust in banks, even among bankers; fewer than one-third of people who worked in banks said they trusted their employer. Similarly, the sexual abuse scandal at Oxfam in Haiti led to a loss of donations not just to Oxfam but UK charities in general.

Individual scandals do damage, but when a large number happen close together the effect begins to snowball and can lead to more long-lasting problems. Historically, events like the South Sea Bubble led to a backlash not just against the South Sea Company but against businesses generally. Left-wing revolutionary movements such as Marxism and anarchism gained traction in the later nineteenth century in part because of abuses by business leaders, and the corruption of 'robber barons' like John D. Rockefeller and Cornelius Vanderbilt eventually turned even moderate Americans against business. There was a similar backlash during the Great Depression of the 1930s. The Occupy movement that emerged in the aftermath of the 2008 financial crisis blamed not just the banks but capitalism more generally, and the climate change protests such as Extinction Rebellion that erupted in 2019 also has an anti-business element.

Protests, strikes and demonstrations, even civil disorder and violence are one manifestation of anger at business disasters and corruption. Government regulation is another. Each wave of failures is usually followed by a similar wave of restriction and regulation, oftentimes lifted or repealed after people's memories of the original crisis begins to fade. Governments, even undemocratic ones, respond to pressure from the people, and when the social climate turns against business, governments tend to respond. Some of the regulations that have been imposed are sensible and reflect what responsible businesses and other organizations should be doing anyway, that is looking after the interests of their stakeholders. Others restrict the ability of businesses to operate, and this in turn hinders economic growth which is harmful to all of us.

Social damage takes other forms too. When companies collapse and employees lose their jobs, there is an impact on tax revenues, and this in turn means governments have less money to spend on essential services such as health, education, policing, arts and culture and so on. Governments must also sometimes contribute directly to supporting failed businesses that are 'too big to fail,' such as the banking bailouts that happened around the world in 2008. The nine years of losses suffered by Royal Bank of Scotland after it was saved by government were funded by the taxpayer.

In his book *World Out of Balance*, former A.T. Kearney chair Paul Laudicina forecast the possibility of a world where business and society are irredeemably at odds and where opposition to business is entrenched within government, the press and the people.[11] If this happens, there is a danger that businesses could develop a kind of siege mentality and become even more removed from their stakeholders, a situation which would be harmful to everyone. Boards have a strong responsibility to maintain relationships of trust with stakeholders and that can only be done if social damage is avoided and minimized.

Boards also have a stake in the performance of governance across their wider sector. The success or failure of governance at one organization can have ramifications for others; the governance failures at some financial institutions in 2008 damaged the reputations of nearly every financial institution to a greater or lesser extent and led to legislation and the imposition of new governance rules. On a more positive note, there is also an opportunity for governance to be strengthened through more collaborative working and information sharing between boards. High-performing boards could be asked to advise other boards on elements of best practice. For example, business schools are accredited through a process of inspection by accrediting associations. The inspection panels usually include deans from other business schools, whose presence on the panel is approved by both the accrediting institution and the business school being inspected. This practice could be usefully copied in other business sectors.

Environmental Damage

Climate change, contamination of seas and rivers with plastic, air pollution, species extinction, the growing scarcity of fresh water are all issues that can be traced to human activity, and corporations and other organizations must bear their share of responsibility. As far back as 2002, the United Nations Environment Programme (UNEP) noted that despite the good intentions expressed at the Earth Summit in Rio de Janeiro, 'there was a growing gap between the efforts to reduce the impact of business and industry on nature and the worsening state of the planet.' The UNEP also highlighted that at the time, only a small number of companies were making any kind of concerted effort to reduce the damage caused by their operations (in fairness, this situation has since improved). In 2012, the Deloitte Water Research Group found that barely half of large companies had board-level oversight of issues relating to water scarcity, and in 2020 a Harvard Business School working paper noted that many managers were still struggling to understand how to measure their environmental impacts.[12]

Boards should be taking the lead on these issues and ensuring that they are at the heart of strategy and the business model going forward. To their credit, many do. However, many others are still lagging behind, and the damage done by polluting companies to the environment can be terrible. The Mariana dam collapse damaged an entire ecosystem for hundreds of miles, and much of the area around the Fukushima Daiichi nuclear power plant is still too dangerous for people to live there. More recently, air pollution caused by cars emitting nitrous oxide and brake dust, already linked to a range of health problems, exacerbated the effects of COVID-19 and led to increased death rates around the world in areas where air quality is poor.[13]

Cleaning pollution can incur huge financial costs. A leak at a BP pipeline at Prudhoe Bay in Alaska in 2006 spilled around 200,000 gallons of oil, which cost the company more than $100 million in fines, settlements of legal cases and clean-up costs. The *Exxon Valdez* oil spill in 1989, where more than ten million gallons of oil were spilled into the waters of Prince William Sound, Alaska, cost Exxon nearly $2 billion in clean-up costs, plus billions more in fines and litigation settlements.[14] Very often, though, these costs incurred by the companies are also just the tip of the iceberg. The long-term externalities in terms of poor health and environmental degradation are paid for by the communities where these disasters happen.

Social damage and environmental damage often overlap. Environmental pollution is also an issue that arouses widespread public anger, particularly in areas where the pollution occurs. Shell's conflict with the Ogoni people in Nigeria is an example of that overlap. The Ogoni were protesting not only at the fact that they were not benefitting from the riches that Shell was extracting from the ground in Nigeria but also that pollution was degrading the environment of their homeland. The environmental damage will take years to clean up.[15] Shell also got caught up in the conflict between the Ogoni and the Nigerian government, which arrested and executed a number of activists. The damage done to Shell's reputation was severe, and even twenty-five years later public opinion of Shell is highly affected by perceptions of what happened in Nigeria.

Companies are increasingly being held to account by a public concerned about issues like environmental degradation and the climate emergency.[16] Even relatively minor transgressions are now being exposed on social media, and issues like the impact of air pollution on COVID-19 fatalities are unlikely to go away any time soon.

Financial and Reputational Brand Damage

Scandals damage personal reputations. Some, like Fred Goodwin at Royal Bank of Scotland, have been stripped of knighthoods and honours; others have been forced from office and fled into exile to escape arrest; some are in prison. Even more importantly, they damage the reputation of corporate brands. A brand is one of the most powerful assets a company has, and any damage to its reputation affects the value of its brand, and reputation, or the 'esteem' in which a brand is held by stakeholders is a key component of that valuation.[17] That esteem once again depends on trust, and people are unlikely to trust an organization whose actions are causing unnecessary harm.

Settling lawsuits, paying fines and clearing the damage after a disaster are an increasingly costly affair. The levels of fines levied by regulators in particular are reaching new heights as governments try to bring home to corporations the consequences of what they do. Slaps on the wrist are increasingly less common. In 2017, Bloomberg News estimated that global banks had been fined over $321 billion, a sum greater than the gross national product of Australia, with Bank of America and JP Morgan Chase among the most heavily penalized.[18]

This is a useful source of income for governments and doubtless replaces some of the money lost through tax evasion, but it is not an ideal way to raise revenue. This is also money which is not spent to the benefit of other stakeholders. Every dollar paid in fines is a dollar lost which could have been spent on innovation to deliver better service to customers and/or reduce prices; which could have been spent on employee benefits, paying them better wages and giving them more training and better benefits to increase productivity and staff loyalty; investing in digital and other new technology to improve reach and, again, increase productivity; or return to shareholders to reward them for their investment and enable them to pay into pension pots and insurance policies.

More importantly, the system of fining rather than prosecuting offending companies is not having enough impact on the problem. The leak of more than 2000 Suspicious Activity Reports from the U.S. Financial Crimes Enforcement Network (FinCEN) in September 2020 revealed a vast array of transactions involving fraud and money-laundering, sometimes linked to organized crime groups. The papers also showed that many of the world's leading banks were apparently aware of these transactions, as was FinCEN itself. The billions in fines that have been paid do not appear to have had any deterrent effect; indeed, one US federal judge in Manhattan argued that the fines 'have become in effect a cost of doing business rather than a real punishment.'[19]

Over the long term, though, this behaviour is not sustainable. As with environmental damage and pollution, the actions of corrupt individuals and institutions are generating increasing levels of public resentment.[20] The reputational damage is hard to quantify, and it may be that some banks are cynically writing-off fines as a cost of doing business, but others like J.P. Morgan and Wells Fargo have recognized the damage these incidents do in terms of public trust and confidence and are trying to turn over a new leaf. Boards need to ensure that these efforts are genuine and not merely an attempt at creating good publicity to counter the bad.

The larger question, though, is why are boards allowing this damage to happen in the first place? It is easy to blame overly ambitious CEOs for leading companies into disaster, but boards are meant to be monitoring the CEO; it is they who make, or at least approve, decisions about strategic direction. Fred Goodwin's decision to buy ABN AMRO may have been the final straw that broke the camel's back at Royal Bank of Scotland, but the takeover decision was discussed and approved at board level. Given the obvious risks this transaction involved, it is hard to understand why the board agreed.

A Stakeholder Perspective

And yet, there are still some managers and leaders who will try to justify almost any behaviour so long as it turns a profit and increases value to shareholders. Amazon's strategy to pay as little tax as humanly possible, for example, is justified in the eyes of many on the grounds that the company's first duty is to maximize shareholder wealth—although even Milton Friedman said that companies must also pay their fair share of tax. In fact, this view rests on morally and legally dubious grounds. 'Nor does any rule of law mandate director obeisance to the ideology of share-price maximization,' argued a recent article in the *Harvard Law School Forum on Corporate Governance*. 'No statute anywhere enshrines or even endorses the objective of share-price maximization. Nor does case law require directors to manage the ongoing business and affairs of the corporation with the paramount goal of maximizing share price.' The same article went on to argue that

> [g]overnments charter corporations—and bestow upon them the remarkable gifts of perpetual life and limited liability—not primarily to make money for shareholders, but rather to promote the economy and opportunity for society at large. The essential obligation of corporate directors has thus historically been to the corporation itself: to nurture long-term economic growth that reaps benefits for, and avoids costly externalities on, the broader society. A corporation that succeeds in that effort will advance the interests of all its stakeholders, not just its shareholders. Conceived in this way, shareholder profit is not the sole objective of the corporation, but rather the by-product of a well-functioning corporate governance regime.[21]

It is as stakeholders—customers, employees, members of communities—that most of us interact with business and are affected by what they do. When companies engage in destructive behaviour, it is very often that larger group of stakeholders who pay the price. As customers, we pay that price through the use of defective goods and services, such as the faulty airbags manufactured by Takata and deployed in Honda cars, believed to be responsible for sixteen deaths and more than a hundred injuries worldwide.[22] Or we pay through the consumption of mis-sold services like the payment protection insurance (PPI) mis-sold by British banks over the course of many years. Sometimes, as in the case of PPI where the banks were forced to repay billions of pounds to customers, we eventually get compensation. Often we do not.

We have already discussed the harm caused by unemployment, including the knock-on effects of further job losses in other firms, but it is also worth discussing the harm that can be caused by employment. The Rana Plaza disaster is an example of how workers are forced to work in what are quite literally deadly conditions, but all around the world people in the garment industry work in sweatshop conditions. During the COVID-19 pandemic, these workers were unshielded and could not maintain social distancing, leaving them highly vulnerable. Front-line healthcare workers in hospitals and nursing homes also had, initially at least, to work in dangerous conditions without adequate personal protection equipment, and around the world thousands died as a result of contracting the virus.

Another example of harm caused through employment is institutionalized discrimination in the form of racism and sexism. We will discuss the sexual abuse scandals at Google in more detail, but Google is hardly unique. The scale of sexual abuse perpetrated by men like Harvey Weinstein and Jeffrey Epstein is shocking, but this too is just the tip of the iceberg.

As members of communities, we are also affected by the failings of companies, sometimes directly through pollution and environmental degradation, as well as indirectly through lost tax revenues and the failure to nurture economic growth. As the authors of the Harvard article observes, businesses exist in the first place because governments and people see them as engines for growth and prosperity.[23] What sometimes gets forgotten is that this means creating growth and prosperity over time. Simply making a fast buck is not responsible business and does not create long-term value for stakeholders. Any short-term gains in prosperity will dissipate quickly, more often than not leaving chaos behind.

And what of shareholders? They are stakeholders too, and their interests matter. They also have more direct authority than other stakeholders; they have the power to remove directors from the board, approve compensation awards and so on. But can bad behaviour by company executives be justified on the grounds that it creates shareholder value? In fact, the reality goes in the other direction. Corporate failures and scandals destroy value for shareholders, very often on a grand scale.

The bankruptcy of Enron cost shareholders $74 billion dollars, although some of this money was later recovered. Lehman Brothers had been valued at $60 billion on February 2007; nineteen months later the firm dissolved. Research suggests that during the crisis of 2008, British and American banks lost about 20 per cent of their value; by 2015 American banks had recovered part of their value but their British counterparts, by then labouring under the burden of billions of pounds in PPI repayments, had not.[24] During the same crisis the share price of Royal Bank of Scotland collapsed to under 12p. Shares in Mitsubishi Motors fell by 40 per cent following reports that the company had falsified fuel economy data, and Volkswagen shares fell by 23 per cent on the Deutsche Börse, representing a decline of $17.6 billion. Does any of this really look like enhancing shareholder value?

One possible answer is that stakeholders need to become more closely involved in governance, either indirectly through forms of consultation (stakeholder engagement) or directly through representation on the board (stakeholder governance). This concept has been under discussion for some time, and forms of governance involving greater direct involvement by stakeholder groups are already practised in some countries in Europe and east Asia, and there is a growing feeling elsewhere that change is needed. Larry Fink, CEO of investment group Black Rock, summarized that feeling in January 2018:

> Without a sense of purpose, no company, either public or private, can achieve its full potential. It will ultimately lose the licence to operate from key stakeholders. It will succumb to short-term pressures to distribute earnings, and, in the process, sacrifice investments in employee development, innovation, and capital expenditures that are necessary for long-term growth. It will remain exposed to activist campaigns that articulate a clearer goal, even if that goal serves only the shortest and narrowest of objectives. And ultimately, that company will provide subpar returns to the investors who depend on it to finance their retirement, home purchases, or higher education.[25]

To fulfil that purpose, it is argued, corporations need to listen to their stakeholders and allow them a voice in decision-making. Some writers have exposed the disconnect between democracy being the preferred model of political governance in many parts of the world and the apparent lack of democracy in business, where 'the governance process is based on controlling organizational members to ensure that they act in the shareholder's interests.'[26] We will come back to the concept of stakeholder engagement later in this book, but for the moment it is worth considering whether opening boardrooms to a greater range of influences and a wider selection of voices would improve governance.

Whether it would or not, the lesson of the past two chapters is surely clear by now. We are facing—and have faced for a very long time now—a global epidemic of board failure. Organizations on every continent and across every sector are affected, and the impacts on all of us—on our prosperity, our happiness, our health, our lives—are growing in severity. This needs to stop, for the sake of all of us. Boards need to be better at their job of leading the business. They need to set not just the strategy but also the culture of the business, and boards need to be independent of the executive, more effective and more responsible. It is time now to go below the waterline of the iceberg and see what lies beneath the surface.

Notes

1. Robert K. Merton, *On Social Structure and Science*, Chicago: University of Chicago Press, 1996.
2. Boivie et al., p. 5.
3. Heidi K. Gardner and Randall S. Peterson, 'Back Channels in the Boardroom: How to Prevent Side Conversations Between Directors From Blocking Progress', *Harvard Business Review*, September–October 2019.
4. https://www.deccanchronicle.com/nation/in-other-news/120520/experts-detect-more-gas-leak-risks-at-lg-polymer-factory-in-vizag.html.
5. https://www.nytimes.com/2012/12/06/world/asia/3-walmart-suppliers-made-goods-in-bangladeshi-factory-where-112-died-in-fire.html.
6. https://www.nytimes.com/2012/03/10/world/asia/critics-say-japan-ignored-warnings-of-nuclear-disaster.html.
7. Jennie E. Brand, 'The Far-Reaching Impact of Job Loss and Unemployment', *Annual Review of Sociology* 2015, https://doi.org/10.1146/annurev-soc-071913-043237.
8. https://www.peoplemanagement.co.uk/news/articles/mismanagement-pension-funds-reckless-bosses-criminal-offence.
9. https://www.financialdirector.co.uk/2019/04/03/pension-deficits-in-uk-companies-what-fds-need-to-know/.
10. https://ethicalfashioninitiative.org/.
11. Paul A. Laudicina, *World Out of Balance: Navigating Global Risks to Seize Competitive Advantage*, New York: McGraw-Hill, 2004.
12. https://news.un.org/en/story/2002/05/35182-efforts-reduce-industrial-effect-environment-uneven-un-agency-reports; https://www2.deloitte.com/uk/en/pages/energy-and-resources/articles/water-tight.html; David Friberg, D.G. Park, George Serafeim and T. Robert Zochowski, 'Corporate Environmental Impact: Measurement, Data and Information', Harvard Business School working paper 20-098.
13. https://www.weforum.org/agenda/2020/04/link-between-air-pollution-covid-19-deaths-coronavirus-pandemic/.
14. https://www.sfgate.com/bayarea/article/SAN-FRANCISCO-Punitive-damages-appealed-in-2523668.php.
15. https://www.theguardian.com/environment/2011/aug/04/niger-delta-oil-spill-clean-up-un.

16. https://www.theguardian.com/environment/2018/sep/07/profits-v-planet-can-big-business-and-the-environment-get-along.
17. Paul W. Farris et al., *Marketing Metrics*, Upper Saddle River: Pearson, 2010.
18. https://www.bloomberg.com/news/articles/2017-03-02/world-s-biggest-banks-fined-321-billion-since-financial-crisis.
19. https://www.icij.org/investigations/fincen-files/6-money-laundering-reforms-that-experts-say-need-to-happen-right-now/.
20. https://uk.reuters.com/article/uk-britain-banks/british-public-dont-trust-banks-10-years-after-crisis-survey-finds-idUKKBN1L11EL; https://www.nasdaq.com/articles/americans-still-angry-big-banks-2014-02-28.
21. https://corpgov.law.harvard.edu/2019/10/25/stakeholder-governance-issues-and-answers/.
22. https://www.caranddriver.com/news/a14499263/massive-takata-airbag-recall-everything-you-need-to-know-including-full-list-of-affected-vehicles/.
23. Ibid.
24. Salah U-Din and David Tripe, 'The Impact of Global Financial Crisis on Shareholder Value and Operational Efficiency of Banks', *SSRN Electronic Journal*, January 2018.
25. https://observer.com/2018/01/blackrock-chief-larry-fink-open-letter-advice/.
26. Edward Dennehy, 'Corporate Governance: A Stakeholder Model', *International Journal of Business, Governance and Ethics* 7 (2), 2012.

4

Causes of Dysfunctional Culture

Understanding the cultural dynamics of boards is critical to understanding why crises emerge and how to make boards more effective at preventing them. Board culture, like any culture, is based on the beliefs and values that board members hold in common, and manifests itself in how board members behave towards each other, how they communicate with each other and, perhaps most importantly, how they make decisions.

This understanding of the importance of culture is beginning slowly to permeate regulators' thinking about board effectiveness. For example, the Financial Reporting Council (FRC) in the UK argued in 2016 that

> [a] healthy culture both protects and generates value. It is therefore important to have a continuous focus on culture, rather than wait for a crisis. Poor behaviour can be exacerbated when companies come under pressure. A strong culture will endure in times of stress and mitigate the impact. This is essential in dealing effectively with risk and maintaining resilient performance.[1]

'Strong governance underpins a healthy culture,' the FRC continues, 'and boards should demonstrate good practice in the boardroom and promote good governance throughout the business.'

In his book *The Independent Director*, Gerry Brown summarizes the role of the independent director as follows:

> The independent director is just that, independent. He or she stands back from the firm and examines it with a critical eye. Through both the main board and various committees, he or she ensures that the company is managed in the best

interest of its stakeholders. ... He or she oversees the company's compliance with all relevant laws and regulations, and that it is governed in a moral way. If the independent director detects failings of governance, then it is his or her duty to speak out and warn the board of what is happening; even if the board does not want to hear it.[2]

Brown goes on to stress the importance of having an independent chair, who guides the culture of the board and plays a vital role in guarding board independence. Difficulties arise in jurisdictions where unitary leadership is permitted and the chair of the board also plays an executive role such as CEO; this often happens in India and the USA.

This results in a great deal of power being concentrated in the hands of one person, and it can be very hard for independent directors to exercise that critical eye and to confront and challenge when needed. Non-executive independence is extremely difficult to maintain under these circumstances. Boards in these cases are—and clearly are expected to be—complicit in whatever the CEO or executive chair wants to do. In the aftermath of a number of corporate scandals in India, including the collapse of Satyam, Deloitte India issued a sharp rebuke to Indian boards with a firm instruction to reform their cultures.

> Indian boards must move away from being a rubber stamp to being a strategic asset for the company. They need to set the tone from the top in promoting a transparent culture that promotes effective dialogues among the directors, senior management, and various function and risk managers. Boards should look beyond the 'old boy network' and select directors with individual areas of expertise, and invest on an ongoing basis on their formal and informal education. Independent directors should significantly contribute to the functioning of the board through requisite understanding of the company and the business.[3]

A strong board comprised of genuinely independent directors, with a positive boardroom culture that allows directors to behave and act independently, will have a much better chance of spotting problems before they arise and requiring corrective action by management, a point we will come back to later in this book. This is difficult but not impossible to achieve when the chair and the CEO are the same person, or in other cases the chair is the most recent CEO. In these cases it is easier for the executive to take control of the board and distort the culture of the business for personal or relatively narrow interests gain.

When board culture becomes distorted, however, there is a strong risk that the board itself will become dysfunctional and cease to do its job of monitoring the executive effectively. In the cases we studied for this book, we found six key types of distortion: *cultural amplification, diffusion of responsibility, missing key voices, groupthink, overly controlled cultures* and *lack of independence from management.* It is important to note from the beginning that many dysfunctional board cultures are subject to more than one of these distortions, and sometimes even to all six. Figure 4.1 shows the theoretical frameworks that describe each dysfunction, how they originate and the problems they create for boards and, finally the role the board has to play in finding cures for the ailments and some suggestions as to what those cures might be. We will come back to those cures in Part III; for the moment, let us concentrate on identifying the dysfunctions and their symptoms.

The Subordinated Board

The dominant logic for the purpose of boards has been the agency perspective, which views boards as a governance and control mechanism for protecting the interests of shareholders from self-serving managers.[4] This is the lens that has dominated the logic of advice and regulation of boards for the past fifty years. Studies point towards board composition (size, insider/outsider ratio, demographics/diversity, functional specialists), board leadership (unitary or duality) and compensation incentives of board members as the factors that predict effectiveness. It is generally argued that higher numbers of 'outside' independent directors will provide better monitoring as per the agency perspective.

This independence and outside perspective can be compromised, however, when powerful individuals dominate or control the board—as is the risk in cases of unitary leadership where the CEO is also the chair of the board. From this perspective, unitary leadership is akin to trusting the fox to guard the hen house. The board becomes less relevant; individual directors lose their independence and fall, more or less willingly, into line with the wishes of the dominant executive chair. The problem becomes even more acute when the executives are also significant shareholders or have dominant, charismatic personalities—or sometimes, a combination of the two.

The key cultural dysfunction happens when the board, including the independent directors, cannot put distance between itself and the executives, meaning the board cannot engage in effective independent scrutiny. At best, directors are resentfully silent, knowing what is wrong but feeling unable to speak; at worst, the board becomes a victim of Stockholm syndrome,

Board Name and Dysfunction	Frame/Theory	Core Problem for Boards	Origin of Dysfunction	Role of the Board	Board Effectiveness Focus
The Subordinated Board Lack of Independence (subordinate to the executive)	Agency (e.g., Daily, Dalton, and Cannella, 2003)	Separation of ownership and management: sometimes managers care about their own interests, not the interests of their organization or its shareholders	When the executive controls the board	Align incentives for individuals to do the right thing for the business versus self-interests	Director independence • More Independent versus executive directors • Stop co-optation of independent by executive directors • Director training on incentives • Outside recruiting agency for selection • More shareholder/stakeholder advocacy
The Imbalanced Board Missing Key Voices	Resource Dependence (e.g., Salancik & Pfeffer, 1978)	Organizations with more resources do better	When board does not see or appreciate that relevant voices or resources are missing or muted	Provide resources to the organization (e.g., advice, networks, etc.)	More advice/bigger boards are better Diversity of perspective is better Broader networks better Monitor turnover of underrepresented groups Focus on belonging (i.e., in addition to selection)
The Distended Board Cultural Amplification	Sensemaking (e.g., Weick, 1995; Westphal, 1999)	The environment is complex and ever-changing so true signals are hard to detect	When the situation changes and culture that was once helpful starts to warp the organization	Choose appropriate organizational performance parameters and culture	Change culture to interpret environment differently Get outside assessment of culture Diversity of experience is better
The Bystander Board Diffusion of Responsibility	Upper Echelons (e.g., Hambrick & Mason, 1984)	Dominant coalitions control boards and organizations	When the rules for achieving status (e.g. pay & promotions) are not clear or do not yield people who will do what is in the interests of the organization	Manage status dynamics in the organization	Structural and role clarity Clear lines of authority Demographic dissimilarity (i.e., coalitions should be on values and performance, not demographics) Chair should be higher status than CEO
The Bureaucratic Board Rule-bound	Group Dynamics (e.g., Zander, 1993)	Directors need to collaborate effectively to make high quality decisions and reduce risk of failure	When the board substitutes rules and procedure for genuine interaction, in order to avoid disagreements	Ensure collaborative culture to make effective decisions (i.e., members talk, listen to others, and respond to their ideas)	Reduce regulations and box-ticking Less majority rule to make decisions Manage (not ignore) conflict Ensure all members have a role in the board (i.e., reduces social loafing) Clear, measurable purpose Group interaction surveys and discussions
The Conforming Board	Group Dynamics: Groupthink (e.g., Janis, 1982).	Directors need to collaborate effectively to make high quality decisions and reduce risk of failure	Strong pressure on organization, highly cohesive group, and directive leadership encourage consensus seeking/rule following	Make effective decisions through rigorous debate	Vigilant decision making • Encourage challenge in the discussion • Use of experts to challenge • Clear problems and goals • Evaluate all options rigorously

Fig. 4.1 Board dysfunctions: theories and concepts

identifying so closely with the executives that they become cheerleaders and supporters rather than monitors.

The problem of tame boards nodding meekly along with owner-managers is well known and is one reason why the idea of a separation between owner-ship and control gained traction in the USA and later in Britain.[5] The idea was that professional managers who had no stake in the company would act in the company's best interests, and further, that boards of directors would be better empowered to monitor and scrutinize their activities. The aim was double independence, of both boards and executives, each working in the best inter-ests of the company. This was always going to be a vain hope, and as the politi-cal philosopher James Burnham pointed out in *The Managerial Revolution*, when the owners of businesses vacated power, managers stepped into the gap.[6] In the modern world this manifests itself in over-mighty leaders like Ferdinand Piëch at Volkswagen or Cees van der Hoeven of Royal Ahold, the architect of his company's failed global expansion who drove his strategy through by dom-inating both his fellow executives and the board.

Nor have owner-managers disappeared. The idea of the separation of own-ership and control never really caught on outside the Anglo-Saxon business world; personally owned or family owned businesses remain the dominant model in many parts of the world. The tech revolution has also seen the rise of new firms where the founding owners are not only senior executives but also wield great power on the board thanks to their shareholdings. Google is one such example; Facebook is another. In these circumstances, it can be very difficult for independent directors to be truly independent and exercise proper scrutiny of executive actions.

Red Flag

Lack of Independence: does the board ever seek advice from outside the execu-tive team, either within the organization or externally? When facing crises or major problems, does the board distinguish between the executive and the inde-pendent directors? Are the latter seen as an important resource in helping to make difficult decisions, or are they expected to rubber stamp whatever the executive puts before them?

The Imbalanced Board

The term 'employee voice' refers to the ability of employees to have a say in the affairs of the business and, potentially at least, to exert influence on man-agement. When the employee voice is strong, that usually means management is listening and the interests of employees are being considered; when it is weak, managers act either in what they think are the interests of others (i.e. if they have positive intent) or they act in their own unfettered interests and do pretty much as they please.

As various researchers have identified, one of the problems with the concept of employee voice is the assumption that employees are homogenous and speak with one voice.[7] One of the consequences is that diverse voices—of women, of minorities, of different interest groups—are drowned by the majority or are absent altogether. They become *missing voices*.

One of the perspectives, or lenses, through which boards are viewed by researchers is the *resource dependence* perspective. Resources are directly linked to board performance; the more resources the organization has, the more effective it will be. Boards are seen as a critical resource for providing advice, counsel, legitimacy and social capital/network resources to a firm.[8] However, the quality of the advice and counsel that boards give depends on their ability to collectively understand and analyse key issues.

To function properly, boards need to be debating chambers. Directors must be able to air a broad range of views, asking genuine questions and stimulating debate in order to ensure that key issues are discussed and dissected. Of course at the end of the day the board should attempt to reach a consensus (although this will not always be possible; sometimes compromises have to be made). But if key voices are unable to be heard, or are absent from the table entirely, the quality of the debate suffers. The wrong decision is taken; or sometimes, no decision is made at all.

One of the big reasons why key voices are absent is lack of board diversity. This is a worldwide phenomenon; Indian and Japanese organizations are just as bad at board diversity as those in the West. Established elites have always been hesitant to open the door to newcomers who might threaten their power base or suggest radical ideas, with the result that boards often represent a very narrow segment of their stakeholders rather than the entire constellation.

Diversity is about much more than gender or ethnicity or disability. Simply putting people who are in some way 'different' into the room is not enough. Four of the directors at Alphabet (the parent company of Google) were female, including two independent directors, and yet that was not enough to prevent a series of sexual abuse scandals in which the board was partly complicit.[9] Boards also need people with diverse backgrounds and lived experience, and different mindsets and ways of approaching and analysing problems. Most of all, though, boards need not just diversity but *inclusivity*, ensuring those people from diverse backgrounds can speak and will be heard. As the old saying goes, diversity is being invited to the party; inclusion means feeling confident enough to get up and dance.

The potential benefits of diversity have long been known. As far back as 2003 the Tyson Report on the Recruitment and Development of Non-Executive Directors noted that boards benefit in two ways:

> First, groups make better decisions to the extent that the information available to the group is more diverse, provided the group understands 'who knows what' and takes advantage of this knowledge. Second, diverse teams can leverage their diversity to reach out more effectively to a broader set of constituencies to help avert problems or solve them when they arise.[10]

The more homogenous the board is, so the argument goes, the less likely it will have the ability to recognize its lack of diversity and understand which key voices are missing. Homogeneous boards are unlikely to realize how homogeneous they are because they do not hear the voices telling them that there are alternative perspectives. One of the results of this weakness is a skewed attitude to risk. Without those missing voices to raise key issues, the board does not know what risks it is facing because there is no one there to highlight the issues and make sure they are aired and discussed. Abuses of power, strategic blunders, accounting irregularities and a host of other sins are able to hide in plain sight. In some quarters, albeit slowly, this is being recognized. Goldman Sachs, an organization which has had a number of well-publicized problems in the past, is not only making a commitment towards greater diversity in-house but is encouraging its clients to do the same. Candidates for IPOs, for example, are being encouraged to promote diversity on their own boards.[11]

Finally, a more diverse board makes it more likely that there will be directors who are prepared to challenge the status quo. As the entrepreneur Malcolm Forbes once said, diversity is the art of thinking independently. As with the subordinated board, we know that lack of independence for the board is risky. That diversity was fatally lacking at Google and Alphabet.

However, there is a real doubt as to whether diversity on its own actually creates much benefit. For example, Katherine Klein, one of the world's leading authorities on the role of women in business, concluded that simply putting women onto boards results in very little measurable difference in corporate performance. Other studies have confirmed this.[12] What really matters is whether those people from diverse backgrounds are able to contribute to the work of the board and have meaningful involvement in decision-making. Without inclusivity, there is even a risk that board cohesion could deteriorate as people from different backgrounds, using different vocabularies, strive to understand each other and make themselves understood.

For key voices to be heard, then, two things are needed. First, the voices must be present in the room to be heard. Second, the culture of the board needs to embrace them, accept their diversity as something to be valued, and make certain the board's values and the values of those individual directors fit together. Recruitment and selection need to focus not just on getting diverse directors but also getting the *right* directors who have an independent mind-set and are able and willing to work with the rest of the board. The chair needs to make sure these diverse directors are heard in meetings and, as we said above, feel comfortable enough to express those differing views. If all this happens, then we do indeed start to see a measurable effect on performance. Although when the culture does not truly embrace diverse voices, the additional diversity makes it harder to understand each other, misunderstandings happen and performance can actually decrease (Fig. 4.2).

> **Red Flag**
>
> *Missing Key Voices*: is the organization the subject of a social media campaign or protests, or negative comments on web-based public chat rooms? If so, are these protests being discussed in the boardroom, or are they being pushed aside? If the latter, it may be that there is no one to represent the dissenters on the board. Or, has the board looked at turnover and/or retention of employees by diversity categories? When these are uneven, that is a strong signal that the workplace, and likely the board, is missing key voices. It may be time to start checking for signs of unconscious bias within the organization.

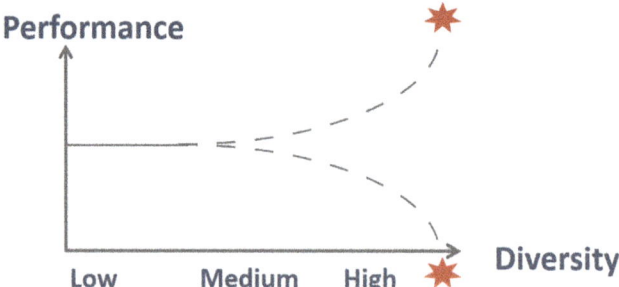

Fig. 4.2 Performance/diversity

The Distended Board

The problem of cultural amplification has its origins in how organizations engage in sense-making, defined roughly by organization theorist Karl Weick as the process by which people give meaning to their collective experience.[13] The world is complex and ever-evolving, and management needs help interpreting the messy signals. Many things can change in an organization or its environment: the business model, the underlying micro-economics, moving from tangible to intangible assets, the parameters for measuring and judging performance and so on. How do we decide what is important and what is not? How do we choose which parameters to focus on, and which to ignore?

We make that choice through a process of sense-making, interpreting the signals we receive, giving them meaning and weighting them according to perceived importance, but that process is also subject to bias. Reality monitoring, for example, means that we distinguish between two types of memories, 'external' memories generated by our perception of things and events, and 'internal' memories which are generated by analysis and rationalization; however, we do not always treat these two kinds of memory as equal.[14] The things that we, collectively, think are important become part of our shared organizational culture.

A robust and positive organizational culture can be a powerful asset. The work of Jennifer Chatman and her colleagues suggests that companies with a strongly cohesive and adaptive culture outperform those that do not by about 15 per cent, and a study from Harvard Business School in 2016 also argued that when employees share common values and a common purpose, this results in superior organizational performance.[15] When everyone shares a common identity and believes in the same values and goals, the organization becomes greater than the sum of its parts and can drive forward towards its goals. Strong cultures enable companies to achieve greatness.

But there is a negative side to this as well. Sometimes, particular elements of the culture start to dominate. Those elements become *amplified*, warping and distorting the original culture into a dysfunctional version of itself, Dr Jekyll transforming into Mr Hyde. Amplification happens particularly in cases where the organization has outgrown its original culture but has not yet evolved a new one. Instead, the sense-making process continues to assert that the same old things are important and/or that new ideas should be shunned. People cling to the original culture, or parts of it, even after it is clear that the culture is no longer working well.

So long as the board is aware of this, it can take corrective steps to guide the culture back onto its original course. Problems arise when the board takes its eye off the game. Amplification can happen with surprising swiftness when no one is watching and turn the culture into something threatening and more dangerous.

Even worse, the board's own culture can become infected. Far from challenging amplification, the board becomes part of the problem. Its sense-making becomes restricted and narrow, focusing on just a handful of measures, like competitiveness or productivity, and ignoring wider issues and strategic threats. Risks are taken without really understanding the nature of risk; alternatively, high levels of risk are accepted because the culture cannot be questioned. The board becomes reluctant to look at anything that is not part of its increasingly narrow focus, and other issues—bullying and sexual harassment, health and safety issues, mis-selling, corruption—are ignored or swept under the carpet. Sometimes abuses are accepted as being the price of success, a kind of transaction cost of rapid growth. Never mind the long hours culture that is undermining employee health, the logic goes; this is how we got to be great, so people just need to be stronger.

When the board fails to challenge cultural amplification, or even notice it, and when board culture itself becomes amplified, the organization itself is increasingly at risk—and when at the same time, the board's ability to recognize risk and deal with it effectively has been compromised—then we have the recipe for a perfect storm. That is more or less what happened at Uber, leading to huge crisis and loss of trust. In this book we have chosen Uber as an example, but it is far from the only case.

Red Flag

Cultural Amplification: would directors tell their most racy tales or 'war stories' about what goes on in the organization to their friends and family? Or would they keep silent because other people 'would not understand'? Do directors have to explain their organization's culture to other people, in order for them to understand what is happening to them?

The Bystander Board

Diffusion of responsibility is a well-known psychological phenomenon. In a famous study from 1968, psychologists Bibb Latané and John Darley found that most people would rush to help in an emergency if they were the only person present, but if they were part of a group they were more likely to hang back and let someone else take responsibility.[16] Latané and Darley also found that the larger the group, the more likely people were to wait for someone else to step forward. As a result, instead of raising the issue for discussion, everyone waits for everyone else to do so, and no one actually does. The moment passes, the agenda moves on and the opportunity is lost.

Other studies have found that in larger groups people are less likely to volunteer to undertake particular tasks or assume positions of leadership. Other factors that can lead to diffusion of responsibility include division of labour (people focus on their own task and forget their responsibilities to the group as a whole), lack of expertise (people don't step up because they hope someone more qualified than themselves will take over) and moral disengagement, meaning that people feel no connection with the problem and therefore feel no compulsion to get involved. The latter is sometimes described as the 'bystander effect.' Another study found that in risky situations, diffusion of responsibility leads the group to transfer risk onto the shoulders of a single individual, absolving the rest from responsibility.[17]

We can also link diffusion of responsibility to the *upper echelons theory* proposed by Donald Hambrick and Phyllis Mason.[18] Upper echelons theory holds that organizations are dominated by a small number of people at the top. The upper echelon, whose culture and ways of working set the tone for the rest of the organization. If the top team works well together, the organization will prosper; if they neglect their duties and turn to factionalism and contests for status, the risks to the organization will correspondingly increase. This can apply equally to conflicts between the board and the executive, or between board members themselves.

One of the features of a healthy board culture is that independent directors are not afraid to challenge the executives, and each other. Healthy debate is very important to avoid problems such as groupthink and the subordinated board. The American governance consultant Nancy Axelrod calls this a 'culture of inquiry,' where mutual respect and constructive debate lead to better decision-making.[19]

At the same time, however, boards need to work collectively and take full ownership of problems, and they must be prepared to move swiftly and in unison when a crisis arises. This may seem like a paradox; how can there be individual challenge and debate and, at the same time, collective decision-making? The problem can be tricky to solve, especially when differing points of view are strongly held. It is up to the chair to bring the different points of view together and build a consensus.

When this does not happen—when there is a lack of collective responsibility and ownership—the problem of diffusion of responsibility arises. Here, the cultural dysfunction manifests itself as an abdication of responsibility for the whole. Key players point at one another, or perhaps at a previously identified fall guy, and collective ownership of major problems goes out the window. As a result, responses to problems and crises become glacially slow because everyone is pushing decisions onto other people.

At board level, diffusion of responsibility is a clear sign that the 'culture of inquiry' is absent and that directors, instead of working collaboratively to solve problems, are failing to engage. At BP in 2010, diffusion of responsibility played a major role in the corporation's deepest ever crisis. We saw how the board failed to respond swiftly or decisively to the crisis, but that diffusion of responsibility had begun long before. Boards are responsible for than just metrics of performance; these are important for monitoring how the organization works, but the real impact is in how the organization shapes its culture around the metrics. Focusing on metrics means that what is measured gets done, and what is not measured is not a priority.

Boards have a primary responsibility for ensuring that the people in the upper echelons of the organization, who exercise control over it, represent the organization's values and serve its legacy. They literally 'set the rules' for who gets rewarded by selecting a CEO and the culture of the business. In BP's case, as with so many others, the board failed in its duty to ensure that the right kind of senior leaders were in the right places.

Red Flag

Diffusion of Responsibility: is the board monitoring how things happen in addition to what happens? How is at least as important as what. Do directors feel uncomfortable when someone else on the board says or does something embarrassing? If not, are they taking enough responsibility? Is silence taken, consciously or unconsciously, as agreement? Remember, boards need to speak to the world with a unified voice; so if someone says something that turns out to be incorrect, it reflects poorly on everyone.

The Bureaucratic Board

Rules-Bound Cultures

The group dynamic perspective on a board dates back to the 1950s as the developing research on group dynamics began to be applied to understanding natural groups such as juries, political cabinets and boards. The insight is that all groups of people working together have to navigate various tensions. We mostly think of task versus relationships, but equally important is the tension between individual autonomy and allowing individuals to engage work as they see fit, versus group rules that allow individuals to coordinate. Boards have strong rules-focus because they demand a unified external voice. The risk is in taking this too far. Rules-bound cultures emerge when the organizational pressure to conform becomes so severe that the organization establishes strict sets of rules and procedures which must be obeyed.

Rules and procedures are of course necessary, especially in highly regulated sectors such as financial services or healthcare. Problems begin when the guardians of the rules are invested with near-total authority, including the authority to impose severe sanctions on anyone who breaks the rules. Rules become sacrosanct. This tends to result not only in conformity of action but also in conformity of thinking. Social identity theory kicks in again, and people conform in order to gain approval and escape punishment. Conformity then becomes embedded in the roles people play and the norms and performance targets they work to; indeed, conformity itself becomes the dominant norm. Rules and procedure replace ordinary human interaction, and individual instinct and judgement are no longer trusted.

In his book *On The Psychology of Military Incompetence*, Norman Dixon observed the dangers of cultures where absolute authority is vested in a few people, without oversight or scrutiny, citing again the British army and navy where rigid obedience to authority means that people lower down in the organization have become immunized against taking risks of any kind. This results in a refusal to meet the demands of the changing world; we convince ourselves that the systems that have worked for us in the past are working now and will continue to work in the future. We found this culture to be particularly embedded in the Big Four accounting firms.

Back in the days of their foundation, audit and accountancy firms led the way in establishing good practice in governance. In 1849 during the height of the railway mania, it was William Deloitte who introduced the practice of external audit at Great Western Railway. Known for his probity and ability, Deloitte did his job so well that the directors of Great Western recommended to the government that the practice of external audit be made universal. Forty years later Edwin Waterhouse, co-founder of Price Waterhouse the Pw of PwC, was one of the leading figures in both Britain and the USA calling for reform of company accounts to ensure greater transparency and honesty. He was also a founder member of the Institute of Chartered Accountants of England and Wales, and worked tirelessly to turn accountancy into a respected profession.

The standards of professionalism Deloitte and Waterhouse developed have spread around the world, but the firms to which they gave their names have not always moved with the times. There is virtually no independent governance; at time of writing the Big Four in the USA still have only three independent directors between them. All four engage in practices which lead to obvious conflict of interests of the kind that has already claimed the fifth global accounting and audit firm, Arthur Andersen. The warning bell from Andersen's fall has not been heard within the profession. The list of blunders, disasters and scandals into which the Big Four have fallen goes on and on, and it is probably only a matter of time before another goes the way of Arthur Andersen. In the end, reform may be forced upon them, at least in the UK where the Financial Reporting Council has instructed the Big Four to separate its auditing and consulting functions by 2024.[20]

One of the problems that besets overly controlled cultures is that rules, and conformity to those rules, become paramount. Performance is judged by how well one executes on the rules, rather than on other criteria such as customer satisfaction or scandals averted. Judgement, which should play an important role in spotting problems before they arise and finding response to them, plays an unfortunately small role; all that matters is following the rules.

Bibb Latané's work on social impact theory suggests that over time, as people work closely together, their ideas affect each other and create greater conformity. This process of consolidation gradually embraces the entire organization, with fewer and fewer people prepared to or able to express dissent.[21] However, this does not mean the minority or critical viewpoints go away. For those who are prepared to take the risk, pathways around the rules can always be found. Ironically, it is under regimes that most value conformity and press for it the hardest, that one finds people who are most likely to walk a fine line on breaking rules by stepping well over the moral boundaries. Overly controlled cultures thus have two potential sources of risk. The first is the blinkered thinking and outlook that comes with adherence to the rules and at all costs. The second is the presence of a few dangerous outliers who can, through their actions, bring the organization down.

Red Flag

Rules-Bound Culture: when a crisis hits, does the board focus first on process, how things are done, or on content, the data or information presented? How difficult is it to challenge or change the process? Are there generalized customs concerning who needs to sign onto what, or are there specified processes/formulas? Does the board pretty much always require a formal vote on key issues?

The Conforming Board

The notion that safety is to be found in numbers is found throughout human history and seems to be hard-wired into our thinking processes. In his book *The Undiscovered Self*, the psychologist Carl Jung noted how we seek the company of others whenever danger threatens; and, further, that we adapt our behaviour in order to fit in with our group in order to be accepted and enjoy the safety the group offers, however illusory it sometimes can be.[22] In organizations this sometimes results in the condition known as *groupthink*—a term inspired by George Orwell's *1984*, though Orwell did not actually use the word. In conditions of groupthink, people make decisions not so much to achieve the best possible result, but to ensure that their own conclusions conform with those of the people around them.

Groupthink is part of the larger phenomenon of group dynamics.[23] Two important elements of group dynamics play a role in the creation of groupthink: social identity and group cohesiveness. Social identity describes how people will modify their behaviour to fit into a group, perhaps suppressing their own personal views and desires in order to be accepted by the rest of the group; cohesiveness refers to the forces that compel members of a group to remain together, including the emotional need for belonging, morale, personal and social attraction. These can be powerful positive forces, leading to high levels of productivity and performance, but they can have negative aspects as well.

'The more amiability and *esprit de corps* there is among the members of a policy-making ingroup,' wrote the psychologist Irving Janis, 'the greater the danger that independent critical thinking will be replaced by groupthink, which is likely to result in irrational and dehumanizing actions directed against outgroups.'[24] Janis studied the impact of groupthink on political, military and business decision-making and concluded that it led not only to domestic and foreign policy disasters—his early work on the attack on Pearl Harbor and the Bay of Pigs fiasco and the abortive American-backed invasion of Cuba in 1961 are particularly good descriptions of groupthink in action—but also to persecution and violence against minorities who do not fit into the main group.

Janis found similar examples of groupthink in a board, notably Ford's introduction of the Edsel brand which proved to be an expensive flop. Fixated on the need to close the gap between themselves and General Motors, Ford executives failed to listen to warning voices suggesting that the market for Edsel which everyone imagined did not actually exist. The board closed its mind to dissenting views and pushed the project through, overriding even the objections of Edsel Ford's son, Henry Ford II.

Groupthink is not a passive phenomenon. As Norman Dixon observed, 'far from diminishing the chances of ineptitude, the group actually accentuates the effects of those very traits which may lead to incompetence in individual commanders.'[25] In other words, groupthink will make an incompetent leader even more incompetent by amplifying the leader's weaknesses.

Studies of groupthink often assume that people willingly sublimate themselves to the group and adapt their behaviour in order to blend. However, George Orwell painted a different picture in 1984, showing the masses cowed into obedience by the overwhelming authority of Big Brother. Psychologist Stanley Milgram also noted how conformity can be enforced by threat.[26] Groupthink often occurs when highly directive leadership is also present.

A further aspect of groupthink that deserves mention is the concept of social loafing. First detected in sporting events such as tug-of-war competitions, social loafing asserts that when people are competing individually they will give their full effort, but when they are part of a team they will often hold back, expending less effort on the assumption that someone else will engage the slack. Sometimes this works, but if everyone is engaging in social loafing at the same time, the end result is significantly less than the sum of its parts.

Boards of directors, working in close proximity to each other and often under conditions of considerable risk and pressure, are particularly prone to groupthink, consciously or unconsciously. This again leads to a heavily skewed version of risk. Janis described how groups take one side of an argument only, dismissing any alternatives as being unworthy of discussion. This position of safety where no one raises questions or concerns, as both Janis and Dixon argued, is an illusion. All too often, the position the board chooses is in fact dangerously risky because no one raises questions. The case of the Royal Bank of Scotland brutally exposes the consequences of groupthink, consequences which the British public is still paying for.

Red Flag

Groupthink: do directors feel under pressure to agree constantly with the rest of the board? Do they hold back from speaking their minds? Do they go along with the majority in public, while secretly wishing they were able to visibly disagree? Or do they feel that if everyone else has taken a position, it is their duty to go along with them and not make waves? Are they challenging people at the right time? Do they have a strong need to be liked, accepted? Are they afraid that if they speak up, they will be ostracized?

It is worth reiterating the point made earlier that many dysfunctional boards suffer from more than one of these distortions. We have chosen these six detailed case studies because they exemplify particular distortions, but these are not the only distortions present; there is evidence of groupthink at BP, of missing voices at Facebook and so on. As the illustration earlier showed, all these distortions exist in close proximity to each other and influence each other (Fig. 4.3).

Why do these distortions appear? What drives them? Before turning to the case studies, it is worth quickly looking at some of the distorting forces that lead to these problems.

Distorting Forces: Cognitive Bias and Risk

Central to board culture is the ability to evaluate and estimate risk in an accurate manner, and here boards suffer from several forms of collective cognitive bias. One of these is optimism bias which, put simply, means that people have a tendency to believe what they wish to believe unless someone presents them with irrefutable evidence to the contrary; and sometimes, even that is not enough. Optimism bias tends to take the form of statements such as, 'everything is fine and we don't have a problem,' 'it can't happen here' or 'if it does happen, it won't happen to us.'

The second form of bias is illusory superiority, often referred to as the Dunning-Kruger effect, in which boards and board members believe themselves to be more capable and competent than they really are. In the words of psychologist David Dunning, 'All of us have pockets of incompetence we don't recognize.'[27] We cannot recognize our areas of incompetence because it takes a degree of knowledge about something to judge the knowledge we do have. Lack of self-knowledge and self-awareness is the curse of many boards and is often the result of a lack of proper, impartial board evaluation including rigorous and honest skills assessments.

The third form is the Langer effect, sometimes known as the introspection illusion or the illusion of control, in which we imagine we have control over a situation because our own self-esteem refuses to allow us to believe that we do not. This is a trap into which even experienced professionals sometimes fall, as they come to believe that their own experience gives them superior knowledge and assume, often rather arrogantly, that *only* they can control the situation. The combination of these biases often leads to *threat rigidity*, 'essentially freezing innovation and resorting to actions that have worked in the past rather than creating crucial new approaches.'[28]

Categorization of Dysfunction: Symptoms/Factors

Distended Boards – Cultural Amplification

Definition: culture intensifies, becoming exaggerated and dysfunctional or misdirected (e.g., Uber).

Symptoms/Factors: Board is so focused on one or two things (such as competitiveness) that it cannot see other board development needs.

General Interventions: Require an outside assessment of organization and engage culture change.

Bystander Boards – Diffusion of Responsibility

Definition: Key players point to everyone else re: problems; no one takes responsibility (e.g, BP).

Symptoms/Factors: Independent directors not stepping up; performance of Chair, including their performance appraisals not get enough attention; individual director effectiveness; the role of the Board.

General Interventions: Requires clear terms of reference, committees, roles.

Imbalanced Boards – Missing Key Voices

Definition: Lack of diversity of background, specific required knowledge, etc. (e.g., Google)

Symptoms/Factors: Quality of IDs - explain skills and experience and personal qualities needed; digital challenges not really addressed.

General Interventions: Focus on belonging and inclusion (i.e., more than new faces).

Conforming Boards - Groupthink

Definition: Identity threat causing directors to go along with others, not raise legitimate concerns.

Symptoms/Factors: Lack of effective annual Board evaluations to focus on performance improvement of boards.

General Interventions: Be more vigilant in decision making, structured decision making, attention to any disagreements, etc.

Bureaucratic Boards – Rule Bound Cultures

Definition: Extreme focus on rules and process results in ignoring or sidelining content or ideas.

Symptoms/Factors: Committee organisation and processes no longer functional; board processes and supporting information and materials (cannot change).

General Interventions: Instinct is to cut costs and tighten belt, which generally backfires; focus on innovation and ideas instead.

Subordinated Boards - Lack of Independence

Definition: Independent directors are not, in fact, independent from the executive (e.g., Facebook).

Symptoms/Factors: Insufficient involvement or concern with strategy or succession planning; insufficient independence in board culture and dynamics and board relationships with CEO (incl combined Chair/CEO); remuneration issues/ excessive bonuses.

Interventions: Director and board training, selection via agency, clear guidelines.

Fig. 4.3 Categorization of dysfunction: symptoms/factors

Taken together, these forms of behaviour can create a lethal combination. They allow boards to believe that all is well, and the situation is under control, when it manifestly is not. Only when the crisis explodes do boards finally spring into action—or not. In many of the cases we will discuss in this book, the board sat like rabbits caught in the headlights, and only much later did they get around to asking those hard questions they should have asked earlier. In other cases, boards did react decisively, but too late. The damage had already been done, and all the board could do was try to mitigate the worst of it.

Crisis, according to an article in *Harvard Business Review*, produces its own biases in thinking. Three in particular have been identified: (1) narrow thinking, or 'falling back on existing remedies' rather than taking the risk of trying something new; (2) deferring to the leader, hoping the latter will come up with magic bullet solutions and (3) conformity, a form of herd instinct that compels directors to seek unity and consensus, when in fact debate and challenge may be urgently required.[29] Going further, the leader may attempt to pressure group members into a false consensus, citing the danger and the need for unity as reason for everyone to toe the line. Needless to say, this is not a good way to make decisions.

Of course, it is not only boards that are guilty of biases in thinking. We all suffer from them to some extent, especially under pressure. As the old saying goes, when you are up to your neck in alligators, it is hard to remember that your original objective was to drain the swamp. And, if we are honest, most of us only start looking for problems and asking questions when things have gone wrong rather than pre-emptively trying to assess board dynamics risk. But the status quo is not good enough; it is not working. As already noted, audits and board evaluations, which are intended to identify problems before they occur, are too often ineffective. We will come back to the issue of board evaluation in more detail later in this book.

Distorting Forces: Ineffectiveness and Complacency

The Harvey Nash/LBS Leadership Institute report for 2019 identified two types of dysfunctional board cultures: *ineffective boards* and *complacent boards*.

Ineffective boards were characterized by a sense of pessimism bordering at times on futility about their ability to function. These boards no longer subscribed to the optimism bias, but had perhaps gone too far the other way. Fewer than half of directors of ineffective boards reported a culture of trust and respect in the boardroom. As a result, directors were severely hampered in their ability to complete their duties. For example,

- 70 per cent felt their boards do not align with the executive team on key issues such as risk management.
- Only 44 per cent said their boards are able to discuss top team performance with the executive team.
- Only 42 per cent felt they are effective at reviewing the top talent pipeline.
- Only 1 per cent believed their directors receive adequate induction training.

While members of ineffective boards tended to be gloomy about their ability to govern, they at least understood that there is a problem. Directors of complacent boards painted a much more rosy picture. Their belief in their own effectiveness, however, may have been subject to the Dunning-Kruger effect. They believed their organizations to be high-functioning and the board excelling at creating value. Two-thirds felt their board had a culture of trust and respect. But when the research began looking at individual board functions and tasks, a different picture emerges. Organizational health and talent management was a particular weakness; only 9 per cent of directors on complacent boards rated themselves as effective at CEO succession planning. Directors of complacent boards also reported a lack of feedback. For example, fewer than one in five said their board engages in regular evaluation exercises, nor do chairs ask for feedback after board meetings. And these were boards that considered themselves to be highly effective!

Both ineffective boards and complacent boards show what happens when a board loses control of its culture. It is easily done, as this book will show. At Uber, for example, the board culture was originally strong and highly engaged. It was the board that drove Uber towards the critical pursuit of scale and growth, and enabled it to challenge the status quo in its industry. But the board lost control. The culture went from aggressive to toxic, promoting growth as an ideal that transcends everything, including the rights of people and the rule of law.

Distorting Forces: Constraints on Independence

Ultimately, many of these problems come back to the issue of director independence. Wherever board dysfunction is found, it is safe to assume that the independent directors have been compromised in some way and are unable to act independently. Research from Henley Business School suggests four types of constraint which can hamper directors' independence: *individual constraints, board constraints, organizational and sector constraints* and *issue-based constraints.*[30]

If directors spend too long with an organization there is a risk that they may become too close to it. Social identity theory posits that people tend over time to take on the characteristics of groups to which they belong, and independent directors are no exception to this. Many directors speak of the difficulties of maintaining true independence over time. For this reason, in many countries, directors are limited to the number of years or terms they may serve with the same organization. Lack of appropriate knowledge and skills can also mean that independent directors lack the confidence to speak and challenge when they should.

The effectiveness of boards also depends heavily on the relationships between board members. When these relationships are asymmetrical, the actions of a few powerful board members may come to dominate proceedings and other board members are squeezed out of decision-making. This is particularly a problem if the board has a dominant and charismatic CEO or chair who dominates proceedings. Another form of board constraint is lack of effective communication between independent directors and executives, meaning the former do not get enough information—or enough of the right information—to evaluate performance and ask questions.

It is more difficult to exercise independence in very complex organizations or sectors unless the independent director already has a deep well of sector experience upon which to draw. Lack of knowledge again can prove a significant constraint; it is difficult to ask hard questions when you do not know what questions to ask. The Henley research also cited examples of dominant stakeholders, for example the owners of sports teams who hold 100 per cent of the shares and insist on interfering in strategy and operations. Challenging these individuals can be very difficult, in part because of the power they have—dissenting directors can be fired—and in part because they are often charismatic individuals who treat the team as their own personal possession and believe their own views should not be challenged.

Finally, reputational issues in particular pose a paradox which can be very difficult for independent directors to resolve. The role of independent director carries with it an obligation to speak the truth, but what if speaking the truth will also jeopardize the reputation of the organization and perhaps put its existence in doubt? Are there times when it is better *not* to challenge? These are difficult moral and ethical questions, and many independent directors struggle with them. It is also rare to find independent directors who have received any training in how to deal with these issues, especially if they do not naturally have the personality attributes required to deal with complex moral decisions.

And so, the answer to the question 'where was the board?' seems to be that the board was physically present, but the independence of its directors was compromised so that they were unable to take effective action. For whatever reason, when independent directors lose their independence, when they are unable to challenge for whatever reason, the risk that the board will sleepwalk into a crisis increases sharply.

Distorting Forces: Lack of Diversity

Another factor impacting on the effectiveness of directors is lack of diversity, still apparent in many boards around the world. There are many initiatives aimed at increasing board diversity, and the evidence suggests that these efforts are having some effect.[31] Nevertheless, many countries are still lagging behind. According to the *Financial Times*, 57 per cent of Japanese companies still do not have a single female director on their boards; worldwide, the percentage of female directors languishes at about 20 per cent.[32] For ethnic minorities the picture is much worse. A review in the UK in 2020 found that 69 per cent of FTSE-250 companies had no ethnic representation on the board at all and that only nine directors from an ethnic minority background held chair or CEO positions.[33] There is a similar lack of diversity in terms of age, with the majority of directors aged sixty-plus, and there is a woeful lack of representation by people with disabilities. In the West, boardrooms are still majority occupied by middle-aged white men, just as in India they are dominated by middle-aged Indian men and in China by middle-aged Chinese men.

The critical problem, however, is not demographics but experience. When recruiting new directors, most boards are looking for corporate experience, preferably as CEO. This means that a preponderance of independent directors are serving or former CEOs and CFOs, with the occasional director with a background in marketing if the organization is in retail or hospitality, or perhaps an operations director if the company is engaged in manufacturing. This makes for a very narrow range of points of view, which tends to stifle debate; when everyone shares the same functional mindset because the best track to CEO is through the CFO role, the range of views is relatively narrow. This point is not made to diminish the important role of finance in any business, but there is so much more to running a successful business. Boards need to recruit from a wider pool, bringing in people with more diverse experience and mindsets, people who are willing to challenge the status quo.

The counter-argument often advanced is that only highly experienced corporate executives have the necessary experience and knowledge to run large and complex corporations. However, the evidence for this claim is not strong. Technical knowledge and industry knowledge are important, but they are not the only assets an independent director needs. Courage, empathy, analytical skills, an open mind and a willingness to admit they do not understand something are also essential. The range of technical skills required is also much broader than many boards possess. Digital skills, for example, are often missing from boards, and yet the importance of digital and of data analytics in modern organizations cannot be overstated. In all sorts of ways, boards need to widen their horizons.

Increasingly, a lack of diversity is no longer acceptable. This is partly because low diversity is no longer acceptable to shareholders, regulators or the general public; increasing diversity is partly a matter of protecting reputation, which a cynic might say is why Goldman Sachs is so keen to push the matter. However, high diversity is also seen as increasingly important in improving performance and reducing risk. Having more of those missing voices in the room is a very good way of making sure more information is fed into the decision-making process and that in turn can make decisions less risky.

However, in saying that, we need to return to the point made above, that diversity will have very little positive impact unless it is also accompanied by inclusion. The diverse voices in the room must be heard, and those who speak must know that they are being heard and their voices are being taken into account. If there is even a hint of tokenism, of an idea that people have been recruited onto the board simply to tick boxes on a diversity assessment form, then directors will quickly become disillusioned and either fall silent or leave the board altogether; a key indicator of a poor culture is turnover of minority members of a board. The white men stay for the camaraderie, the women and racial minorities leave because they are not having any impact. Diversity is not just a matter of collecting people from different identities and putting them on show. It must be real.

Notes

1. Financial Reporting Council, 'Corporate Culture and the Role of Boards: Report of Observations', July 2016.
2. Gerry Brown, *The Independent Director: The Non-Executive Director's Guide to Effective Board Presence*, Basingstoke: Palgrave Macmillan, 2015, p. 2.
3. https://www2.deloitte.com/in/en/pages/risk/articles/board-of-directors.html.

4. C.M. Daily, R. Dalton, and A. A. Cannella, Jr. (2003) 'Corporate governance: Decades of Dialogue and Data. Introduction to Special Topic Forum', *Academy of Management Review* 28, 371–382.
5. Brian R. Cheffins (ed.), *The History of Modern US Corporate Governance*, Cheltenham: Edward Elgar, 2011.
6. James Burnham, *The Managerial Revolution*, London: Putnam, 1941.
7. Adrian Wilkinson, Jimmy Donaghey, Tony Dundon and Richard B. Freeman (eds), *Handbook of Research on Employee Voice*, Cheltenham: Edward Elgar, 2020.
8. For example, Gerald R. Salancik and Jeffrey Pfeffer, *The External Control of Organizations: A Resource Dependence Perspective*, New York: Harper and Row, 1978.
9. https://boardofdirectorssalary.com/alphabet-inc/;   https://www.nytimes.com/2018/10/25/technology/google-sexual-harassment-andy-rubin.html.
10. Laura Tyson, 'The Tyson Report on the Recruitment and Development of Non-Executive Directors', London Business School/Department of Trade and Industry 2003, p. 6.
11. https://www.goldmansachs.com/what-we-do/investing-and-lending/launch-with-gs/pages/commitment-to-diversity.html.
12. Katherine Klein, 'Does Gender Diversity on Boards Really Improve Corporate Performance?', 18 May 2017; Elizabeth Mannix and Margaret A. Neale, 'Diversity at Work', *Scientific American*, August–September 2006; Corinne Post and Kris Byron, 'Women on Boards and Firm Financial Performance: A Meta-Analysis', *Academy of Management Journal* 58 (5), 2015.
13. Karl E. Weick, *Sensemaking in Organizations*, Thousand Oaks: Sage Publications, 1995.
14. M.K. Johnson and C.R. Raye, 'Reality Monitoring', *Psychological Review* 88 (1), 1981, pp. 67–85.
15. Jennifer A. Chatman, David F. Caldwell, Charles A. O'Reilly and Bernadette Doerr, 'Parsing Organizational Culture', *Journal of Organizational Behavior* 35, 2014; Jenny Chatman and Francesca Gino, 'Don't Let the Pandemic Sink Your Culture', *Harvard Business Review*, 17 August 2020; Claudine Gartenberg, Andrea Prat and George Serafeim, 'Corporate Purpose and Financial Performance', Harvard Business School working paper, 2016.
16. Bibb Latané and John M. Darley, *The Unresponsive Bystander: Why Doesn't He Help?* New York: Appleton-Century-Croft, 1970.
17. Allan I. Teger and Dean G. Pruitt, 'Components of Group Risk-Taking', *Journal of Experimental Social Psychology* 3 (2), 1967, pp. 189–205.
18. Donald C. Hambrick and Phyllis A. Mason, 'Upper Echelons: The Organization as a Reflection of Its Top Managers', *Academy of Management Review* 9, 1984, pp. 193–206.
19. Nancy R. Axelrod, *Culture of Inquiry: Healthy Debate in the Boardroom*, Washington, DC: BoardSource, 2007.

20. https://www.bloomberg.com/news/articles/2020-07-06/u-k-asks-big-four-firms-to-separate-auditing-units-by-june-2024.
21. Bibb Latané, 'The Psychology of Social Impact', *American Psychologist* 36 (4), 1981; D.R. Forsyth, *Group Dynamics*, New York: Wadsworth, 2009.
22. C.G. Jung, *The Undiscovered Self: The Dilemma of the Individual in Modern Society*, New York: Berkley, 2006.
23. Alvin Zander, *Making Boards Effective*, San Francisco: Jossey Bass, 1993.
24. Irving L. Janis, *Victims of Groupthink*, Boston: Houghton Mifflin, 1982.
25. Norman Dixon, *On the Psychology of Military Incompetence*, London: Cape, 1976.
26. Stanley Milgram, *Obedience to Authority: An Experimental View*, New York: HarperCollins, 2009.
27. https://www.ted.com/talks/david_dunning_why_incompetent_people_think_they_re_amazing.
28. Heidi K. Gardner and Randall S. Peterson, 'Executives and Boards, Avoid These Missteps in a Crisis', *Harvard Business Review*, 24 April 2020, p. 2.
29. Ibid.; see also Barry M. Staw, Lance E. Sandelands and Jane E. Dutton, 'Threat Rigidity Effects in Organizational Behavior: A Multilevel Analysis', *Administrative Science Quarterly* 26 (4), 1981.
30. Brown et al., 2020.
31. Harvey Nash/LBS Leadership Institute report, 2019; Deloitte/*Wall Street Journal*, 'Women and Minorities on Fortune 500 Boards: More Room to Grow.'
32. https://deloitte.wsj.com/cfo/2019/03/21/women-and-minorities-on-fortune-500-boards-more-room-to-grow/; https://timesofindia.indiatimes.com/business/india-business/india-lags-in-female-board-members/articleshow/71532170.cms.
33. https://www.ey.com/en_uk/news/2020/02/new-parker-review-report-reveals-slow-progress-on-ethnic-diversity-of-ftse-boards.

Part II

5

The Subordinated Board: Facebook

A board is a board that is incapable of acting independently of the executive. As we noted earlier, this subordination sometimes happens when the organization has a dominant CEO with a strong character, but sometimes it happens because of the way power within the organization is structured, for example if the chief executive is also a dominant shareholder and/or has the power to control appointments to the board. When this happens, it becomes hard—if not impossible—for the executive to exert proper scrutiny and call the CEO to account.

Facebook is an example of a company where the board has consistently struggled to make any impact or rein in the senior executive team. Other dysfunctions can be observed at Facebook too, including amplification of culture and diffusion of responsibility, but the extent to which Facebook's board operates in a kind of strait-jacket imposed by its ownership and governance structure is remarkable.

As founder, CEO and chairman of Facebook, Mark Zuckerberg wields immense control over the company's governance, despite its publicly owned status. Under Facebook's dual-class structure, each share of Class A stock (which is held by individuals and institutional investors) has one vote. Zuckerberg, executive management and directors hold Class B stock, where each share equals ten votes. And because Zuckerberg owns 75 per cent of the Class B stock, he controls 58 per cent of the vote.[1]

Zuckerberg is, in the words of investor and shareholder advocate James McRitchie, 'a dictator,' even if a benevolent one.[2] This view is hardly unique; the *Financial Times* ran an op-ed piece entitled 'Facebook's Dual-Class Share Structure is Akin to a Dictatorship' in May 2018, in which the authors

© The Author(s), under exclusive license to Springer Nature Switzerland AG 2022
G. Brown, R. S. Peterson, *Disaster in the Boardroom*,
https://doi.org/10.1007/978-3-030-91658-9_5

endorsed the 'one share, one vote' principle because 'every share of a public company's common stock should have equal voting rights.' They argued that excessively powerful shareholders (like Zuckerberg) can all too easily isolate the board from problems, prevent the passing of shareholder proxy proposals and repel activists.[3]

A London School of Economics business review analysis by Gerry Brown, fellow of the Institute of Directors and visiting fellow at Henley Business School, similarly highlighted the dangers of Facebook's voting mechanisms and the risks created by permitting the executive to effectively control the board. Sharply criticizing Facebook's 'light to non-existent touch approach to corporate governance symbolized by the combined chair and CEO role,' Brown described the company's decision to ignore best practices for splitting the chair/CEO roles as an 'arrogance borne of a management bubble with almost zero effective regulation, supervision and oversight.'[4]

Facebook, however, flatly disagreed with the notion that Zuckerberg's over-whelming control of the board contributed to complacence and missed (or ignored) signals while data privacy issues spiralled out of control in the years leading up to the Cambridge Analytica scandal. Instead, the company responded to suggestions of a problematic board structure by stating that 'our capital structure is in the best interests of our stockholders and … our current corporate governance structure is sound and effective.'

Cambridge Analytica

In March 2018, *The Observer*, the UK's *Channel 4 News* and *The New York Times* simultaneously broke a shocking data privacy news story by following a major collaborative investigation led by the British journalist Carole Cadwalladr. At the heart of the scandal was the evidence of a whistleblower, who was persuaded by Cadwalladr to reveal how Facebook had allowed political consulting company Cambridge Analytica to surreptitiously harvest Facebook user data, in direct contravention of individual, user-controlled privacy settings within the Facebook platform. The impact of the story was immediate and included a massive public outcry and plummeting market value. The US and UK governments quickly opened investigations into the company's conduct.

The key events began in 2015. Aleksandr Kogan, then a data scientist at Cambridge University, had developed an app called 'This is Your Digital Life.' Kogan, through his company GSR, used Facebook to organize a survey completed by nearly 300,000 Facebook users, who agreed to consent terms indicating that certain personal data would be collected and used for purely academic purposes. In reality, however, Facebook allowed the app to amass a wide range of personal data from both the original survey-takers *and* from their Facebook 'friends,' regardless of what privacy settings had been selected. Facebook thus released data for nearly 87 million Facebook users,[5] the vast majority of whom had never consented to having their personal information shared.[6] Kogan provided this information to Cambridge Analytica.

Cambridge Analytica then used this massive data set—which included birthdays, photos, location information, phone numbers, private messages and more—to develop 'psychographic profiles' of the users. The profiles relied on data about user interests, activities and opinions to predict likely values, attitudes and even feelings. These profiles can then be combined with traditional demographic data points like age, gender or race to create a deeper understanding of what will likely motivate or influence a particular consumer or set of consumers.[7] The psychographics that Cambridge Analytica created based on the Facebook user data were designed to enable political campaigns to deliver precisely targeted advertisements to people who might be more readily swayed in their voting intentions. The company then directed these ads towards the original Facebook data providers and their online friends.

As early as December 2015, Facebook learned that the data provided to Kogan via the company's platform had been shared with Cambridge Analytica. In that same month, *The Guardian* published a story claiming that US presidential candidate Ted Cruz's campaign had used data harvested from millions of Facebook users without their consent.[8] Mark Zuckerberg later stated that upon learning of this, Facebook immediately banned Kogan and demanded that he and Cambridge Analytica 'certify' that they had destroyed any residual data in their possession. Zuckerberg also stated that certifications had been given, although it is not at all clear that they had; later events confirmed that Cambridge Analytica had in fact retained and continued to use the data.[9] Facebook made no disclosures to its users or anyone else at this time.

Chris Wylie, the former Cambridge Analytica employee turned whistle-blower, later provided both the US and the UK governments with copies of a letter he received from Facebook's lawyers, requesting the destruction of any data that had been collected by Kogan's company, GSR. Wylie, who was travelling at the time, did not respond to the letter. Facebook did not pursue the matter, nor did it seek any forensic checks of his computers. 'That to me was the most astonishing thing,' Wylie said later. 'They waited two years and did absolutely nothing to check that the data was deleted. All they asked me to do was tick a box on a form and post it back.' In 2016 Facebook made legal claims against GSR and Cambridge Analytica for misappropriation and misuse of data, claims which were allegedly resolved in a private settlement in November 2018.

In February 2018, both Facebook and Cambridge Analytica assured the UK parliament that Cambridge Analytica did not have or use private Facebook data. Facebook's UK policy director testified that Cambridge Analytica 'may have lots of data but it will not be Facebook user data' and that 'it may be data about people who are on Facebook that they have gathered themselves, but it is not data that we have provided.' Similarly, the CEO of Cambridge Analytica advised lawmakers that 'we do not work with Facebook data and we do not have Facebook data.'[10] Meanwhile, reporters were busily gathering evidence that would ultimately establish that neither of these claims was true.

On 16 March 2018, the day before the Cambridge Analytica stories were set to be published, Facebook threatened to sue *The Guardian* (owners of *The Observer*) if the story was published, asserting that the investigation results were 'false and defamatory.'[11] Campbell Brown, head of news partnerships at the company, later said that this was 'not our wisest move.' Cambridge Analytica also sought to prevent the story from coming to light, threatening a defamation suit.[12] Despite the legal threats, the story went live the next day.

Facebook's Response

As the Cambridge Analytica exposé dominated the headlines, Facebook spent the initial days picking over the minutiae of the claims rather than issuing a formal response. For example, the company argued that the media's use of the term 'data breach' was incorrect because 'no systems were infiltrated, and no passwords or sensitive pieces of information were stolen or hacked.'[13] This was true, but the statement missed the point by a considerable margin. No Facebook user data had not been 'stolen' or 'hacked' because Facebook had essentially sold it (without users' permission and in violation of users' privacy choices). Indeed, one commentator noted that the Cambridge Analytica debacle was troubling precisely because it was *not* a data breach. Instead, 'what happened with Cambridge Analytica was not a matter of Facebook's systems being infiltrated, but of Facebook's systems working as designed: data was amassed, data was extracted, and data was exploited.'[14]

Facebook also claimed that 'friends' information, like photos, was only accessible on devices when people made a decision to share their information with those friends. We are not aware of any abuse by these companies.'[15] The company later argued (unsuccessfully) in a shareholder lawsuit that there was no basis to probe the board's actions, since any breach was due to the actions of 'third parties.'[16]

As the scandal gained steam and users became increasingly outraged, Facebook remained embroiled in the technicalities of the situation, maintaining its insistence that there was no 'data breach.' The company stated Kogan had received the user data 'in a legitimate way and through the proper channels' and explaining that the fault actually lay with Kogan; it was his decision to share information with third parties that violated Facebook's rules. Facebook itself, however, was not at fault; instead, it was a victim of 'a serious abuse of our rules.'[17]

Government Investigations, Penalties and 'Board Reform'

In July 2019, the UK's Information Commissioner's Office announced it was fining Facebook £500,000 on the basis that the company had violated the law through its failure to safeguard customers' private information. The fine was the maximum allowed by law.

On 24 July 2019, the Securities and Exchange Commission (SEC), the Federal Trade Commission (FTC) and the Department of Justice (DOJ) jointly announced the conclusion of a year-long investigation that had been triggered in large part by the Cambridge Analytica scandal.[18] The US government accused Facebook of deceiving consumers in violation of both a 2012 FTC administrative order and the Federal Trade Commission Act. The DOJ indicated that, beginning in 2015, the company had notice of Cambridge Analytica's actions, with more than thirty employees knowing what was happening. Yet in 2016 and 2017, Facebook responded to press inquiries by stating that it had found no evidence of wrongdoing, and the company made only generic disclosures to investors.[19]

The investigation further concluded that Facebook had a pattern of employing deceptive disclosures and using account settings to essentially trick users into sharing personal data, often in contravention of their privacy choices.[20] The company knowingly misled tens of millions of customers about the use of their personal information (including phone numbers, photos and more, as well as similar data about their Facebook friends). Facebook had also led customers to believe that they had explicitly 'turned off' data sharing. However, regardless of the settings a customer chose, their data was still collected based on settings chosen by those users' friends, and Facebook then provided data to developers. Despite being made aware of the issue as far back as 2015, Facebook had continued to deliver the 'turned off' data to a set of whitelisted developers in direct contravention to individual user privacy selections.[21]

To resolve the FTC investigation, Facebook agreed to a $5 billion fine. FTC Chairman Joe Simons explained the significance of the settlement:

> Despite repeated promises to its millions of world-wide users that they could control how their personal information is shared, Facebook took steps to undermine consumers' choices. The magnitude of the $5 billion penalty and sweeping conduct relief are unprecedented in the history of the FTC. The relief is designed not only to punish previous violations but, more importantly, to change Facebook's entire privacy culture to decrease the likelihood of continued violations. The Commission takes consumer privacy seriously, and will enforce FTC orders to the fullest extent of the law.

Despite the government's strong words, the settlement did not actually change the company's corporate structure or its ability to continue collecting user data, which led people to question whether the fine had any real impact on how Facebook operates.[22] Zuckerberg was permitted to continue his dual role as CEO and chair while also controlling 60 per cent of the voting shares. He retained his right to appoint independent directors (and to remove them with or without cause, raising the obvious question of how 'independent' they could be).

The settlement did require the establishment of a privacy committee comprised independent board members whom Zuckerberg would not be allowed to remove, although it was not entirely clear how this requirement would interact with his existing appointment/removal rights. It also mandated access for an external privacy auditor and required Zuckerberg to certify compliance with the new requirements, with criminal and civil penalties for any false statements.[23] However, there was and is considerable doubt as to whether this committee will be effective. The FTC hailed the settlement as meaningful progress in protecting consumer privacy, but critics observed that all the changes were entirely internal and there was no public accountability mechanism. Former Facebook security chief Alex Stamos commented that 'Facebook paid the FTC $5 billion for a letter that says "You never again have to create mechanisms that could facilitate competition."'[24] Others noted that the $5 billion fine was trivial for an organization whose 2018 revenue exceeded $55 billion.

Challenges to the Corporate Governance Structure

At Facebook's 2019 annual shareholders' meeting, Zuckerberg was criticized by activist investors who cited ongoing negative press about Facebook's governance and management and asserted that he held too much power to effectively manage the company. Sixty-eight per cent of outside shareholders supported a proposal to split the role of CEO and chair—and to make the chair an independent position—and an overwhelming 83 per cent of outside investors voted in favour of eliminating the dual-class share system and replacing it with a 'one share, one vote' structure. Despite the mass of investors ranged against him, Zuckerberg remained protected by his 60 per cent control and was never likely to vote against himself.[25] Facebook's unified CEO/chair role and its Class A/Class B voting structure remained intact.

Although investors lost that battle, they won another a few days later when a Delaware Chancery Court judge granted a shareholder demand for access to internal Facebook information that might support their claim of corporate wrongdoing in connection with Facebook's provision of data to Cambridge Analytica. The shareholders asserted that Facebook's conduct breached a 2012 data privacy consent decree with the FTC. Ruling that internal communications (including data privacy-related emails from both Zuckerberg and COO Sheryl Sandberg) should be disclosed, the court found that the shareholders had provided 'a credible basis to infer the board and Facebook senior executives failed to oversee Facebook's compliance with the consent decree and its broader efforts to protect the private data of its users.'[26] An expansion of the shareholder investigation was warranted because evidence suggested the board of directors had failed in its duty to protect data privacy.

Asymmetries of Power

One of the results of these asymmetries of power and the consequent loss of director independence is that, once again, analysis of risk becomes badly skewed. In effect, it is the executive who determines what is risky and what is not; the board has no power to stay or alter any executive decision. At Facebook, this meant that Zuckerberg and his senior executive team were allowed to conduct their response to the Cambridge Analytica crisis in their own way; and in doing so, arguably made a bad situation even worse.

Rather than coming clean, apologizing fully and making real and genuine reforms, Facebook chose a strategy of delay and obfuscation. The company's response was to highlight technicalities, for example, arguing again and again that the Cambridge Analytica affair was not a 'data breach,' which of course it was not, but again that misses the point. The next step was to insist that 'bad acts' by third parties had violated Facebook's rules, but the company was not at fault. Considerable effort was spent trying to spin that line before falling back to the next position: the company did not know about the situation and, later, that it had already ensured destruction of the files. This too was proven false. All these defences failed to address the central issue.

Zuckerberg and his executives were enabled by their complete control of the board. There was, and remains, no oversight. Attempts by shareholders and the FTC to change the board and impose more oversight have failed. Even the FTC's imposition of the 'privacy committee' has been widely met with scepticism; Zuckerberg still controls the board and chooses who is on it and who is removed.

Whenever we see a board with such obvious asymmetries of power, alarm bells should sound. Facebook is far from an isolated case. We can refer again to the reputational scandal at Samsung, which has had even more dramatic and far-reaching consequences. Although the scale of the bribery revelations in 2017 was enormous, the practice was clearly not a new one. An investigation by *Bloomberg Businessweek* found that 'for years the Lee family and its top strategists have coordinated interactions among subsidiaries, dealt with the government, and approved large expenditures out of a department alternatively called the corporate strategy office, the restructuring office, and the control tower.'[27] Although the Lee family's control over Samsung was nowhere near as absolute as Zuckerberg's over Facebook—*Bloomberg* described their control as 'rather fragile'—a complex web of cross-holdings and special voting rights meant that they could usually get their own way. Lee's charismatic father had been venerated not just inside the company but across the nation, and the political classes had endorsed him on the notion that 'what is good for Samsung is good for Korea,' meaning that people's respect for the company was so great that those who might have been inclined to challenge felt constrained and kept their mouths shut. As a result, there was no effective scrutiny of the actions of Lee and his allies, and they led the Samsung group into disaster. Following his own conviction in 2017, Lee has indicated that he will step down and hand over control of the group to professional managers.

Sometimes it is personality rather than control that allows executives to dominate. At Volkswagen, for example, Ferdinand Piëch exercised near-total control over the board through force of personality rather than ownership.

His 'reign of terror' ensured that directors did not challenge or scrutinize his decisions. Cees van der Hoeven of Dutch supermarket group Royal Ahold is an example of an executive who dominated his board and ensured that there was little or no dissent. Van der Hoeven's style of leadership concentrated on setting and hitting growth targets, and so long as the company continued to do so, no one questioned the company's performance. Royal Ahold's strategy for becoming the world's largest supermarket group was eventually ship-wrecked, like so many before and since, by a failed attempt to expand into America. The company collapsed with massive debts, and van der Hoeven faced criminal charges (which were later dropped). By the time the board of Ahold had become aware of the problem, it was too late.

The same was true at Satyam Computer Services. The founder, Byrraju Ramalinga Raju, served as both chairman and CEO; he was also well-connected with local politicians in the state of Andhra Pradesh and enjoyed wide respect and high status inside the company and without. Raju was able to manipulate the company's finances as he pleased, until he realized that his cover-up of the company's poor financial performance could no longer be sustained. It was only when he submitted his resignation that anyone realized the scale of the problem. Raju later admitted his guilt in full, explaining the situation in which he found himself:

> What started as a marginal gap between actual operating profit and the one reflected in the books continued to grow over the years. It has attained unman-ageable proportions as the size of the company's operations grew over the years. … It was like riding a tiger, not knowing how to get off without being eaten.[28]

There are plenty of other examples of firms that failed to ride the tiger. Founded in January 2018 with coffee shops in Shanghai and Beijing, the Chinese start-up Luckin Coffee enjoyed dramatic growth: 1300 stores by October that year, 3680 by the end of 2019, 6500 by April 2020, a listing on Nasdaq and a position as the largest coffee shop chain in China, outstripping even Starbucks. Starbucks had been the company's target right from the start; beating their American rival was Luckin's most important goal, subsuming everything else.

In January 2020, American investment firm Muddy Waters Research pub-lished a report accusing Luckin of overstating its profits. The firm first denied everything, but in April the full story began to emerge, and Luckin finally admitted overstating profits by $310 million. Shares were suspended on Nasdaq and the firm was delisted; the CEO and COO were fired in an attempt to blame them for the scandal, but the chair, Guo Jinyo, now faces charges of instructing staff to commit sales fraud. Subsequent investigation found that the chair also served as chair of the remuneration and compensation committees, held a large proportion of stock and had compromised the independence of the non-executive directors.[29] No one on the board had the power to call the chair to account and the stakeholders of the company all paid the price.

Lack of Independence

The case of Facebook shows in sharp relief the absolute necessity of independent directors who have the power to challenge the executive. Asymmetries of power at board level must be addressed. At Facebook, at Satyam, at Lehman Brothers and in many other cases, the concentration of power in the hands of a few, largely unaccountable people led to disaster (and at Facebook, the problem was compounded by the fact that share ownership structure was concentrated in the hands of the executive, rendering them virtually immune to monitoring).

Unitary leadership, combining the posts of chair and CEO in one person, can be a source of strength, but only so long as that individual remains accountable to the independent directors on the board. Separating the roles is not necessarily the answer—in the UK where the roles are required to be separated, there are plenty of examples of dominant executives who domesticated their chairs and boards of directors, like Fred Goodwin of Royal Bank of Scotland and Mike Ashley of Sports Direct—but whatever structure is chosen, the board must have the ability to bring over-mighty CEOs to heel.

Once again, of course, this is easier said than done. This is particularly the case when the CEO is also an iconic figure, typically the founder of the organization, and when they also have a large shareholding, all of which is true of Mark Zuckerberg. As owners of capital, they of course have a right to make their voices heard. But should that give them an unfettered right to dominate? When all is said and done, shareholders are only one class of stakeholder in a business; there are many others who also have rights. The notion that having a controlling interest in a company gives one the right to do as one pleases, including abusing the trust and good faith of customers and the community, is as dangerous as it is false.

The best counterweight to the power of the CEO, and the best way of ensuring that the board remains independent, is to have a strong and effective chair. An effective chair/CEO relationship is a bit like a good marriage: a partnership of equals, where each party complements the other and the two work together in harmony. In cases where the two roles are combined, the same is true of the chair/CEO's relationship with the senior independent director. Of course there is a risk that chairs can also become overly powerful, and it is the duty of the rest of the board to ensure that they do not. But chairs set the tone for the rest of the board. They have a strong influence on board culture and can help to dilute the presence of the charismatic executive. However, it should be added that chairs are rarely able to do this on their own, and expecting the chair to be the sole influencer of culture is another example of diffusion of responsibility. Chairs and directors must work collaboratively in the interests of the business.

This again highlights the importance of board evaluation, which should have the effect of forcing the board to take a look in the mirror and see whether it is indeed independent or whether some of that independence may have been compromised. It is also important for periodic evaluation to be facilitated by external consultants, rather than simply leaving the board to conduct its own internal evaluation year after year. This is not to suggest that all internal evaluations lack rigour, but over time there is a danger that the directors will begin to mark their own homework. In the UK, external evaluation in every third year is now mandatory for FTSE-350 companies—though not for charities, for whom it is only a recommendation—but in many other countries there is not even a recommendation. We would encourage all boards to engage a rigorous external review at least once every three years, and they should see evaluation as an opportunity for development and not just a matter of compliance.

As the cases of Facebook and Google also highlight, the structure of the board can also work against board independence. At both companies, key figures are able to dominate the board through their shareholdings which give them additional voting power, and attempts to reform the board are simply voted down. Breaking the power of those dominant individuals will require alliances such as one we will see in the case of Google, between investors and other stakeholders. The Google attempt failed, this time, but future alliances bringing in more key stakeholders—and supported by independent directors—might well have more success.

Notes

1. https://www.forbes.com/sites/betsyatkins/2019/06/07/facebook-strong-arms-investors-who-want-zuckerberg-out/#11168dc15901.

2. https://variety.com/2018/biz/news/facebook-alphabet-corporate-governance-1202869861/.
3. https://www.ft.com/content/d22eb6e8-52b4-11e8-b24e-cad6aa67e23e.
4. https://blogs.lse.ac.uk/businessreview/2018/05/01/facebooks-light-approach-to-corporate-governance/.
5. The original reporting indicated that 50 million users had been affected, but the number was quickly revised to reflect a total of 87 million. https://www.theguardian.com/technology/2018/apr/08/facebook-to-contact-the-87-million-users-affected-by-data-breach.
6. https://www.nytimes.com/2018/03/17/us/politics/cambridge-analytica-trump-campaign.html?referringSource=articleShare.
7. https://www.cbinsights.com/research/what-is-psychographics/.
8. https://www.theguardian.com/us-news/2015/dec/11/senator-ted-cruz-president-campaign-facebook-user-data.
9. https://www.techrepublic.com/article/facebook-data-privacy-scandal-a-cheat-sheet/.
10. https://www.theguardian.com/news/2018/mar/17/cambridge-analytica-facebook-influence-us-election?CMP=Share_iOSApp_Other.
11. https://twitter.com/carolecadwalla/status/974995682124804099.
12. https://www.techrepublic.com/article/facebook-data-privacy-scandal-a-cheat-sheet/.
13. https://about.fb.com/news/2018/03/suspending-cambridge-analytica/.
14. https://www.theguardian.com/technology/2019/mar/17/the-cambridge-analytica-scandal-changed-the-world-but-it-didnt-change-facebook.
15. https://newsroom.fb.com/news/2018/06/why-we-disagree-with-the-nyt/.
16. https://www.wsj.com/articles/court-tells-facebook-to-open-its-records-on-data-privacy-11559335755.
17. https://www.theguardian.com/news/2018/mar/17/cambridge-analytica-facebook-influence-us-election?CMP=Share_iOSApp_Other.
18. https://www.justice.gov/opa/pr/facebook-agrees-pay-5-billion-and-implement-robust-new-protections-user-information.
19. https://www.wsj.com/articles/facebook-agrees-to-pay-5-billion-in-ftc-settlement-11563971400?mod=hp_lead_pos3&mod=article_inline.
20. https://www.wsj.com/articles/facebook-agrees-to-pay-5-billion-in-ftc-settlement-11563971400?mod=hp_lead_pos3&mod=article_inline.
21. https://www.wsj.com/articles/facebook-agrees-to-pay-5-billion-in-ftc-settlement-11563971400?mod=hp_lead_pos3&mod=article_inline.
22. https://www.wsj.com/articles/facebook-board-to-tighten-oversight-as-zuckerberg-keeps-control-11563982646.
23. https://www.wsj.com/articles/facebook-agrees-to-pay-5-billion-in-ftc-settlement-11563971400?mod=hp_lead_pos3&mod=article_inline.
24. https://www.wsj.com/articles/facebook-agrees-to-pay-5-billion-in-ftc-settlement-11563971400?mod=hp_lead_pos3&mod=article_inline.

25. https://www.forbes.com/sites/zakdoffman/2019/05/31/facebook-loses-in-court-over-privacy-emails-as-zuckerberg-votes-to-keep-full-control/#12b51c85560c.
26. *In re Facebook Inc.*, Memorandum Opinion, C.A. No. 2018-0661-JRS (Del. Ch. May 30, 2019).
27. https://www.bloomberg.com/news/features/2017-07-27/summer-of-samsung-a-corruption-scandal-a-political-firestorm-and-a-record-profit.
28. https://www.nytimes.com/2009/01/08/business/worldbusiness/08satyam.html?_r=0.
29. Lindsey Zhang, 'Governance in China', *Governance*, 2020.

6

The Imbalanced Board: Google

The phenomenon of missing key voices on board is widespread and, as already noted, links directly to a lack of diversity, not just of ethnicity, gender and so on but also background and lived experience. The inability of boards to listen to voices from outside the boardroom and the C-suite means that boards often overlook evidence of everything from widespread fraud to sexual harassment and abuse going on almost under their noses. The sexual misconduct scandals at Google are a case in point.

In 2017, the US Department of Labor, as part of an ongoing investigation, asserted that tech giant Google was engaged in 'systematic compensation disparities against women pretty much across the entire workforce.' These claims were vehemently denied by the company.[1] In early 2018, however, a class action discrimination action was brought against Google by women engineers, managers, sales people and early childhood educators.[2] The company continued to deny wrongdoing, but by the autumn of 2018 Google's treatment of women—and, relatedly, the men who harassed them—was a major news story. Allegations of misconduct, cover-ups and pay-offs dominated media headlines.

Protecting the Powerful

In October 2018, the *New York Times* ran an investigative report entitled, 'How Google Protected Andy Rubin, the "Father of Android",' which detailed accounts of not only Rubin's conduct but that of several other prominent male leaders in the company.[3] Hailed as a departing hero when he left the company in 2014, Rubin, the creator of the widely used Android operating platform, was publicly praised by CEO Larry Page who wished him well in his next venture. Earlier that year, though, a Google employee had filed a misconduct complaint against Rubin, stating that the two had had an undisclosed relationship (in violation of company policy) and that it had ended when he had forced her to perform oral sex in a hotel room. Google commenced an investigation, but just weeks into the inquiry the board made Rubin an unusually generous share grant valued at $150 million. Share grants to high-level executives were normally based in part on Larry Page's recommendation, and the grant was also approved by the board's leadership development and compensation committee.

The company's misconduct investigation resulted in a determination that the claim was credible, and Page was notified of the investigation's outcome. Rubin was not fired, although Google's sexual harassment policy clearly stated that violators could be terminated. Instead he was asked to resign and his departure was spun in a positive light, complete with praise for his contributions to the company. Nor were there any financial consequences from his misconduct; Rubin left with an exit package valued at approximately $90 million. The company also invested millions of dollars into his new venture firm, Playground Global, and delayed his repayment of a $14 million loan that Google had given him to buy a beach house. Rubin had arrived at Google in 2009 with a net worth of approximately $10 million. When he left the company, it was estimated at $350 million.

The 2018 *New York Times* article also shed light on the story of David Drummond, then chief legal officer and a member of the board at Google's parent company, Alphabet. In 2004, when he was chief legal officer at Google, Drummond engaged in an extramarital affair with a direct report, Jennifer Blakely. This was in direct violation of company policy. Three years into the relationship, the pair had a child and Drummond disclosed the relationship to the company. 'One of us would have to leave the legal department,' Blakely recalled. 'It was clear it would not be David.'[4] Drummond retained his role in the legal department; Blakely was relocated to sales, an area where she had no experience. She exited the company within a year, after being asked to sign paperwork confirming that she had left voluntarily. Explaining that she signed 'whatever' waivers and releases she was asked to, Blakely noted that it 'felt like *I* was the liability.'[5] Drummond, who was still married, later began a relationship with a different Google employee, breaking off the relationship with Blakely and setting the stage for a bitter custody battle characterized by a significant power imbalance.

The next year, 2015, Drummond became the chief legal officer for Alphabet. In 2018 he and his wife finally divorced, amidst allegations that he had had a number of extramarital relationships including with women at Google. In 2019, he married a different Google legal team member (because he was now at Alphabet, she was not his direct report).[6]

After a long history of personal involvement with his subordinates, Drummond left Alphabet in January 2020 with some suggestion that he 'was seen as one of the last major links to [Google's] past culture problems.' In a marked difference from Rubin's treatment a few years earlier, he did not receive an exit package, but he did sell $222 million worth of company stock in the months leading up to his exit.[7] The message to ordinary workers, as Blakely explained, was clear: 'for a select few, there are no consequences.'

The company showed similar tolerance to Rich DeVaul, a former director in an R&D division known as Google X, in connection with an incident that also came to light in the 2018 investigation. In the course of a 2013 job interview with twenty-four-year-old hardware engineer Star Simpson, DeVaul explained that he and his wife were polyamorous and invited her to the Burning Man Festival, a radical arts festival held in the Nevada desert. Believing that attending the festival presented an opportunity to talk about a possible job at Google, Simpson agreed. When she met DeVaul, he asked her to remove her shirt for a backrub. She declined, and he continued to pressure her; she finally agreed to let him rub her neck, later explaining that 'I didn't have enough spine or backbone to shut that down as a 24-year old.' She found out a few weeks later that she did not get the job at Google; no explanation was given. Simpson did not report the incident to Google for two years. When she did, an HR representative told her that they believed her story to be more likely to be true than not and that the company had addressed the issue. When the *New York Times* exposé was published, Google declined to explain its response to the allegations, except to advise that it had taken 'appropriate corrective action.' DeVaul left Google X on 30 October 2018, five days after the story broke. Although he did not receive an exit package, he remained in his senior position for a full three years after the complaint (and five years after the incident).[8]

The Workers Walk Out in an Attempt to Be Heard

Following the disclosure of Google's shielding of senior executives accused of sexual misconduct, on 1 November 2018 over 20,000 Google workers around the globe walked out of their offices in protest. They presented a specific list of demands including greater transparency regarding the company's response to sexual harassment claims and pay/opportunity disparities, and demanding an employee seat on the board.[9] In June, a handful of employees had also attended a shareholders' meeting to demand that Alphabet adopt a proposal by an investor, Zevin Asset Management, calling for executive compensation to be tied to diversity metrics. Alphabet recommended that shareholders vote against the proposal because, it claimed, the company already incorporated diversity measures (further evidence if needed that diversity without inclusion makes very little impact). The company's dual-voting structure, which gives the founders greater control, ensured that the proposal failed.[10]

Before the walkout, CEO Sundar Pichai sent a memo to employees explaining that the company had been taking a harder line on inappropriate workplace conduct and that forty-eight people had been fired in the last two years and had not received exit packages.[11] He did not appear to notice any irony in the fact that rank-and-file employees had been summarily dismissed while executives at the highest level had already received extreme deference and rich compensation packages, although he did state that 'any executive' (without saying whether there *were* any) who departed voluntarily during a sexual harassment investigation had not received an exit package. Pichai later offered a further response to the protests, noting that Google was committed to making progress and wanted to turn employees' 'feedback into action.' Company leaders also conducted a town-hall meeting with employees to better understand their concerns.[12]

Further Fallout for the Board

In January 2019, shareholder James Martin brought suit against the Alphabet board of directors for the alleged cover-up of sexual misconduct claims against two executives.[13] Raising claims of breach of its fiduciary duty, abuse of control, waste of corporate assets and unjust enrichment, the suit claimed that the directors were 'knowing and direct enablers of the sexual harassment and discrimination.' Martin's lawsuit was quickly followed by a similar case by two other shareholders who alleged that, among other things, the board's 'culture of concealment' concerning sexual misconduct was a breach of its fiduciary duty to shareholders.[14]

Both lawsuits relied on similar factual allegations, arguing that the board approved of sizeable severance packages for accused executives in order to keep them quiet, resulting in ongoing harm to Google's women employees. The Martin case specifically asserted that

[i]f you were a high-level male executive at Google responsible for generating millions of dollars in revenue, Google would let you engage in sexual harassment. And if you get caught, Google would keep it quiet, let you resign, and pay you millions of dollars in severance. … On the other hand, if you were a low-level employee at Google and were accused of sexual harassment or discrimination, you would be fired for cause with no severance benefits. In this way, Alphabet and the Board were able to maintain optics and superficial compliance with its code of conduct, internal rules, and laws regarding sexual harassment.

The complaint relied in part on internal board minutes obtained under state corporate record inspection laws. According to the suit, the board intentionally paid off harassers in order to keep the peace. For example, the minutes allegedly show that the board was afraid that terminating Andy Rubin for any cause would result in an ugly public dispute that would reveal the details of sexual misconduct by multiple Google executives. According to the plaintiff's counsel, the board minutes indicate 'a free for all' where the board's view was that 'people who are not at the top are going to receive retribution, and everyone else gets a free pass.'[15] Martin sought significant monetary damages, including the return of at least $90 million that was paid out in exit packages, and also the elimination of Alphabet's dual-class voting structure, which means Google's founders retain voting control despite not owning a majority of shares.

Failures to Speak, Failures to Listen

Tales of sexual discrimination and abuse in the tech industry are nothing new. In her book *Brotopia*, American journalist Emily Chang paints a picture of Silicon Valley where women are systematically discriminated against and marginalized. While Wall Street banking firms now insist on a 50–50 gender ratio, fewer than 25 per cent of jobs in tech firms are held by women, and very few of these reach senior executive positions. According to Chang, this has an impact not just on corporate culture but on the products and services tech firms produce. Twitter co-founder Evan Williams told Chang that he deeply regretted not having women on the team that developed Twitter; if they had been present, online abuse and trolling of women might have been reduced.[16]

The real storm at Google centred around the double standard of behaviour. Those guilty of breaching the company's code of conduct at lower levels of the company were summarily dealt with; those at the highest level had no penalty and were sometimes even rewarded. The extreme deference shown to these high-level offenders caused deep resentment. Employees felt like they were not being heard. Women who had been the subject of unwanted overtures from senior executives could not obtain justice or redress. Employees who were uncomfortable, to say the least, by the blatant abuse of power by these executives had their complaints brushed aside.

The employees have attempted to fight back. As noted, 20,000 of them walked out in protest. In an attempt to widen diversity and make sure that the missing voices were heard, they demanded a seat on the board for an employee representative. With the support of an investor, they suggested that executive compensation should be tied to meeting diversity objectives. All was in vain. The dual-voting structure meant that the founders on the board had a disproportionate share of power and could silence dissenting voices.

The contents of board minutes (which are not publicly available) are particularly troubling. If these accounts are correct, then it appears the board may have knowingly given preference to the elite/powerful harassers with full awareness that the voices of victims and 'regular' employees were either not heard or intentionally ignored. Most astonishing of all is the $150 million grant to Andy Rubin, along with deferred loan payments and a massive investment into his new enterprise, all of which took place during an active sexual misconduct investigation—one that ultimately resulted in a finding against him.

If fear of a backlash was the board's motivation for compensating the executives, then the move has backfired badly. Public exposés, constant press attention, the drawn-out departures of top executives, a worldwide protest by employees, shareholder lawsuits against the board—all these have been a high price to pay.

Google is by no means the only example of a company where missing voices have led to disaster and sometimes even to complete collapse. Few corporate failures have been as sudden and spectacular as that of British construction company Carillion, which went bankrupt in January 2018 with a loss of thousands of jobs and debts of nearly £7 billion. Suppliers lost more than £2 billion in unpaid bills, and some of them were forced into insolvency as well. A subsequent parliamentary inquiry pulled no punches:

> Carillion's rise and spectacular fall was a story of recklessness, hubris and greed. Its business model was a relentless dash for cash, driven by acquisitions, rising debt, expansion into new markets and exploitation of suppliers. … Long-term obligations, such as adequately funding its pension schemes, were treated with contempt. Even as the company very publicly began to unravel, the board was concerned with increasing and protecting generous executive bonuses. Carillion

was unsustainable. The mystery is not that it collapsed, but that it lasted so long.[17]

Carillion's board included four experienced non-executive directors, two of whom had accounting backgrounds, and an independent chair, although none had experience of the construction industry. The inquiry found that the finance director of Carillion probably concealed the company's increasingly desperate financial position from the board, a claim the finance director denies. But even if this were to be true, the board had no excuse. As early as April 2017 the chief financial officer of one of Carillion's subsidiaries, Emma Mercer, had raised concerns about how the business was accounting for work on a number of major projects. Receiving no satisfactory answer from either the CEO or the finance director, Mercer in effect blew the whistle and went directly to the board. The minutes of that meeting show that no director had any idea about the scale of the crisis facing the company. This raises two questions. If the board really did know, why did they not take action? And if they did not know, why not?

Even a cursory look at performance would have shown that Carillion's construction projects were nearly always late and over-budget. The company kept itself afloat by grabbing more and more construction projects and using the up-front fees to finance ongoing projects that were swallowing money. Mercer continued to make her views heard, but the board effectively rejected her findings and called in auditors KPMG instead. When the auditor said there was no need to make any public restatement of the accounts based on Mercer's findings, the board agreed. By this point it was probably too late to rescue the company, and the entire house of cards collapsed a few months later.

The mystery of why the board ignored clear warnings has never been resolved and may never be. But it is clear there was a missing voice: Mercer's. Had she been empowered to speak earlier, and even more, if there had been others like her on the board who would have added their voices to hers, the whole mess might have been avoided and the largest corporate insolvency in the UK history—so far—could have been averted.

The situation at Lehman Brothers, the investment bank that collapsed in September 2008 and precipitated the global financial crash of that year, was different but yielded similar outcomes. Most of the 'independent' directors at Lehman Brothers owed their places to the patronage of Richard Fuld, the long-serving chair and CEO. Few had any prior banking experience—others included a retired admiral and a theatrical producer. The rest of the board seems to have been largely unaware of Fuld's reckless overexpansion of the bank, which left it badly stretched when the financial crisis began to unfold earlier in the year.[18] Certainly there was no voice on the board that was ready to confront and call Fuld to account.

The crisis at Mitsubishi Motors has some similarities to that of Lehman Brothers, although the consequences were not quite so severe. In 2016 Mitsubishi Motors was accused of falsifying fuel consumption figures for several of its popular lines. The company eventually admitted to having used misleading testing systems for the past twenty-five years.[19] The result was a collapse in public confidence in Mitsubishi Motors. Sales of cars in its home market collapsed by 40 per cent, and the company, already struggling financially, predicted losses of $1.4 billion. Several key executives including the president were forced to resign. A bailout arrived in the form of a $2.2 billion investment from Nissan, but that relationship struggled to flourish and in 2020 a second Mitsubishi Motors president was compelled to resign.

The picture of Mitsubishi Motors that emerges between 2016 and 2020 is one of a company struggling to cope with the scandal and its aftermath. A supportive board might have perhaps made a difference, but the Mitsubishi Motors board lacks crucial experience of the auto industry. Of the twelve outside directors (as independent directors are known in Japan) at the time of writing, two have industry experience and two more come from elsewhere in the Mitsubishi corporation. The others include accountants, lawyers and academics, and their CVs indicate no previous experience with the auto industry.[20] Many of these directors have been appointed since the scandal, but it seems reasonable to assume that the board at the time of the scandal was similarly inexperienced.

Missing Voices

The problem of missing voices takes two forms. The first is a board that lacks diversity; the second is a board that has diversity in theory, but for various reasons its members will not challenge the status quo. Those reasons can include lack of competence and experience, lack of confidence or the presence of overly powerful board members—including but not always limited to the CEO and the chair—who stifle dissent and disempower others from confronting.

Not every board wants diversity. Research completed by Henley Business School found examples of boards purposely recruiting from their own networks, choosing directors 'who they think will give them a less challenging time.'[21] Even when the decision is not deliberate, unconscious bias can play a significant role. When recruiting to fill places on a board, nominations committees look for particular sets of skills and competencies, but they also tend—often subconsciously—to look for people who will 'fit in.' As a result, they often appoint directors who look and sound very much like the directors who are already on the board.

The point needs to be made again that diversity alone is not enough. Even when a board does recruit from a wide range of backgrounds, sticking twelve or fourteen diverse people into a room does not itself make for a diverse board. That board needs to also be capable of working together, with open debate as part of the dynamic. As noted, four of the fourteen directors at Alphabet, including two independent directors, were women. That did not stop the board allegedly colluding with men who abused women at the very top of the company. At Mitsubishi Motors and Lehman Brothers there were no voices to challenge the executive; at Carillion, the board ignored the one voice that did appear, the internal whistleblower.

To prevent this from happening, boards need to conduct a stakeholder analysis to see whose voices are represented and whose are missing and consider why those missing voices are important. Once they have been identified, those voices can then be added to the board. Employees at Google were well aware that their voices were not being heard, which is why they requested employee representation on the board. Presumably, this is also why the dominant figures on the board rejected the idea—perhaps they knew this voice was missing and did not want to hear it. This looks like wilful blindness, especially considering that employees and investors were openly making common cause against the company.

Board audits and evaluation, properly implemented, should be telling the board whose voices are present and whose are absent from the room. If representatives of missing voices cannot be found, then it is up to the independent directors to fill the gap. This in turn requires a board culture where directors *can* become dissenters without fear of reprisal. Freedom to speak honestly and to represent all points of view is essential if the missing voices are to be brought into the discussion. This means real and genuine inclusion, bringing all the different and diverse voices together to scrutinize, debate, discuss and, ultimately, speak with one voice.

Notes

1. https://www.theguardian.com/technology/2017/apr/07/google-pay-disparities-women-labor-department-lawsuit.

2. https://techcrunch.com/2018/01/03/google-faces-revised-gender-pay-lawsuit/.

3. https://www.nytimes.com/2018/10/25/technology/google-sexual-harassment-andy-rubin.html.

4. Ibid.

5. Ibid.

6. https://www.cnbc.com/2019/09/03/google-legal-chief-david-drummond-marries-employee.html.

7. https://www.nytimes.com/2020/01/10/technology/david-drummond-google.html.

8. https://www.axios.com/executive-accused-of-harassment-at-alphabet-x-unit-is-out-6f583d1e-91e3-4a8b-ae2b-51fd4517ec74.html.

9. https://www.cnbc.com/2018/11/03/google-employee-protests-as-part-of-new-tech-resistance.html.

10. https://www.cnbc.com/2018/06/06/google-employees-presenting-zevin-shareholder-proposal-at-meeting.html.

11. https://www.cnbc.com/2018/11/01/google-employees-walk-out-in-protest-of-sexual-misconduct-handling.html.

12. https://www.cnbc.com/2018/11/08/google-ceo-sundar-pichai-memo-on-changes-sexual-misconduct.html.

13. *Martin v. Page et al.*, Cal Superior Ct., 10 Jan 2019.

14. *Northern California Pipe Trade Pension Plan v. Hennessey et al.*, Cal. Superior Court, 9 Jan. 2019.

15. https://www.theguardian.com/technology/2019/jan/10/google-sexual-harassment-shareholder-lawsuit-alphabet.

16. Emily Chang, *Brotopia: Breaking Up the Boys' Club of Silicon Valley*, New York: Portfolio, 2018.

17. *Carillion: Second Joint Report from the Business, Energy and Industrial Strategy and Work and Pensions Committees of Session 2017–19*, London: House of Commons, 2018.

18. Peter Chapman, *The Last of the Imperious Rich: Lehman Brothers, 1844–2008*, New York: Portfolio, 2008.

19. https://in.reuters.com/article/us-mitsubishimotors-regulations/mitsubishi-motors-says-cheated-on-mileage-tests-for-25-years-idINKCN0XN0DV.

20. https://www.mitsubishi-motors.com/en/company/director/.

21. Brown, Kakabadse and Morais, *The Independent Director in Society*.

7

The Distended Board: Uber

In business, as in sport and many other human endeavours, a certain level of ambition and aggression can be a good thing. This is especially true in start-up organizations, which need to force their way into the market and establish a position quickly. Looking at the history of most successful organizations, we can see how ambitious leaders with a strong vision played a key role in getting the venture off the ground. The problem comes when the vision begins to fade, and ambition and aggression take over and become, not a means to an end, but the end themselves. This is what we mean by amplification of culture: the distortion of the original healthy, vibrant culture into something much darker and malign.

From its inception in 2009, Uber was an assertive, ambitious organization, keen on dominating the newly evolving ride-sharing industry. This ethos permeated interactions within and outside the company, and propelled Uber to an astonishing expansion that saw it established in 53 countries and over 250 cities in under four years. High-profile investors flocked to the company, and in 2019 Uber's pre-IPO valuation hit $72 billion. At IPO, it offered shares at $45 each, for a total valuation of $82.4 billion. The next day the share price was down almost 8 per cent, trading at $42—but Uber now had $8.1 billion in new capital. But the IPO was successful thanks only to some intensive rebuilding work, after a series of scandals that left the company's reputation in tatters.

At the beginning, people could not find enough good things to say about Uber. The company was lauded as a 'disruptor' overturning established categories and transforming the world taxi market forever—although some observers, notably Harvard Business School professor Clayton Christensen,

G. Brown, R. S. Peterson, *Disaster in the Boardroom*,
https://doi.org/10.1007/978-3-030-91658-9_7

argued that Uber was not a true disruptor. Business school academics wrote cases about the company and promoted it to their students as an example; ironically, just as they had with Enron a decade earlier. Forbes praised the company to the skies, arguing that 'if you want to build your own disruptive company, there is a good lesson to learn here.'[1]

Uber made no secret of its aggressive culture, which was seen as one of its strengths; and indeed, in those foundation years it probably was. Uber was trying to establish an entirely new market model in a highly regulated industry, no mean feat at the best of times. The company described its culture as 'hard-charging,' the connotation being that it would not let obstacles stand in its way. That in itself was no bad thing. An element of aggression is an important asset in highly competitive environments and that almost certainly played a role in Uber's early and rapid success.

But Uber pushed the boundaries to breaking point and then beyond. The culture of aggression became amplified to the point where the company's aggressive tendencies encourage other forms of behaviour and led Uber to break moral and ethical limits, with consequent damage to its reputation. That same cultural amplification permeated the culture of the board as well, with aggressive figures like Kalanick and his supporters dominating the boardroom and denying other stakeholders a voice.

As the company moved into territory previously held by licenced and regulated taxi and car services, it tangled repeatedly with state and local governments. In its home city of San Francisco, Uber defied cease and desist orders issued for alleged violation of city and state regulations to its benefit. In New York it increased driver numbers even as officials were scrambling to cap the number of rideshare vehicles. All around the world, Uber continued to build its customer base aggressively. In major European cities including London, Paris and Berlin, taxi drivers engaged in protests and strikes, giving Uber the opportunity to add even more riders as people turned to the company for transport. Uber officials in Paris and South Korea were indicted for violating transportation laws, risking fines and even prison sentences.[2] None of this deterred the founder CEO, Travis Kalanick, who explained that he ignored cease and desist instructions because 'we don't think we should' stop.

Why did the board not intervene when the company started to engage in illegal activities or hold Kalanick personally to account? The answer rests partly on the composition of the board and partly on the character of some its directors. As is often the case with tech firms, the board members were not equal, or at least, some were more equal than others. In 2017 the board consisted of eleven members, a minority of whom were independent directors. The rest were either co-founders like Kalanick himself or company insiders, or representatives of key shareholders. Kalanick and two others, Garrett Camp (one of the co-founders who contributed the original seed money to establish Uber) and Ryan Graves (senior vice-president of global operations and one of Kalanick's most important allies) held so-called supervoting rights which gave them multiple votes per share. Kalanick also had the right to nominate directors to the board, a right he continued to exercise even after his resignation as CEO.[3] Some investors, including the venture capital firm Benchmark, were unhappy with this arrangement and wanted to get rid of supervoting rights; others supported Kalanick and his colleagues, claiming that supervoting made the company more accountable and that taking away rights without consent would be unfair. The board was factional and fractious, but no one yet had the power to effectively challenge Kalanick.

Then, in 2017, a series of events took place that put Uber's 'growth at all costs' approach squarely in the spotlight.

Aggression and Harassment at Uber

During the years of growth, and possibly as a result of the concerted opposition it faced from local governments and competitors, Uber's combative culture became more and more entrenched. The company's stated values included ideas like being '*superpumped*' and 'always be *hustlin*'.' Another later value which became infamous was 'meritocracy and toe-stepping,' which was intended to promote ideas from across the ranks, but instead resulted in a bitterly competitive culture where getting to the 'top' was the first priority.

By 2017 the company had developed what some called a 'Hobbesian environment,' in which workers were pitted against one another and where top performers engaged in bad behaviour while management looked the other way. Reported incidents included a manager groping a female employee, a director shouting a homophobic slur at a subordinate and a manager threatening to beat an employee's head with a baseball bat.[4] Matters came to a head in February 2017 when a female Uber engineer posted on a blog describing her two-year experience of gender discrimination and sexual harassment. The post went viral, and Uber's culture was suddenly under the public microscope. By this time the company was already facing sexual harassment or abuse lawsuits in multiple countries.

Kalanick opened an investigation and hired outside law firm Covington and Burling to manage it. While some praised his concern, others argued that Kalanick himself had set Uber's combative, truculent tone both inside and outside the company. Kalanick's position was undermined still further in March 2017 when a video emerged of him shouting at and swearing at an

Uber driver who complained about pay and conditions.[5] Not every Uber driver agreed with the man's complaints, but many were shocked by Kalanick's attitude and language and there were reports of drivers defecting to rival firms such as Lyft.

The wave of sexual harassment claims continued to grow. Multiple employees reported reaching 'dead-ends' with human resources, as harassers were shuffled around the company or women's complaints were simply ignored. Current and former employees spoke repeatedly of how an 'A-Team' of executives, all personal friends of Kalanick, were consistently protected from any ramifications of their actions. Kalanick's ex-girlfriend described an executive team outing with Kalanick and other Uber managers who selected numbered women at a Korean escort bar.[6] When a female passenger filed rape charges against an Uber driver in India, the executive team took the decision to obtain medical records from the victim in order to discredit her.[7] It emerged that the company's head of engineering had been the subject of a sexual harassment claim in his prior position at Google although he denies the allegation.[8]

And if that was not enough, people were reminded of the CEO's comment to *GQ* magazine in 2014 where he called the company 'Boob-er' because it enabled him to attract so many women.[9] Some board members seem to have regarded this culture as normal. In June 2017, director David Bonderman resigned after telling fellow director Arianna Huffington during a board meeting that women talked too much.[10]

In 2017, the US Equal Employment Opportunity Commission (EEOC) began a federal investigation into Uber's toxic workplace culture. The Commission ultimately 'found reasonable cause to believe that Uber permitted a culture of sexual harassment and retaliation against individuals who complained about such harassment' and launched a federal case against the company.[11]

The *Greyball* Scandal

In early 2017, on the heels of Uber's sexual harassment scandals, the *New York Times* uncovered the company's use of an internal data tool called '*Greyball*' to secretly pull internal and external customer data to deny rides to certain individuals. Uber defended the programme, claiming that it was merely denying rides to 'fraudulent users,' but it became clear that *Greyball* was also being used against investigators and those suspected of working for city agencies to run sting operations against Uber. The programme was deployed in cities where the company was not authorized to operate, denying rides to government officials in France, Italy, Australia, China, South Korea and several major US cities. Uber quickly scaled back its use of *Greyball* as the news broke, but the scandal contributed to Uber's loss of its London licence later that year as severe doubts were raised about its commitment to corporate responsibility and lawfulness.[12]

By June 2017, at least five major investors were demanding that Kalanick resign as CEO. Kalanick had earlier claimed that he 'needed leadership help and would get it,' but in fact very little had changed. It was becoming increasingly clear that Kalanick himself was at the heart of the problem. One public relations expert claimed that what Uber needed was 'a colonic, not a Kalanick.'[13] Kalanick resigned as CEO that same month but remained on the board.[14]

Data Breach Cover-Up

Greyball was soon to be the least of Uber's worries. In November 2017, the company revealed that its IT systems had been hacked, resulting in a massive theft of personal data that affected over 57 million riders, including drivers' licence information for 600,000 American drivers. That was bad enough, but it then emerged that the data breach had occurred nearly a year earlier, in 2016. Rather than advise affected customers and drivers—or the applicable regulators—that their personal data had been compromised, Uber had instead chosen to pay the hackers $100,000 to destroy the stolen information. Former CEO Kalanick was aware of and approved the payment, and the company then hid the incident. When the cover-up was finally disclosed the company's chief security officer, who had also worked to keep the incident quiet, was terminated.

In 2018, Uber finally reached a settlement with the fifty US states and the District of Columbia on the data breach claims, paying fees of $148 million.[15] In the UK, the company was fined only £385,000 for the same breach, having narrowly missed the timing for significantly higher fines under the new GDPR rules.[16] At the same time as the data breach scandal broke, Uber was also facing *multiple* criminal investigations for bribery, impermissible software use to evade law enforcement, suspect pricing and theft of trade secrets, all issues that could be traced back to its 'hard-charging' approach that had changed from competitiveness to a culture of winning at the expense of anything and everything.

But as Uber's pay-off of data thieves dominated news headlines, one thing was markedly different: the tone of corporate leadership. Dara Khosrowshahi, the new CEO, openly discussed both the data breach and the company's attempt to hide it, using this as an opportunity to apologize and take responsibility. 'None of this should have happened, and I will not make excuses for it,' he stated. 'While I can't erase the past, I can commit on behalf of every Uber employee that we will learn from our mistakes. We are changing the way we do business.'[17] His attempt to 'get skeletons out of the closet during the first months of his tenure' won him approval in some quarters and signalled that change was coming at Uber.[18]

Arrogance and Aggression

The amplification of Uber's culture that occurred between the company's foundation and the blow-up in 2017 took that culture well beyond the bounds of normal competitive behaviour. How much of this change was due to the intense opposition the company faced wherever it tried to do business, and how much was down to the personalities of the 'A-team' coterie of executives around Kalanick is not clear; both probably played a part. Certainly, values like 'always be hustlin'' and 'stepping on toes' seem expressly designed to promote a culture of confrontation. Kalanick did make reference to the notion of 'principled confrontation,' but looking at the company's behaviour it is difficult to see what 'principles' he was referring to.

Arrogance and aggression were the hallmarks of Uber's distorted culture, and both these attributes create significant risks for a company. The aggressive behaviour of executives towards customers, drivers and each other can be compared to the 'reign of terror' at Volkswagen under the leadership of Ferdinand Piëch, who threatened his staff with dismissal unless they met his demands, or Richard Fuld of Lehman Brothers threatening to 'cut out the hearts' of short-sellers. In both cases, aggression created a culture where people were unwilling or unable to stand up to their leaders. In Volkswagen, this created a scandal for which the company is still paying; at Lehman Brothers, it brought the house down. Compared to this, Uber got off lightly, and the bloggers and whistleblowers who made accusations against their leaders may well have helped to save the company.

Aggression was also a key feature at Enron where CEO and later chairman Kenneth Lay and his successor as CEO, Jeffrey Skilling, presided over a hard-nosed culture where failure was not tolerated and success was the only thing that mattered. According to Bethany McLean and Peter Elkind in their book *The Smartest Guys in the Room*, Skilling believed that fear and reward were the only things that motivated people. Executive were rewarded according to the amount of money they generated for the firm and were dismissed if they failed to generate enough. People were graded according to performance on a scale from one to five, and Skilling ordered that 10 per cent of the workforce should always be graded five, the lowest on the scale. Those who scored five were given two weeks to find another job within the company or were fired.[19]

This system of performance review was known in the firm with grim humour as 'rank and yank.' Skilling described it as being of vital importance to the company, probably because it too created a 'reign of terror' that kept executives silent and compliant. The corruption at Enron finally came to public notice and the company imploded. Skilling and Lay were both sentenced to prison, and former CEO Lay was named by broadcaster CNBC as the third-worst American CEO of all time—Richard Fuld of Lehman Brothers was awarded the top spot.[20]

A certain level of aggression can be a positive factor in leadership, so long as it is accompanied by a degree of integrity. Coca-Cola's long-serving CEO Paul Austin once described himself as 'playing my executives like a violin' in order to get the most out of them. But while a degree of stress can be a useful spur to creativity and innovation, putting people under incredible strain for long periods—as we learned during the pandemic—does not bring out the best in them. The first thing that Austin's successor, Roberto Goizueta, did was to bring the culture back to a place where people could trust each other and work collaboratively without fear.

Kalanick went too far. As psychologist Adrian Furnham has pointed out, early success—which Uber clearly had—can turn initial confidence and toughness into arrogance.[21] More generally, as has often been observed, success all too often carries with it the seeds of future failure. Companies and their leaders begin to believe their own publicity. In the early years, business academics and journalists saw Uber as a shining example of how to re-invent not just a business but an entire market. The 'A-team' at Uber began to believe their own publicity. They were the best; they too were the smartest guys in the room, and no one could touch them.

A less toxic example but one which still shows clearly the dangers of believing one's own publicity is IBM. In the 1950s and 1960s, IBM dominated the emerging computer industry. It was held up as a beacon of corporate success, and its chairman, Thomas Watson, was a national hero. To many people—including its own employees—IBM was synonymous with computers in the same way that Levi's was with denim jeans.

Part of IBM's success was down to the fact that the company had invested heavily in developing a powerful and cohesive culture, which in turn played a major role in driving the company. IBM was particularly proud of its strong identity. Staff referred to themselves as IBMers; they wore identical suits and ties to work and regarded themselves as part of an IBM family. Another important element of the culture was innovation. IBM staff were encouraged to think outside the box, designing and creating new products and re-imagining the future of technology. Thomas Watson praised people who questioned the status quo and went beyond the limits of conventional think-ing, referring to them as 'wild ducks.' There are similarities here to Uber's 'meritocracy and toe-stepping' concept; people were supposed to be free to say what they liked, no matter where they were in the hierarchy. 'Treasure the wild ducks' became one of the organization's mantras, and these free-flyers and free-thinkers were seen as one of the reasons behind IBM's success.

Unfortunately, as time wore on, the reality on the ground in IBM no longer matched the perceptions of those at the top. The board and senior manage-ment continued to believe that the 'wild ducks' were driving innovation at IBM. In reality, at lower levels the corporate culture had ossified. The empha-sis on identity was still there, stronger than ever, dominating everything else. But out-of-the-box thinking was no longer allowed. People who challenged accepted authority were side-lined or pressured to leave. 'What happened to all the wild ducks?' people asked. The answer was, 'They all got shot.'

This is a slightly different take on the idea of amplification of culture, with one form of amplification happening at the top of the organization—we are the best in the world—and another form happening lower down—confor-mity is all that matters. Inevitably, with a culture that focused on conformity but denied challenge and innovation, IBM ground to a halt while newer, more agile competitors eroded its position in the marketplace. The company was eventually re-invented and new life was breathed into its old culture of innovation, but the process was a long and painful one.

For all these companies, aggression and undiluted competitiveness coupled with arrogance and a false sense of superiority led them into a trap. Their view of risk, especially reputational risk, became badly distorted. They felt that the rules no longer applied to them; either they could get away with it because they were cleverer than everyone else or, particularly at Volkswagen and IBM, they deemed themselves too big to fail. They were wrong, because as soon as news of their transgressions was exposed, the trust of stakeholders—employ-ees, customers, investors, regulators and society at large—began to erode.

With hindsight, the aggression and arrogance at Uber, which were never concealed, should have been warnings signs for investors and the board. And therein lies the problem, because investors and the board had been similarly blinded by Uber's early success. There is no evidence that anyone seriously tried to hold the board to account until 2017, when the scale of the scandals began to turn public opinion and a real reputational threat began to emerge. Then the board did act, and reasonably swiftly, securing Kalanick's resignation in a matter of days. He lasted for another two years on the board, however, which must have made for uncomfortable board meetings, a little like having Banquo's ghost sitting at the boardroom table.

But why did the directors not act sooner? The aggressive style, the flouting of laws and regulators, the 'macho' culture were widely known within the company and in many cases outside it, but until things began to go wrong, no one thought it necessary to challenge Kalanick and his team. They were delivering value and growth; did it matter how? Illegal software and sexual harassment could be dismissed as the transaction costs of success. One cannot make an omelette without breaking eggs.

Certainly the board failed, initially at least, in its duty to shape the culture of the business in a way that served the business. The directors failed to scrutinize the company appropriately and failed to challenge illegal and immoral behaviour. Had they done so and asserted their authority over Kalanick, they might have been able to pull the culture back on track and avoid the entire sorry mess. The one positive thing to take from this is that at least the board *did* act. But it was nearly too late.

When the Board (Finally) Asserted Itself

When the board finally did take action, it showed itself willing to act and to confront the huge cultural problem Uber was confronted with. Replacing Kalanick with a CEO whose leadership style and values were diametrically opposed to his was a major step. This helped to restore trust in the organization and established a platform from which a more general cultural turnaround could be launched.

Tackling that dysfunctional culture directly was the right thing to do, but we must not underestimate the magnitude of the task the board and the new CEO faced. Of critical importance was the recognition and public admission that the focus on aggressive growth at all costs was no longer suited to the company's needs. Uber still had growth plans, of course, but a new approach was needed. The removal of special voting rights meant a more even distribution of power on the board, which should encourage the board to assert itself and become more independent. The eventual removal of Kalanick from the board must have been useful as well.

Amplification of Culture

At Uber, amplification of culture manifested itself in aggressive, uncooperative behaviour towards stakeholders, a sense of arrogance and superiority and an emphasis on competition and 'winning' as the primary goal. We saw too how aggression and that same focus on winning at all costs pervaded the cultures of other companies including Volkswagen, Lehman Brothers and Enron, among others. At IBM there was less aggression but more arrogance, with justified pride in past accomplishments turning into a close-minded belief that the company was invulnerable, compounded by the fact that the board and the executive both had lost touch with the rest of the organization.

Another common warning sign is lack of transparency. No matter how many key figures in the organization may believe that what they are doing is right, a corner of their mind warns them that not everyone will agree. The outside world may have a very different perception. So, even as those key figures continue to proclaim that their actions are justified, they also conspire to sweep evidence of their actions under the carpet. Overly amplified cultures can also be secretive, with an inner cabal controlling information and refusing to share it with outsiders.

Whenever these behaviours are present, there is a strong possibility that the culture is going off the rails. Directors are no longer scrutinizing the actions of the executive, or each other. Instead, they have absorbed the dominant narrative. A kind of mass delusion descends in which everyone believes—or pretends to believe—that the amplified culture is somehow true and real. Directors subordinate their independence to the greater culture, and the interests of stakeholders are also subordinated or trampled underfoot.

The first priority for any board on spotting warning signs is to scrutinize and analyse the culture for themselves, and not just accept the CEO's word that everything is well. Boards should be running culture audits, using tools such as rigorous culture assessments and employee engagement surveys, to try and understand what the real situation is. Most companies have these surveys, but they do not always ask the right questions or allow employees to speak in their own voices. For example, sorting results by level or function within the organization, ethnicity or gender can reveal patterns that aggregated data do not show. The 'small group of unhappy employees' might just be a key underrepresented group. Surveys also should use open-ended questions where employees can speak freely and answer questions the survey does not ask. Key indicator data such as turnover, unpaid leave, average salaries compared to benchmarks and so on can also be useful in establishing the truth, and boards also need to see the organization for themselves, talk to the workforce and to other stakeholders directly and listen to their views.

A key difference lies in espoused values versus enacted values: what does the organization think its values are, or claim its values are, and how are those values perceived by employees, customers and others? Does the organization live its claimed values, or does employee behaviour indicate that its true values lie somewhere else? Analysing the gap between the two can tell the board a great deal about the real situation.

And finally, of course, boards need to scrutinize themselves and ensure their own cultures are fit for purpose. This requires honest discussions around the issue, and the chair in particular has a vital role in determining the culture and ensuring it is strong and independent. A robust and independent system of board evaluation also has a strong role to play.

Notes

1. https://www.forbes.com/sites/kevinharrington/2014/06/19/the-uber-disruptor-what-ride-shares-can-teach-you-about-disrupting-the-market/#4cdf540e7b01.
2. https://corpgov.law.harvard.edu/2018/01/20/governance-gone-wild-misbehavior-at-uber-technologies/.
3. https://boardmember.com/corporate-governance-lessons-learned-ubers-board/; https://www.reuters.com/article/us-uber-board-directors-idUSKCN1C72CK.
4. https://www.nytimes.com/2017/02/22/technology/uber-workplace-culture.html.
5. https://www.washingtonpost.com/news/innovations/wp/2017/03/01/what-uber-drivers-think-about-ceo-travis-kalanick-yelling-at-one-of-their-own/.
6. https://www.theinformation.com/uber-groups-visit-to-seoul-escort-bar-sparked-hr-complaint.
7. https://www.bloomberg.com/news/articles/2017-06-07/uber-workplace-probe-extends-to-handling-of-india-rape-case.
8. https://www.vox.com/2017/2/27/14745360/amit-singhal-google-uber.
9. https://www.gq.com/story/uber-cab-confessions?currentPage=1.
10. https://www.huffingtonpost.co.uk/entry/david-bonderman-sexist-joke-uber_n_59404db6e4b09ad4fbe3d96e?
11. https://www.nytimes.com/2019/12/18/technology/uber-settles-eeoc-investigation-workplace-culture.html.

12. https://www.theguardian.com/technology/2017/mar/03/uber-secret-program-greyball-resignation-ed-baker.
13. Ibid.
14. https://www.nytimes.com/2019/12/24/technology/uber-travis-kalanick.html.
15. https://www.npr.org/2018/09/27/652119109/uber-pays-148-million-over-year-long-cover-up-of-data-breach?t=1585311081316.
16. https://www.telegraph.co.uk/news/2018/11/27/uber-fined-385000-watchdog-hackers-stole-sensitive-details-27m/.
17. https://www.uber.com/newsroom/2016-data-incident/.
18. https://www.ft.com/content/ed66a21a-cf0e-11e7-9dbb-291a884dd8c6.
19. Bethany McLean and Peter Elkind, *The Smartest Guys in the Room: The Amazing Rise and Scandalous Fall of Enron*, New York: Portfolio, 2003.
20. https://www.cnbc.com/2009/04/30/Portfolios-Worst-American-CEOs-of-All-Time.html?slide=19.
21. https://www.managers.org.uk/insights/news/2017/november/the-three-personality-disorders-of-failed-ceos.

8

The Bystander Board: BP and *Deepwater Horizon*

We have seen what happens when a strong culture goes wrong, but sometimes a weak board culture can be equally dangerous. This is the case with bystander boards, where the board fails to work together and no one steps up to take responsibility at a critical time. As noted, diffusion of responsibility is a particular risk when key board members—especially the chair—are new in post and have not had time to form strong relationships. The *Deepwater Horizon* disaster and the BP board's response to it are an example of this dysfunction in action.

The *Deepwater Horizon* was a floating, semi-submersible drilling unit operated by a contractor employed by BP in the Gulf of Mexico in 2010. The US Department of Interior had granted the company an exemption from filing the usual detailed environmental impact study because a massive spill was deemed unlikely. The rig was actually owned and operated by another firm, Transocean, under contract with BP.

On 20 April 2010, the *Deepwater Horizon* was drilling an exploratory well when an explosion occurred on the rig, leading to eleven deaths and seventeen injuries, and an ongoing spill that poured oil into the Gulf waters for eighty-seven days. The rig itself ultimately burned and sank.[1] By the time the underwater well was finally capped, an estimated 168 million gallons of oil had been pumped into the water, creating a 25,000-square mile oil slick that stretched along the US Gulf Coast from Mississippi to Florida.

The spill halted the Gulf fishing and tourism industries, which were worth $3.5–4.5 billion per year. Millions of pounds of oily residue coated the coastlines of Alabama, Louisiana, Mississippi and Florida for hundreds of miles, and untold damage was caused to sea and wetland life, including damage to

G. Brown, R. S. Peterson, *Disaster in the Boardroom*,
https://doi.org/10.1007/978-3-030-91658-9_8

fish at the cellular level, massive reductions in fish stocks, severe lung damage to the bottlenose dolphin population and rapidly rising rates of sea turtles, dolphins and whales being stranded on land.[2]

President Barack Obama ultimately convened the US National Commission on the BP Deepwater Horizon Oil Spill and Offshore Drilling to investigate the incident. The Commission concluded in its 300-plus page report in September 2011 that the disaster was 'an overarching failure of management,' finding that the failures leading to the explosion were systemic, likely to recur, and arose almost entirely from decisions that saved time and money for BP and its collaborators in the drilling project.

At the time of the accident, BP had an entrenched culture of 'costs first' according to employee reports, not, as the company itself claimed, 'safety first.' At each turn in the path to the *Deepwater Horizon* disaster, individual decisions prioritized cutting costs and reducing employee hours, often at the clear expense of safety protocols and systems, and in the face of warnings from workers on the ground. These systemic flaws, when combined with lax US regulatory policies and set against an industry backdrop that valued speed and economic efficiency above all, were lethal.[3] However, the Commission's report was criticized by some for its failure to evaluate what the BP board and corporate leaders did—and did not—do at a governance level to resolve a previously identified culture that had historically prioritized safety over profit.[4]

BP faced a stream of civil and criminal lawsuits including, ultimately, charges of corporate manslaughter, to which the company later pleaded guilty. At time of writing, BP has paid over $65 billion in fines, compensation and legal damages as a result of the *Deepwater Horizon* disaster.[5] In addition to direct economic and environmental costs and plummeting stock value, the incident was also a public relations nightmare, with offhand comments and a perception of callousness by BP's leaders contributing to a negative public opinion of the company. Among other missteps, CEO Tony Hayward—who, ironically, had been elevated in 2007 in part to bring a renewed focus to the company's safety efforts—was quoted as asking his executive team, 'what did we do to deserve this?'[6]

The Myth of the 'culture of safety'

There was significant evidence of systemic issues concerning safety management and the absence of a culture of safety at BP as early as 2001. In that year, outside lawyers and an internal committee prepared a series of investigative reports focusing on BP's Alaska operations but covering other areas as well, including operations in Texas and California. These reports highlighted an alarming pattern of a company-wide culture that disregarded safety rules and led to increased risk.[7]

In 2005, an explosion at a BP refinery in Texas killed 15 people, injured 180 others and caused massive damage to the refinery itself. The refinery, built in 1934, had been acquired as part of BP's takeover of Amoco in 1999. Amoco is alleged to have neglected making safety improvement to the facility, and BP failed to rectify the problems.[8] The incident resulted in a record-breaking $87 million in fines as a result of BP's failure to correct identified safety violations. A comprehensive internal analysis found several primary causes for the accident, including unclear expectations of supervisory and management behaviours that in turn led to inconsistent adherence to rules; an environment in which workers and managers were not encouraged to suggest improvements; and a lack of clear safety, operations performance and systematic risk reduction priorities across the organization. In particular, the report found several cultural problems that contributed to the explosion, noting that the existing organizational culture simply did not treat 'safety and basic operations as a priority.' After extensively reviewing records and interviewing personnel, BP's internal report noted that

> safety did not seem to be a priority, particularly as compared to cost management, for example. Although leadership stated 'safety first,' this was not evidenced or believed by many of the workforce. Lack of leadership visibility and poor communication through the complex, siloed organization did not assist in delivering the right messages.[9]

BP also appointed an independent panel, headed by former US Secretary of State James Baker, to examine safety at all its American refineries. The panel focused on refineries, but its conclusions were much broader. The Baker report found that 'BP has not provided effective process safety leadership' and that 'leadership from the top of the company, starting with the board and going down' was required. The report describes the lack of leadership as 'systemic, touching all levels of BP's corporate management' and concluded that 'BP's board did not ensure, as a best practice, that management implemented effective safety practices.'

> The BP board was on notice that the corporate culture of 'saving over safety' pervaded BP. They were on notice that the mechanisms for informing the board were dysfunctional. The board had an affirmative duty to understand the risks involved in the drilling of [the Texas] well.[10]

In March 2006, while the Baker panel was still working on its safety analysis, a BP pipeline in Prudhoe Bay, Alaska, spilled 212,000 gallons of oil. Fines of $25 million were levied as a result of the company's failure to repair the corroded pipeline, and BP was ordered to develop a system-wide programme to assess and manage pipeline integrity at an anticipated cost of $60 million.[11] The company was later ordered to pay a further $66 million in connection with a civil lawsuit, and BP also pled guilty to a federal investigation which found that the company exhibited a cost-cutting mentality that contributed to the failure to safely maintain the pipeline.

Less than a year later, BP hired an external panel of experts to assess employee complaints that equipment and safety systems were not being maintained. The panel found 'systemic problems in maintenance and inspection programmes' and warned that a chronic lack of accountability on the part of senior management had created a 'fundamental culture of mistrust' on the part of BP workers.[12]

However, despite internal and external analysis after both the lethal Texas refinery explosion and the Alaska 2006 pipeline leaks, there is very little to suggest that the company, at a governance level, focused on how to correct the cultural and process problems around safety. In 2007, Tony Hayward was promoted from head of exploration and product to CEO. He took the job in the wake of the two disasters, with a supposed focus on safety.

BP's Response to *Deepwater Horizon*: Missing the Mark

From the outset, BP failed to be honest or transparent about the explosion and ensuing oil spill. The BP board did not even meet for several days after the accident, in part because the board felt the problem was nothing to do with them because the rig belonged to Transocean; therefore they believed the liability was with Transocean. Only once the scale of the threat and BP's name was invoked repeatedly did the board meet to discuss BP's response. The company downplayed the severity of the leak, minimized the volume of oil being pumped into the sea and wildly over-estimated the speed with which the well could be capped. Worse, BP came across as both oblivious and heartless to the massive devastation caused by the accident. The company quickly lost credibility with the media, the public and the President of the USA. Among the incidents which contributed to this were:

- CEO Hayward, who took personal charge of the operation to cap the well, famously complained that he 'wanted his life back' and described the spill as 'tiny' when compared to the size of the ocean. In June, he provoked outrage when he was photographed yachting off the Isle of Wight, just two days after testifying before the US Congress about the explosion.[13]
- BP initially insisted that fishermen who volunteered their time to help with the clean-up, despite having just lost their livelihood, had to agree in advance to a cap on any damages owed by BP. The company refused to compensate fishermen who couldn't show proof of 'normal earning,' despite the fact that the vast majority kept no such records.[14] BP also angered Alabama's attorney-general, Troy King, by encouraging coastal residents to forfeit their right to sue in exchange for payments of just $5000. Hayward commented that BP would pay all 'legitimate' claims arising from the accident and then went on to say that many claims would be 'illegitimate' because 'this is America.'[15]
- Chair of the BP board Carl-Henric Svanberg, while attempting to express empathy (and in fairness, while being interviewed off-script and in his second language), noted that BP cared about the 'small people.' Along with Hayward's comments, this quickly became part of a public narrative depicting an uncaring, unaccountable organization and board.[16]

Where was the board-level guidance and crisis management? In public, at least, they were notably lacking; to all appearances, the board was keeping its head down. On one occasion Svanberg commented that Hayward should be the one to be publicly dealing with the issues, as 'there was no crisis that was ever made better by having two different people talk about it.'[17] As we saw earlier, one manifestation of diffusion of responsibility is the loading of risk onto a single individual, and Svanberg's remark suggests that was exactly what happened at BP.

'Culture of safety' Revisited

In 2013, Bob Bea, a former BP consultant and expert in catastrophic engineering failures, gave evidence in a civil lawsuit against BP. Bea stated that over time he had become more and more concerned that BP's risk management systems and protocols were not fit for purpose. He had warned the company in 2007 that 'you still don't get it. Process safety is deadly serious and now you've turned it into a travelling road show.' Bea testified that 'cost-cutting' drove the failure to implement proper safety systems on the *Deepwater Horizon*, citing a BP mantra of 'every dollar counts.' The system failure encompassed much more than just the failed safety mechanisms on the rig itself; it extended right across the organization and all the way to headquarters in London.[18]

BP's leaders, managers, engineers and workers consistently made decisions that favoured speed over safety, eventually falling prey to an effect known as 'normalization of deviance.' As anomalies arose in their testing data, they incrementally adjusted standards to redefine the anomaly as within the range of acceptable error. The presidential commission of inquiry concluded that a shared ethos of cost-cutting between BP and its partners contributed to the disaster.[19] This resulted in multiple alarm systems on the *Deepwater Horizon* rig being disabled or poorly maintained as the quickest (rather than the safest) path was chosen again and again.[20] These choices, fed by the culture of 'every dollar counts,' gradually pushed the rig towards the series of small failures that led to disaster.[21] Despite this, Tony Hayward testified before the US Congress that 'there is nothing I have seen in the evidence so far that anyone put costs ahead of safety.'

Everyone at BP from the board on down knew that deep water drilling that was inherently dangerous but also that, if all went well, it would be extraordinarily profitable. There was an inherent contradiction between this high level of operational risk and an organizational culture focused on cost-cutting and making every dollar count. But there is virtually no indication that the board, as the organizational leadership, ever considered this crucial issue. Analysis from the University of California-Berkeley's Center for Catastrophic Risk Management determined that the disaster was preventable had existing guidelines and practices been followed.[22] Instead, BP and its partners continued to focus on costs and efficiency over risk which led, and in the words of one observer, to 'a slow, unchallenged drift into less safe processes and procedures because "we haven't had a problem yet".'[23]

The Board's Response

At the time of the explosion, the board of directors was in a weak position. There had been a number of recent changes in board membership, and some directors had not yet got to grips with the complexities of leading an organization the size of BP. Svanberg, the chair, had been in post for less than four months. Perhaps for this reason, from the outset, the board backed Hayward, despite increasing concerns about BP's culture and a series of public relations blunders. In a June 2010 investors' call, 'The chairman expressed full support for [Hayward], and there isn't anything more supportive they could have said at this time.'[24] Despite this, Hayward was replaced as CEO by Bob Dudley in October of that year. Otherwise, the BP board appears to have taken little to no other public action in response to the Deepwater Horizon crisis. As one commentator noted, the board's response to the tragedy was 'deafening silence.'[25]

In some ways, though, asking why the board did not make a more positive response during the crisis is asking the wrong question. The diffusion of responsibility at BP goes back a long way. The board had plenty of opportunities to intervene and ensure that BP really did have a culture of safety. As early as 2005 (and likely earlier), the board had detailed reports indicating an embedded culture that prioritized costs over safety. If the board did make any attempt to deal with this issue, there is little evidence to support it. It is true that Tony Hayward was promoted to 'focus' on safety. But the board continued to ignore key information that should have shown them safety was still not a priority. Where was the collective responsibility of the board for what was clearly a deeply rooted organizational culture issue? Although he did not create the cost-cutting culture, Hayward owned it in the end. When the Deepwater Horizon disaster happened, the board was silent, and Hayward was effectively hung out to dry.

Lack of Inquiry and Scrutiny

What happened at BP is symptomatic of the deeper problem of diffusion of responsibility, but why does this happen? The fault lies with the directors, especially the independent directors. Taking responsibility is one of the most important responsibilities of a non-executive director, and if directors fail to do so, then their effectiveness is compromised. As a result, the organization and its staff and contractors are put at risk, and in the case of *Deepwater Horizon*, eleven people were killed.

The diffusion of responsibility can manifest itself in a number of different ways, but two of the most important that we saw in the BP case are the lack of challenge, inquiry and scrutiny, and the failure to take responsibility in a crisis. Scrutiny is one of the most important duties of an independent director, and boards need to do their utmost to foster that culture of willingness to challenge. When we look at other scandals and disasters, we see a similar failure to take action, even though issues are well known and, in some cases, already in the public domain.

As we saw in Chap. 4, a lack of scrutiny and failure to hold the executive team to account has been a feature in many cases. Tyco was described as having a lack of governance and accountability, and the board of BHP Billiton seems to have overlooked the poor environmental and safety record of Vale when they partnered with them in the Mariana dam project. The mining company Glencore had a long track record of 'sailing close to the wind,' in the words of one industry observer, but the board seems to have remained silent. And, as highlighted in Appendix 1, the chair of the board during the Project Caesar scandal was none other than Tony Hayward.

Looking further afield, the board of Goldman Sachs is full of illustrious names serving as independent directors, powerful people with international connections in the business, politics and higher education. Yet since 2008, Goldman Sachs has rarely been out of the news. Accusations of share price manipulation, insider trading, gender bias, dealings with repressive regimes such as the government of Venezuela are just some of the scandals the bank has been dealing with. The most recent, and costly, was its involvement with the Malaysian sovereign wealth fund, 1Malaysia Development Berhad (1MDB). The bank was already under investigation by American authorities for failure to report suspicious transactions when it emerged that two former Goldman executives had siphoned around $200 million from transactions with 1MDB. Both executives were charged with money-laundering and Goldman Sachs paid the Malaysian government $3.9 billion in compensation, forcing the company to downgrade its earnings forecasts.[26]

There have been repeated accusations that something is broken in the culture of Goldman Sachs. One insider, Steven Mandis, described in detail the process of 'organizational drift' whereby the organization has deviated from its original principles. According to Mandis, insiders either cannot or will not recognize that this drift is taking place. Another senior executive, Greg Smith, resigned from Goldman Sachs citing a toxic and destructive culture in the bank as the reason for his departure.[27]

When looking at 1MDB, then, we come back to the eternal question: where was the board? If people are writing books about the company describing its culture as toxic and in a state of drift, we hope that someone on the board is taking these accusations seriously, but why have we not seen evidence of action? Why was the drift allowed to continue and the 1MDB fiasco allowed to happen? And will this finally be enough to wake the board and compel them to demand real change?

Like the board of BP, the board of Goldman Sachs has been largely silent about the affair. The Glencore board, too, declined to publicly apologize or take responsibility for Project Caesar. In these and many other cases, individuals are identified as the culprits, blame is shifted onto their shoulders and the board stands back, not taking any responsibility. Far from being independent directors demanding accountability and accepting responsibility, the directors in these cases are like mourners at a funeral; except in this case, the funeral may be their own.

Why does this diffusion of responsibility happen? It seems to be hard-wired into the culture of some boards. Many boards are quite large, large enough to be unwieldy, and as Latané and Darley showed in their research, diffusion is more likely to happen in larger groups—put simply, there are more people to hide behind. Another issue in some cases, at least, is the lack of diversity. Both before and after the disaster, the BP board was composed largely of older white men with minimal diversity in professional or personal experience; almost all members are/were from the oil and gas industry or the financial services sector. There was a definite lack of independent outside voices such as retail who might have been more willing to confront and challenge.

Diffusion of Responsibility

One of the key symptoms of diffusion of responsibility is silence. If there are issues that are clearly going wrong within the organization but no one is willing to confront, to raise concerns and complaints at board level, to rock the boat if necessary, then clearly people are not accepting their responsibilities as independent directors, which means their independence is compromised. We saw at BP, Goldman Sachs, Glencore and others how the board remained largely silent, even as the company was experiencing a major crisis. There are other examples too. The board of Oxfam was nearly invisible during the Haiti sexual abuse scandal, even though the affair had been an open secret within the organization for several years.

Another sign to look for is gatekeepers. If all interactions between directors and executives need to go through the CEO, or through the chair or board secretary or senior independent director, then the board is not functioning correctly. Directors need to be able to roam around the organization, asking questions and learning about issues. High-functioning boards require independent directors as part of their contracts to undertake site visits and report back on what they find. In this way, the board can proactively inform itself as to what the true situation is on the ground—rather than relying on the opinions of the CEO and senior executives—and spot problems with culture hopefully before they happen.

Another important mechanism is the establishment of appropriate board committees with clear terms of reference and a remit to inquire into the workings of the organization. Each committee should have a designated chair who is also an independent director, and committees should present reports at each board meeting. These reports need to sum up not only the decisions each committee reached but also how it reached those decisions, whether there were dissenting voices, general feelings around key issues and any learning that emerged as a result of the discussions. The number of committees and their focus depends on the activities in which the organization is engaged. For example, if health and safety is a priority issue, the board should have a health and safety committee; in an educational institution where the safeguarding of young people is of paramount importance, then the board should have a safeguarding committee; and so on.

As an alternative, boards could consider the dual assurance model adopted by some organizations including the University of Exeter. In dual assurance, the board appoints leads in key functional areas who are paired with the executive leads for those same functions. The independent director lead and the executive lead meet regularly and the director lead then reports back to the board.

Whatever method is used, the point is to make sure that board responsibilities are met and true challenge to the executive happens. Many board members do not see their boards as a group, but rather as a collection of individuals all ostensibly working to help the organization. That aim is laudable, but the problem is that by focusing on their own role, board members are unaware of the group dynamics that we are talking about in this book. Directors need to understand that they work together as a unit; only thus will they meet their goals. Therefore, as well as holding the executive to account, the board also needs to hold itself to account, and assigning directors with formal responsibilities means they will find it harder to dodge those responsibilities even if they wish to. Meanwhile, the board culture should be reinforced in order to make clear that responsibility is not an option—it is a duty imposed on each and every independent director.

Notes

1. Much has been written about the series of technical errors and misjudgements that led to the explosion and about BP's consistent series of safety-related problems over the past twenty years. Those will not be revisited in detail here.
2. https://www.thebalance.com/bp-gulf-oil-spill-facts-economic-impact-3306212.
3. https://www.bbc.co.uk/news/world-us-canada-12124830.
4. http://www.law.harvard.edu/programs/corp_gov/articles/Heineman_BusinessWeek_07-27-10.pdf.

5. https://uk.reuters.com/article/uk-bp-deepwaterhorizon/bp-deepwater-horizon-costs-balloon-to-65-billion-idUKKBN1F50O6.
6. https://www.theguardian.com/business/2010/jun/20/tony-hayward-bp.
7. https://www.propublica.org/article/years-of-internal-bp-probes-warned-that-neglect-could-lead-to-accidents.
8. https://www.kraftlaw.com/mesothelioma/job-site/bp-amoco-oil-refinery-in-texas-city-texas/#:~:text=The%20enormous%20BP%20Amoco%20Oil,of%20Standard%20Oil%20of%20Indiana.&text=An%20investigation%20by%20the%20U.S.,been%20responsible%20for%20the%20explosion.
9. https://web.archive.org/web/20060525213547/http://www.bp.com/liveassets/bp_internet/us/bp_us_english/STAGING/local_assets/downloads/t/final_report.pdf.
10. https://www.hse.gov.uk/leadership/bakerreport.pdf.
11. https://www.theguardian.com/environment/2011/may/04/bp-25m-north-slope-oil-spill.
12. https://www.propublica.org/article/years-of-internal-bp-probes-warned-that-neglect-could-lead-to-accidents.
13. https://www.theguardian.com/business/2010/jun/20/tony-hayward-bp.
14. https://www.theguardian.com/business/2010/may/13/bp-boss-admits-mistakes-gulf-oil-spill.
15. http://www.ethicalcorp.com/business-strategy/bp-and-gulf-mexico-oil-spill-how-create-corporate-accountability.
16. https://www.ft.com/content/3e09d84a-489f-11e8-8ee8-cae73aab7ccb.
17. https://www.ft.com/content/4e228e56-84ae-11df-9cbb-00144feabdc0?shareType=nongift.
18. https://www.theguardian.com/environment/2013/feb/26/deepwater-oil-spill-trial-bp-failure.
19. https://www.theguardian.com/environment/2011/jan/06/bp-oil-spill-deepwater-horizon#:~:text=BP%20cost%2Dcutting%20blamed%20for%20'avoidable'%20Deepwater%20Horizon%20oil%20spill,-This%20article%20is&text=The%20oil%20spill%20in%20the,House%20oil%20commission%20has%20concluded.
20. https://slate.com/technology/2016/09/bp-is-to-blame-for-deepwater-horizon-but-its-mistake-was-actually-years-of-small-mistakes.html.
21. https://chemical-materials.elsevier.com/chemical-manufacturing-excellence/deepwater-horizon-normalization-deviance/.
22. http://ccrm.berkeley.edu/pdfs_papers/bea_pdfs/dhsgfinalreport-march2011-tag.pdf.
23. https://chemical-materials.elsevier.com/chemical-manufacturing-excellence/deepwater-horizon-normalization-deviance/.
24. https://www.forbes.com/2010/06/04/bp-hayward-energy-markets-equities-oil-spill.html#5276ac194be6.

25. http://www.ethicalcorp.com/business-strategy/bp-and-gulf-mexico-oil-spill-how-create-corporate-accountability.
26. https://www.wsj.com/articles/goldman-sachs-restates-earnings-after-3-9-billion-malaysia-settlement-11596796982.
27. Greg Smith, *Why I Left Goldman Sachs*, New York: Hachette, 2014; Steven G. Mandis, *What Happened to Goldman Sachs: An Insider's Story of Organizational Drift and Its Unintended Consequences*, Boston: Harvard Business Review Press, 2013.

9

The Bureaucratic Board: The Big Four

Boards can also become prisoners of their own culture. In Chap. 4 we referred to 'explicit rules' cultures, where all actions are governed by formal procedures with sanctions for those who fail to follow them. At board level this results in bureaucratic boards dominated by overly controlled cultures, psychic prisons where thinking and acting are constrained by the need to conform. In many cases, board members are fully aware of the problem; they know the psychic prisons exist, they know they are constrained and inhibited, and as a result many are deeply unhappy and frustrated. They just cannot see a way out. This is the trap that the Big Four accounting firms are falling into, pushed in part by conflicts of interest that are embedded in the heart of their business models.

The repeated failures by the Big Four—Deloitte, Ernst & Young (EY), KPMG and PricewaterhouseCoopers (PwC)—to spot financial problems during audits have jeopardized businesses across the globe, risking investor funds, pension plans and even the existence of the audited companies themselves. It has also called into question whether 'audited' financial statements in today's world can be trusted by those seeking to understand a company's true financial footing.

The problem is compounded by the fact that the Big Four rarely seem to accept their own failings and repeatedly insist that no real wrong has been committed by the auditors themselves. In September 2020, for example, Deloitte responded to a record £15 million fine for its role in auditing the accounts of software firm Autonomy in advance of its takeover by Hewlett-Packard (HP) by stating that it 'regretted' the decision and that 'We remain committed to playing our role in delivering change that embraces audit quality, improves choice and restores trust in the profession.'[1] PwC also denied responsibility when handed a two-year audit ban in India after the collapse of Satyam: 'The SEBI order relates to a fraud that took place nearly a decade ago in which we played no part and had no knowledge of.'[2]

The Big Four emerged essentially unscathed from the financial crisis of 2008, suffering no serious consequences, although in 2010 they did agree to add (in the UK and Europe) independent directors to their boards in response to a post-Enron audit governance code. In a UK inquiry into the Big Four's role in the collapse, the House of Lords noted in 2011 that 'we do not accept the defence that bank auditors did all that was required of them. In the light of what we know now, that defence appears disconcertingly complacent. ... It may be that the Big Four carried out their duties properly in the strictly legal sense, but we have to conclude that, in the wider sense, they did not do so.' The committee concluded that complacency and dereliction of duty on the part of auditors was a 'significant contributory factor' in the global financial collapse.[3]

Three years after the devastation of the initial crisis, the accounting firms pushed back, citing technical compliance in support of the view that they had done their jobs. Ian Powell, then chair of PwC, responded by saying, 'I am surprised by the committee's claim that there was a "dereliction of duty", given their stated view that auditors fulfilled their legal duties.' Similarly, a Deloitte spokesperson, while supporting the report's suggestions, stated that 'We reject the suggestion of "complacency" or "dereliction of duty".'[4]

At the time of the crisis, the Big Four were responsible for auditing ninety-nine of the FTSE 100 as well as nearly all major banks. The firms' combined global revenue was almost $95 billion, making them equal to the fifty-fourth largest economy in the world.[5] At the same time, each firm also provided consulting services to their audit clients, expanding services to increase revenue in way that tests the limits of conflict of interest. Auditor compensation and bonuses are typically paid based on the firm's total profits, including revenue from consulting work, resulting in a dynamic where tough, accurate audits could jeopardize lucrative consulting projects. Corporate risk to the accountants increased but went unevaluated. This conflict of interest goes to the heart of the supposed independence of auditing firms and the value they are intended to deliver.

That conflict of interest had already seen another major accounting firm, Arthur Andersen, collapse in the aftermath of the Enron scandal, but the Big Four seem to have ignored this risk and continued as before. Rather than develop objective assessments of client compliance with accounting standards in setting valuations and presenting liabilities and assets, or examining internal controls and communications, the auditors turned a blind eye, a practice that continued well after the events of 2008–2009.

For example, a UK tribunal examining Deloitte's 2009–2011 audit work for the technology firm Autonomy issued a scathing finding that Deloitte had committed 'serious audit failings,' had lost objectivity and had been reckless by misleadingly presenting the company's financial performance to investors. Hewlett-Packard (HP) then acquired Autonomy in 2011 for $11 billion and was promptly involved in civil and criminal court proceedings in the USA and the UK, a fraud investigation, and an $8.8 billion write-down on the sale. The FRC asserted that Deloitte, rather than assessing the company's finances in the way an audit is meant to do, 'advocated' for Autonomy and that the audit partners were too close to Autonomy executives. Autonomy was Deloitte's most important client in Cambridge.[6]

By 2016, the EU had introduced legislation to restrict the consulting services that auditors could provide, but that did not slow the flow of auditing oversight failures. Audit-related scandals continued unabated and seemingly with no geographic limits. The full list is too extensive to provide here, but we can describe a few examples:

- In 2017, KPMG International's own audits in South Africa found that the firm's audit teams had 'failed to apply sufficient professional scepticism and to comply fully with auditing standards' as it was revealed that KPMG failed to detect widespread corruption related to multiple companies owned by its wealthy client, the Gupta family, during fourteen years of auditing the family's businesses. The Guptas were accused of misusing state funds and improperly influencing the government.[7] As KPMG's failures came to light, it terminated its relationship with the Guptas and lost multiple other clients, and the leadership team in South Africa were sacked. KPMG South Africa stated that 'despite the deficiencies in the audit work, KPMG International found no evidence of dishonesty or unethical behaviour' by the partners who handled audits for the Gupta companies.

- In 2019, a whistleblower alleged that one of Germany's largest publicly traded companies, payment and financial services entity Wirecard—a client of EY for more than ten years—was engaged in money-laundering and fraud. By 2020, it came to light that EY had failed to report a missing $2.13 billion in connection with its audit work for Wirecard.[8] Financial records had been falsified, and EY had failed to take basic steps such as verifying bank statements. The debacle resulted in the arrest of Wirecard's CEO and insolvency for the company. EY defended its audit, claiming that Wirecard's fraud was 'elaborate and sophisticated' and that 'even the most

robust and extended audit procedures' could not uncover such a 'collu-
sive fraud.'[9]

- We noted earlier the scandal with Satyam Computer Services, where the
  company's chair had blatantly falsified accounts. The chair—who, along
  with nine co-conspirators, was sentenced to seven years in jail—admitted
  to inflating profits via fictitious assets and non-existent cash, as well as mis-
  reporting debts owed to the firm. The regulator found that PwC had fallen
  far below acceptable accounting standards, overlooking multiple red flags
  that 'were all too obvious for any reasonable professional auditor to miss.'
  The result was a two-year ban on PwC auditing listed companies; its client
  went out of business.[10] PwC responded to the decision by insisting that
  there was no evidence of 'intentional wrongdoing' by its auditors.
- The collapse of Carillion in 2018 (see above) sparked a lengthy investigation into KPMG's auditing practices. Four months after the auditor signed
  off Carillion's accounts, the company suffered an £845 million write-down,
  triggering a profit warning and, and nine months later, its collapse. This
  series of events also resulted in all the Big Four—who had done £72 million of auditing and advisory work for Carillion in the decade leading to its
  failure—being called into question by members of parliament (MPs). MPs
  found that KPMG had signed off on 'increasingly fantastical figures' and
  that Deloitte, as internal auditor, had not identified key risk management
  and financial control failures—or had 'too readily ignored them'.[11] In
  response, KPMG's chairman defensively denied responsibility for Carillion's
  downfall, arguing that 'while a company might fail following issuance of an
  unqualified audit opinion, this does not automatically mean the auditor
  did a bad job.'[12]

In 2018, in what could be a cause for a bit of optimism, or perhaps, a cynical play to stop the consultancy from being split from the accountancy,
Deloitte did agree that final say over auditor compensation and bonuses
would be given to the company's non-executive directors.[13] Also in 2018,
KPMG appointed its first US independent director, although it still declined
to identify its full board roster or to answer interview questions about the
board's composition. PwC had two independent US directors. EY and
Deloitte at that time had none, making a grand total of *three* independent
directors across the Big Four's US boards.[14]

In July 2020, however, the UK's FRC announced that the Big Four, now
responsible for over 95 per cent of FTSE 350 audits,[15] had agreed that by
2024 their auditing and consultancy groups would be split in the UK. This
move was criticized by many as inadequate. It was noted that, even with the

separation, supposedly independent auditors could still sell consulting work to clients, could earn up to half of their revenue from consulting and could even switch back and forth between auditing and consulting roles. Additionally, both auditors and consultants would remain under the same point of control, the CEO, and importantly, the agreement was entirely voluntary and arguably not enforceable by government.[16]

The pattern that emerges from this narrative of the Big Four is twofold. First, there is a heavy emphasis on rules and process, with the result that any idea or concept that is outside the process seems to simply get ignored. The widespread dismissal of any notion of conflict of interest is simply ignored. For example, KPMG was appointed to advise the Grenfell Tower inquiry, a public body established to examine the causes of a disastrous fire in a London high-rise block in which seventy-two people died. This was despite the fact that KPMG also served as auditor for the Royal Borough of Kensington and Chelsea, which managed the building; the Rydon Group, which carried out a renovation of the building in 2015–2016 and was responsible for fixing a highly flammable form of aluminium-based insulation which contributed to the rapid spread of the fire, and the parent company of the firm that made the insulation. When news of the appointment broke, there was widespread anger and demands for KPMG to recuse itself from the inquiry. The firm did so, but denied to the end that there was a problem. 'We are confident that no conflicts exist between our role advising the inquiry and our work for other clients,' said a spokesperson.[17]

Second, there continues to be a culture where revenue is prioritized over the principles of sound auditing. The scandals mentioned above could have been avoided if the Big Four had cultures that were focused around professional service rather than profit. Why did KPMG bosses think it was appropriate for them to advise an inquiry into a disaster in which three of their current clients were already heavily implicated? The answer could well be that the subject was never discussed. When profits are prioritized and there are established rules for dealing with potential conflicts of interest, professional judgement can get subordinated to making money.

There is, of course, a subsidiary question of why auditors get it wrong, and the *Financial Times* was quite right to ask, in the aftermath of the Wirecard collapse, who guards the guardians. Who audits the auditors? The answer seems to be, no one. The collapse of Arthur Andersen should have been a warning sign to the entire profession, but it seems to have gone unheeded.

The case of the Big Four illustrates the desperate need for independent governance and oversight in this sector, as well as an equally urgent need for cultural change in many big professional service firms. But the dangers of an overly controlled culture where there is no challenge to authority and no independent scrutiny can be found in other sectors as well. The danger is particularly acute where ownership and control are heavily vested in the same person or small group of people.

Another example of this is Samsung, which in 2017 became embroiled in a scandal that shook the South Korean state and society. The company's interim leader, Lee Jae-yong—standing in for his father, who had suffered a heart attack a few years earlier—was found to have paid $17 million in bribes to Choi Soon-sil, a close friend and aide to President Park Geun-hye. The money apparently came from a slush fund controlled by Lee and an inner circle of managers, the existence of which was known only to a few. President Park was impeached and forced to resign, and she and Choi were both convicted of criminal charges and sent to prison. Lee and four other Samsung executives were also indicted on charges including bribery, embezzlement and perjury.[18]

Here again, there was no effective oversight. The board of Samsung was both bureaucratic *and* subordinated. Lee and his cadre of close followers controlled everything that mattered in Samsung; their word effectively was law. There are other examples too. At ITT, Harold Geneen presided over the board as chairman and CEO for more than twenty years and ruled with an iron hand. Even when ITT began channelling funds through the CIA to support a military coup d'état in Chile, the board made no objection. Staggering under a huge weight of debt and unable to innovate or reform its structures, ITT was finally broken into several constituent parts in 1995. Here too the board of directors had no voice and no power.

Rules-Bound Cultures

The signs of an overly controlled, rules-bound culture are first, inflexibility of thinking. Second is an absolute insistence that the process is all that matters. Third is an equally adamant belief that there is nothing wrong with the process and that any problems are something else wrong, but not the rules in your own organization, because they are tried and true. This stems from a culture where the people at the top have absolute control and there is little or no oversight. In social science research, this is known as *inattentional bias*. At best, people fall into a trap of thinking that the world they see is all there is to see; like the people in the cave in Plato's *Republic*, they see the outside world only as flickering shadows on the wall, while the cave around them is their sanctuary and safe space. At worst, overconfidence in the rules leads them into the kind of arrogance and hubris that allowed the leaders of Samsung to destroy the reputation of their own firm and bring down their country's government.

Breaking down the walls of these monolithic institutions and forcing them to reform their governance is extremely difficult, as regulators in Europe, the UK and the USA have all been discovering. But are we perhaps expecting too much of regulators, and indeed of auditors? They are professionals, but by and large they sit outside the structures and firms of the industries they are assessing, and for the most part they also typically have the power to act only after things have gone wrong.

Audits are meant to be preventive medicine, providing independent data that can help to spot problems before they go wrong, but auditors too are outsiders and they cannot catch every problem. Having 'insiders,' poachers turned gamekeepers, as part of the assessment process is in our view essential. Research has shown that the only effective way to find clever fraud is to follow the lead of someone inside who knows what is really happening and show which threads should be pulled. We argue that these industry insiders should be a part of the process of assessing other firms, rather like using deans of business schools to certify other business schools as we described earlier.

Bringing in these insiders, however, requires that monolithic institutions like the Big Four and others need first to break down their walls and admit that their own rules-based systems need reform. This should not be difficult. Most auditors are well aware of the problems in their industry; most probably want to do something about it. The barriers to reform are structural rather than personal; although the ego needs of individuals may be one of the things that keeps them in place. If the Big Four can take the lead and reform their own cultures to become more flexible and better focused on the problems they face rather than protecting their own reputation, there is every reason to believe that the audit process can be made more effective, and more corporate disasters would be avoided. The giant disasters where massive companies go bankrupt like Samsung, Carillion and Satyam should be especially the type that effective audit ought to prevent, or at the very least become rare events, rather than the almost monthly occurrences we see today.

Notes

1. https://news.sky.com/story/deloitte-fined-15m-for-audit-failures-ahead-of-autonomy-sale-12074182.

2. https://www.accountancyage.com/2018/01/23/pwcs-appeal-2-year-audit-ban-india-rejected/.
3. Auditors Criticised for Role in Financial Crisis. *The Financial Times* (20 March 2011).
4. Ibid.
5. The Audit Industry Should Serve Society … Not Themselves. *Herald Scotland* (23 Nov 2009).
6. Deloitte Faces Record £15m Fine for 'Serious' Failures in Autonomy Audit. *The Financial Times* (9 July 2020).
7. McKinsey Drawn into South Africa's Sprawling Corruption Scandal. *CNN Money* (19 Sept 2017).
8. Critics Say UK's Proposed Big Four Auditing Reforms are Toothless. *Organized Crime and Corruption Reporting Project* (8 July 2020).
9. Wirecard Auditors Face Legal Action After Collapse of Payments Firm. *CNBC* (26 June 2020).
10. India Bans PwC from Auditing Listed Firms over Satyam Case. *CNN Money* (11 Jan 2018).
11. 'Decline in Quality': Auditors Face Scrutiny over String of Scandals. *The Guardian* (1 Feb 2019).
12. KPMG Chairman Defends Audit of Carillion. *The Times* (12 July 2018).
13. Deloitte Hands Control over UK Auditor Pay to Non-Execs. *The Financial Times* (18 Nov 2019).
14. Only Three Directors Across Big Four Boards are Independent. *Compliance Week* (9 Oct 2018).
15. The UK's Big Four Accounting Firms Keep Failing. Now They're Being Forced to Change. *CNN* (6 July 2020).
16. How U.K. Audit Scandals Pushed Big Four Toward Split. *Bloomberg Tax* (17 July 2020).
17. https://www.theguardian.com/uk-news/2018/jan/07/grenfell-inquiry-cuts-ties-kpmg-following-complaints.
18. https://www.bbc.co.uk/news/business-41033568.

10

The Conforming Board: Royal Bank of Scotland

The impacts of groupthink are well-documented, but it is worth considering another case in order to see how groupthink relates to other types of board dysfunction. In the case of Royal Bank of Scotland (RBS) we can see several dysfunctions coming together, including lack of independence, amplification of culture, missing key voices and lack of independence from management. Taken together, these dysfunctions laid the foundation for another and greater dysfunction, groupthink, which led ultimately to the collapse of a large and powerful organization.

The Royal Bank of Scotland's fall from grace began in October 2007 with its ill-fated £49-billion takeover of Dutch bank ABN AMRO, but the seeds of the disaster had been sown much earlier. Chief Executive Fred Goodwin, who took over in 2001, committed the bank to an ambitious programme of expansion. Far from being afraid of taking risks, Goodwin appeared to thrive on them: by 2007, RBS had made twenty-six acquisitions in seven years, including the hostile and extremely lucrative takeover of British bank NatWest. The overconfidence of the bank as a whole—while perhaps justified in light of what the firm had achieved—may have led the board to overlook the risks involved in any new proposals.

In April that year, ABN's management had pleaded with investors to keep the bank together and not take the deal with RBS. 'Price isn't the only thing that counts,' said chief executive Rijkman Groenink.[1] Activist shareholders, however, thought differently. They had already blocked a move by management to sell its American subsidiary LaSalle, which would make ABN a far less attractive target for RBS. The takeover eventually went ahead, with RBS defeating a rival bid by Barclays.

© The Author(s), under exclusive license to Springer Nature Switzerland AG 2022
G. Brown, R. S. Peterson, *Disaster in the Boardroom*,
https://doi.org/10.1007/978-3-030-91658-9_10

Barclays had been having quiet merger talks with ABN for over a year and had clearly been the preferred option of the ABN board. When RBS got wind of this, it quickly made a rival offer, joining forces in a consortium with Belgian-Dutch group Fortis and the Spanish bank Santander. A bidding war developed, from which Barclays eventually withdrew. Barclays CEO John Varley later said that Fred Goodwin, Chief Executive of RBS, had paid too high a price to take over ABN. 'We weren't prepared to secure a win at any price,' he said.[2]

Goodwin, it seems, was willing to do just that. But the decision to go ahead with a major acquisition is a specific responsibility of the board. The newly appointed chairman of the RBS board, Philip Hampton (who had succeeded Tom McKillop) stated publicly in 2010:

> I don't think there can be any doubt that the key decision that led RBS to its difficulties was the acquisition of ABN AMRO. That is the painful reality that we can now do nothing to change. With the benefit of hindsight, it can now be seen as the wrong price, the wrong way to pay, at the wrong time and the wrong deal.[3]

The board's role is to monitor, scrutinize and challenge major decisions such as this acquisition. This move was an instance where the board should have played a much bigger part and scrutinized the potential deal far more closely. According to the Financial Services Agency (FSA) 2010 report into the failure of RBS, four features made the acquisition far riskier than a 'normal' transaction:

- It was exceptionally large and complex.
- The bid comprised primarily debt rather than shares, and RBS's decision to raise most of that debt on the short-term wholesale markets increased its reliance on short-term wholesale funding and its consequent vulnerability as the financial crisis developed.
- There was considerable uncertainty in the market arising from the consortium structure, under which RBS would consolidate the whole of ABN AMRO on its balance sheet before the transfer of assets to other consortium partners.
- RBS undertook extremely limited due diligence, especially considering the size of the acquisition.

The review team for the FSA report found no holes whatsoever in the board's processes throughout the acquisition period, stating that meetings were inclusive, continuous and frequent. They did however find that the board's decision-making processes reflected 'an inadequate and seriously flawed assessment of relevant issues, above all in relation to risk.'[4]

Dramatically Negative

Goodwin had shown no interest in ABN—other than LaSalle—until Barclays attempted to buy it. There is no evidence of anyone at RBS asking why ABN suddenly appeared so attractive. One former RBS manager said later that he and his colleagues knew the bank could not bid for all of ABN. The acquisitions Goodwin had already made in his seven-year reign as CEO had already raised eyebrows in financial circles.

But Goodwin decided to form a consortium to challenge Barclays, bringing in first Fortis and then Santander, who had also helped RBS win the lucrative NatWest takeover in 1999. On 11 April the consortium held its first meeting, and shortly thereafter ABN received a letter from the banks outlining their intention to bid. All had gone well for Goodwin, and finally LaSalle was within his reach.

A few days later, he was startled to receive the news that Bank of America had just bought LaSalle for $21 billion. Incensed, Goodwin called John Cryan, one of the men who had helped broker the deal, but who had been a close adviser of his in the past. Cryan had always told Goodwin that buying ABN was a bad idea for RBS and that ABN's exposure to the subprime lending market was risky. 'There's stuff in here that we can't even value,' he said in one note to Goodwin. 'Stop being such a bean counter,' Goodwin replied.[5]

Now LaSalle was gone, there seemed little reason for RBS to pursue the bid for ABN. The situation called for a full meeting of the RBS board to discuss whether to go ahead. Johnny Cameron, an executive director and chairman of global banking, said that ABN's investment banking operations made it worth their while, and presented a reasoned argument to continue. At a dinner with forty of RBS's most senior GBM (global banking and marketing) staff, Goodwin told them that investment banking was now the main focus of the merger. This came as a surprise to most of the investment bankers, who could not remember ever seeing him on the trading floor.

Cameron would later admit in an interview with the FSA that neither he nor anyone else on the board did any due diligence on the acquisition of ABN. 'It was part of doing a hostile acquisition,' he said.

After we bought NatWest, we had lots of surprises, but almost all of them were pleasant. And I think that lulled us into a sense of complacency around that. The fact is that the acquisition of ABN was also hostile. We got bits and pieces of information but fundamentally it was hostile. There's this issue of did we do sufficient due diligence. Absolutely not. We were not able to do due diligence.[6]

The FSA concluded that 'the outcome of the RBS board's decision-making was dramatically negative.'[7] They reported that they found no evidence that the board discussed in enough depth the risks involved in the acquisition, including its complexity, scale or how it was to be financed, without the opportunity to do due diligence. Instead, the board focused on potential synergies and cost-cutting, and reasoned that because ABN was regulated by various official bodies, had good reports by ratings agencies and had been pursued by Barclays, it was a good idea to acquire it.

Goodwin provided 'background to the project' in a board meeting in March 2007, and is recorded in the minutes as warning that the bid should not be seen as a 'must-do deal.' He advised the board that 'execution risk would be high' and that 'any bid and subsequent integration would be more difficult than previous transactions.'[8] Despite this, the board did not undertake any deep analysis of the risks. While there is no doubt that they discussed the plans, one board member said in an FSA interview that 'at no stage did any board member propose that we should not proceed.' Another even said that there was an element of groupthink in the board's decision to acquire ABN and that they could not remember any board member ever saying they were worried about the deal. As the FSA commented, 'it is very difficult to reconcile this approach with the degree of rigorous testing, questioning and challenge that would be expected in an effective board process dealing with such a large and strategic proposition.'[9]

The RBS strategy at the time, which the board believed was responsible for their success thus far, was a mixture of acquisition and organic growth. The bank wanted to be open to opportunities for growth away from the core UK retail business and allow expansion into other businesses and regions. A board is responsible for assuring that a strategy is accompanied by sufficient attention to risk, but given the scale of RBS's ambitions for growth, it is clear that the board did not fulfil its role. The FSA said that it is possible that, in the absence of the global financial crisis, RBS would have continued to be successful, but it was 'clearly and demonstrably the case' that the board did not sufficiently examine the risks that an acquisition of that size—in any type of financial climate—would represent. But nobody on the board—and very few in the wider world—had predicted what was about to happen to the global economy.

As summer came and Barclay's share price fell, the RBS takeover looked ever more likely for ABN, whose staff council had identified blasé attitudes among senior RBS staff. Mark Fisher, head of RBS's operations division, was openly laughed at when he told the ABN council that he estimated the integration of the merged firms would take forty-five days. At RBS, doubts were mounting as the financial downturn began to take hold. In September, when the bank Northern Rock asked the UK government for emergency funding, the ABN staff council visited the RBS headquarters outside Edinburgh. None of the RBS managers could give robust indications of their plans to develop the business after integration. According to eyewitnesses, Goodwin looked just as shocked as the council at his executives' lack of preparation.

Barclays withdrew its offer on 5 October, and RBS bankers began to look at what their organization had bought. When RBS credit traders first visited ABN's offices in London, they were appalled. 'Once you started to look around ABN's trading books you realized that a lot of their businesses, particularly what you would call model businesses, where valuations were based on assumptions, were based on forecasts that were super aggressive,' said one senior former RBS trader.[10] Staff reported a stream of never-ending problems, while former ABN employees were often obstructive.

The consortium began to flounder. Fortis ran into financial problems and was forced to sell its stake in ABN. Suddenly, the future for RBS began to look bleak.

What Happened?

In January 2009, RBS posted a loss of £28 billion. The share price had collapsed from £6.03 to just 11.6p. Once hailed as Scotland's economic miracle, the billions that the bank had borrowed for its acquisitions over the preceding seven years had brought the bank to its knees.

In an article in the *Daily Telegraph* in January 2009, journalist Gordon Rayner commented that the demise of RBS can be summarized in just one word: greed. 'Sir Fred became so obsessed with his quest to make RBS a titan of world banking, and had such an overbearing personality that none of his staff had the clout to stop him, even when some of them began to have concerns that the bank was overstretching itself.'[11] David Buik, partner at City firm BGC Partners, said the fall of RBS was 'all down to a degree of arrogance the like of which you will never see again in your lifetime.'

RBS never had a chance to digest anything they bought and so they've never delivered shareholder value. It's a combination of relentless greed and an inability to deliver shareholder value. … They were buying companies when their share price was at its peak, rather than when shares were at rock bottom, and they clearly got involved with things they just didn't understand. The ABN Amro takeover was the zenith of their stupidity, but the die was cast before that. … There were people in that boardroom during the ABN Amro takeover who must have thought 'this is madness,' but no one was prepared to stand up to Sir Fred. I know people who worked for him, and it was a case of 'yes sir, no sir, three bags full, sir.'[12]

After the takeover of NatWest—a bank three times RBS's size—Fred Goodwin was named businessman of the year by *Forbes* magazine, which described the acquisition as a 'brilliantly strategized hostile takeover.' He slashed 18,000 jobs in the ensuing merger and won huge praise from investors for delivering efficiency. Buoyed by his accolades and undeniable success, Goodwin went on to mastermind the takeovers of Royal Insurance, Churchill Insurance and Charter One, among others. In 2003 alone there were seven acquisitions. RBS opened offices in Asia, continental Europe, the Irish Republic and the USA, and bought 5 per cent stake in the Bank of China.

His spending went largely unquestioned until the end of 2006 when shareholders became concerned. Goodwin publicly promised that there would be no more major deals until he heard that Barclays were negotiating to buy ABN AMRO. On deciding to challenge Barclays, he reassured the world that 'the key to good deal making is knowing when to walk away.'[13] But he failed to take his own advice. When the banking crisis of 2008 happened, RBS had become so frail as a result of its excess borrowing that it had to accept a government bailout, and the true cost of all its acquisitions became public knowledge. They were worth up to £20 billion less than the bank had paid for them.

Where Was the Board?

Fred Goodwin has always been seen as the central figure in the demise of RBS. Despite his much-maligned style and the grave mistakes he made, he remains the man primarily responsible for turning a once conservative high street institution into the world's largest bank, until it became the UK's biggest financial failure. But chief executives do not rule alone. They co-exist with a senior leadership team, shareholders and, perhaps most importantly, a board of directors whose job it is to ensure the company's prosperity and monitor the chief executive.

'The board was fully briefed and gung ho,' said one of the advisers to the RBS board in 2007.[14] They added that Sir Tom McKillop, chairman at the time, had privately expressed misgivings about such a large and complex deal but felt that saying no would be seen as a *de facto* move to replace Goodwin. 'He felt he had to back the chief executive,' the advisor said. With a clear lack of countervailing voices on the board, Goodwin was given free rein to wield his considerable power.

RBS may have bought ABN for the wrong price at the wrong time, but this was just one in a series of disastrous boardroom decisions. Although there is no evidence for a failure of procedure at the top of RBS, the excesses of the bank were sanctioned by those whose job it is to ensure the company's prosperity. The ABN bid does not appear to have been independently checked by anyone on the board and there was no effective due diligence. It was arguably masterminded on the back of the momentously successful takeover of NatWest which left RBS thinking of itself as untouchable.

One of Goodwin's colleagues described him as an optimist, who had 'often in his life been proved right.' Financial incentives for Goodwin and his leadership team—created by the board—which encouraged the building of assets, profits and leverage rather than capital, liquidity and asset quality likely helped that 'optimism' permeate throughout the whole organization. The FSA report noted that 'the board was much more focused on revenue and profit than on the size of the balance sheet.' Acting in the interest of the business and its stakeholders is a primary function of any board. The optimism of the RBS board, in their support—wilful or otherwise—of short-term objectives, crossed over into the territory of negligence, with the FSA surmising that 'the acquisition [of ABN] was not characterized by the degree of moderation and sensitivity to strategic risk appropriate to a bank.'[15]

With seventeen directors, the board was large. How big is too big for effective discussion and challenge? It is possible that a board with so many people made it difficult for individuals to raise their voice. The average size of a FTSE-100 board is 10.5 members.[16] Most executives agree that to create effective debate, a critical mass of diverse expertise, background and opinion is needed, but if there are too many people, that critical mass can get lost.[17]

A board also needs people who will not avoid dissent at the critical time. In an article for Reuters in 2011 Lucy Marcus, CEO of Marcus Venture Consulting, argues that 'it is essential, at a time when everyone seems to be agreeing even though there's something niggling at the back of their heads, that people speak up.'[18] She goes on to say that she thinks of RBS every time she gets 'the look' for being the one to ask the question that holds up everyone going for dinner. Richard Lambert, former editor of the *Financial Times*, commented in 2011 that the RBS board seemed to have been 'badly infected by groupthink' and that 'the number of establishment figures in the board-room meant that the group as a whole were not "boat-rockers".'[19] The hiring of a group of advisers—whose full fees were only to be paid if their advice to go for the risky ABN bid proved lucrative—cannot have helped their objectivity.

Herd Behaviour

One of the main functions of a board is to challenge the executive. Even if Goodwin's style discouraged robust and effective challenge, as the FSA report states, it was the board's responsibility to create and maintain a psychologi-cally safe environment where people were free to challenge and speak their mind. There are no outright answers as to why that did not happen, but groupthink appears to play a large role. The Seven Pillars Institute, a think-tank for research, education and promotion of financial ethics, observed that 'while the strong and dominant personality of Fred Goodwin may well have contributed to a culture of appeasement within RBS, it is questionable that this was the most significant cause of RBS's poor decision-making. The more likely cause is human susceptibility to "herd behaviour": the groupthink bias.'[20] The fundamental causes of groupthink include directive leadership, stress. Both were clearly present here.

The RBS board took seven meetings, between March and September 2007, to reach a decision to acquire ABN, and the bid team based their judgements on materials in two lever arch files and a CD containing electronic docu-ments. The FSA found no evidence that the board discussed the risks involved in sufficient depth. Nor did they appear to acknowledge the exceptional com-plexity, unprecedented scale or the question of the deal, or how it was to be financed.

The FSA admits its own failings and argues that had the current regulatory system been in place, the bank would not have failed. That may well be true. But many have identified governance as the core underlying problem. The purchase of ABN was symbolic of RBS's broader approach and attitude. The bid was just one of a whole series of ill-judged acquisitions, all of them sanc-tioned by the board and the shareholders. Richard Lambert summarized the matter in 2011: 'A forceful chief executive in a complex business and with the wrong incentives is unlikely to be constrained by an over-large board of directors drawn from the same establishment pool.'[21]

Over-Mighty Executives

The problem of the over-mighty CEO domesticating the board and getting them to do whatever the CEO wants has been seen many times. One particularly spectacular fall from grace was the American investment bank Salomon Brothers, which in the 1980s was the most profitable investment bank in America. Its CEO, John Gutfreund, was known as the 'King of Wall Street.' As Michael Lewis described in his book *Liar's Poker*, Gutfreund created a culture of winning at all costs, rewarding success with bonuses and firing traders and bankers who failed to hit their targets.[22] Traders rejoiced in nicknames such as 'the Human Piranha.' Famously, the culture of Salomon Brothers was the inspiration for Tom Wolfe's novel *The Bonfire of the Vanities*.

Just as with RBS, the board did not challenge Gutfreund or his methods. When profits were tight in the aftermath of the 1987 financial crisis, Gutfreund and his executives overstepped the mark. In 1991 it emerged that a Salomon trader had been submitting fraudulent bids to purchase US Treasury Bonds. The bank was fined $190 million, and Gutfreund was forced to resign and was barred from acting as chief executive of a brokerage firm.[23] Even after the scandal became public, Gutfreund was unrepentant, telling his senior executives, 'I'm not apologizing for anything to anybody. Apologies don't mean [expletive]. What happened, happened.'[24] No one contradicted him.

This refusal to admit wrongdoing even in the face of overwhelming evidence to the contrary is evidence of groupthink which, combined with the egotism of the chief executive, led to disastrous results. Lacking direction and leadership after Gutfreund's departure, Salomon Brothers was bought out, passed from one owner to another. It finally disappeared in the aftermath of the collapse of Long-Term Capital Management.

Very similar was the fate of brokerage firm E.F. Hutton, like Salomon Brothers a venerable firm with a long history. Robert Fomon had risen through the ranks of the firm to become chairman and CEO of Hutton in 1970. He was originally chosen for the top job as a compromise candidate, after factions on the board failed to get agreement for their own choices. Despite this, Fomon successfully managed the factions and over time became the firm's most powerful voice, especially after he oversaw its successful listing on the New York Stock Exchange. Fomon had near-total control over the bank and few on the board, or elsewhere, questioned or argued with what he said and did. In 1984, a criminal investigation found that for more than two years various branches of the firm had engaged in a form of fraud known as 'check kiting,' writing checks based on non-existent funds in one bank and then depositing them with other banks in order to create the illusion of a positive balance, in effect giving themselves free loans without paying interest. According to one estimate, this gave the bank an estimated $250 million of free credit every day.[25]

The writing of bad cheques, which is essentially what the company was doing, is of course unethical, but Hutton executives justified their behaviour on the grounds of financial expediency. As one researcher put it,

> [t]his line of thinking supports financial success as the only value to be considered. It promotes short-term solutions that are immediately financially sound, despite the fact that they cause problems for others within the organization or the organization as a whole. It promotes an unrealistic belief in some organizational groups that everything boils down to a monetary game. As a result, such rules on ethical conduct are merely barriers, impediments along the way to bottom-line financial success.[26]

Hutton initially challenged the investigation, but when evidence emerged that senior executives knew about the practice and tacitly endorsed it, the bank was forced into a plea bargain. Pleading guilty to 2000 counts of fraud, the bank paid a fine of $2 million plus costs of the investigation and a further $8 million in restitution, in exchange for which no Hutton executives faced criminal charges. Fomon was forced to resign, and E.F. Hutton was acquired by another banking group.

Fomon and Gutfreund escaped prison, but executives at food producer the Beech-Nut Company were not so fortunate or so well represented by legal counsel. In 1987 the company was found guilty of selling apple juice drinks for babies that had been adulterated with other products, including cherry juice and sugar syrup. The company had been under severe financial pressure, and Beech-Nut senior executives decided that adulterating the product was the only way to get costs down. They justified their actions on two grounds: (1) most other food producers were also selling adulterated products (there was no evidence of this) and (2) the adulterated juice was perfectly safe and could cause no harm to babies.[27] The top leadership of Beech-Nut persuaded themselves to believe what they wanted to believe.

While the product was not deliberately harmful, the US Food and Drug Administration still deemed there to be a health risk to babies.[28] Vice-president for operations John Lavery was sentenced to a year in prison and CEO Niels

Hoyvald was given six months community service; both men were also heavily fined. Just as with RBS, the board was unable to think independently and did not seek to challenge or scrutinize the actions of the company too heavily—until it was too late.

Groupthink

Following on from the work of Irving Janis referred to earlier, in *On the Psychology of Military Incompetence*, Norman Dixon described the symptoms of groupthink as follows:

1. An illusion of invulnerability that becomes shared by most members of the group.
2. Collective attempts to ignore or explain away anything that might challenge currently shared assumptions.
3. An unquestioned belief in the group's own inherent morality, meaning members can overlook the ethical consequences of their actions.
4. Stereotyping the opposition as stupid, weak, evil and so on.
5. A shared illusion of unanimity among the group, meaning silence is often taken as consent.
6. Self-appointed guardians who protect the group from information that might challenge their current beliefs.[29]

To these can be added an element of self-censorship, where people who might disagree with the sentiments being expressed in the room keep quiet, preferring not to rock the boat and thus giving an illusion of consensus.

Our case studies found signs of all these things, particularly a lack of debate and discussion at board meetings, and a lack of any spirit of inquiry among the directors. Another potential sign of groupthink is lack of diversity, directors coming from the same or very similar backgrounds and sharing the same sets of beliefs and experience. According to Marianne Jennings in her book *The Seven Signs of Ethical Collapse*, the presence of a charismatic CEO can sometimes amplify the problem.[30] The rest of the board coalesces around this dominant individual and adapt their own thinking to match his or hers. Directors who start as independent free-thinkers are gradually subsumed into the cult of personality.

It is critically important that the board remembers its duty to analyse and, where necessary, challenges the executive instead of merely nodding along. Unfortunately, not every board does this, and far too many boards are characterized by groupthink. A study by McKinsey & Company found that more than 70 per cent of American company directors were prepared to nod strategy through, rather than undertake any form of real debate.

Avoiding groupthink and corollary behaviour like social loafing means independent directors must (a) maintain their independence and (b) remember their purpose. Why are they on the board? To get a free lunch once a quarter and claim back travel expenses? To satisfy power or ego needs? Or to give meaningful service to the organization and its stakeholders? Being an independent director carries with it duties of care and responsibility, and those duties will not be discharged by simply agreeing with the dominant minority. Breaking the shackles of groupthink, speaking out and challenging authority can be difficult, and does require courage, but that is a very important part of the job. On the other side of the coin, directors also need to remember to ask themselves: by contributing to groupthink, what are the personal benefits to me? And what, in ethical and moral terms, are the costs?

Notes

1. https://www.forbes.com/2007/04/27/abn-amro-closer-markets-equity-cx_po_0427markets10.html#3dacda2c671d.
2. https://www.theguardian.com/business/2007/oct/07/money1.
3. www.cnn.com/2009/BUSINESS/04/03/rbs.goodwin.pension.jobs/index.html.
4. Financial Services Authority Board Report 2011, 'The failure of the Royal Bank of Scotland'.
5. https://www.telegraph.co.uk/finance/newsbysector/banksandfinance/8947530/RBS-investigation-Chapter-2-the-ABN-Amro-takeover.html.
6. https://www.theguardian.com/business/nils-pratley-on-finance/2011/dec/12/what-rbs-board-thinking-abn-amro.
7. Ibid.
8. Ibid.
9. Ibid.
10. https://www.telegraph.co.uk/finance/newsbysector/banksandfinance/8947530/RBS-investigation-Chapter-2-the-ABN-Amro-takeover.html.
11. https://www.telegraph.co.uk/finance/newsbysector/banksandfinance/4291807/Banking-bailout-The-rise-and-fall-of-RBS.html.
12. Ibid.
13. Ibid.

14. https://www.telegraph.co.uk/finance/newsbysector/banksandfi-nance/8947530/RBS-investigation-Chapter-2-the-ABN-Amro-takeover.html.
15. http://blogs.reuters.com/lucy-marcus/2011/12/19/rbss-board-lessons/.
16. Elisabeth Marx, Randall Peterson, Vyla Rollins and Brent Hamerla, 'A View at the Top: Boardroom Trends in Britain's Top 100 Companies', ICSA Report 2019.
17. See for example the Walker Report of 2009, http://www.hmtreasury.gov.uk/walker_review_information.htm.
18. Ibid.
19. https://www.ft.com/content/c91ca412-24b6-11e1-ac4b-00144feabdc0.
20. https://sevenpillarsinstitute.org/wp-content/uploads/2017/11/RBS-Case-EDITED.pdf.
21. https://www.ft.com/content/c91ca412-24b6-11e1-ac4b-00144feabdc0.
22. Michael Lewis, *Liar's Poker*, New York: W.W. Norton, 1989.
23. https://www.nytimes.com/1994/08/19/business/ex-salomon-chief-s-costly-battle.html.
24. Ronald R. Sims, 'Linking Groupthink to Unethical Behavior in Organizations', *Journal of Business Ethics* 11, 1992, p. 658.
25. https://www.nytimes.com/1985/05/03/business/ef-hutton-guilty-in-bank-fraud-penalties-could-top-10-million.html.
26. Sims, 1992, p. 657.
27. Sims, 1992.
28. https://www.washingtonpost.com/archive/politics/1987/11/14/beech-nut-guilty-in-juice-fraud/aed8287d-6c41-4e09-bb27-dd70a234074a/.
29. Dixon, *On the Psychology of Military Incompetence*.
30. Marianne Jennings, *The Seven Signs of Ethical Collapse*, New York: St Martin's, 2006.

Part III

Part III

11

Changing Board Culture

Regulators, when they do take action against failing boards, usually do so retrospectively, once the damage is done. We need to move towards a system based much more on preventive medicine, where the 'cure' is put in place before the problem ever arises. As far back as 1992, Martin Lipton and Jay Lorsch argued that reforming board culture is essential if we are to see improvements in corporate governance and performance. Regulation was not the answer, they argued; regulation had been tried and had done everything it could. The responsibility now lay with boards themselves. Boards had to *want* to change and be serious and genuine about reform.[1] Subsequently Sir David Walker, author of a report on corporate governance in the UK banking industry, has noted that culture was a major omission from the report; if writing it again today, he said, culture would most certainly be included.[2]

We continue to agree that changing board culture to make boards more robust, independent and effective is the best way to prevent the catastrophic damage that is being inflicted on companies, shareholders, workers, customers, society at large and the global environment. So, how do we go about doing so?

Defining Board Culture

Charles O'Reilly and Jennifer Chatman, two of America's leading analysts of corporate culture, described culture as norms in the organization that shape behaviour. If an organization has an adaptable, flexible culture, people within the organization will be more likely to behave in adaptable, flexible ways; if

© The Author(s), under exclusive license to Springer Nature Switzerland AG 2022
G. Brown, R. S. Peterson, *Disaster in the Boardroom*,
https://doi.org/10.1007/978-3-030-91658-9_11

the culture is risk averse, this will manifest itself in risk-averse behaviours and so on. O'Reilly and Chatman also argued that few managers have much understanding of what culture is or how it is managed. 'You'll see culture mostly talked about as stories or anecdotes,' they said. 'It's a vague concept that people know is important, but they don't quite know how to apply.' 'Citing a survey showing that 94 per cent of executives believed a strong culture was important to business success,' they added, '[b]ut if you asked them who was responsible for managing culture or how they would manage it, most wouldn't have a clue.'[3]

Recruitment consultants Spencer Stuart, who specialize in board recruitment, define culture as follows:

> A board's culture is defined by the unwritten rules that influence directors' interactions and decisions. These include the mindsets, hidden assumptions, group norms, beliefs, values and artefacts (such as the board agenda) that influence the style of director discussions, the quality of engagement and trust among directors, and how the board makes decisions. Board culture also is influenced by the style of the board chair and/or the CEO.[4]

The Spencer Stuart report also notes that organizational culture will reflect board culture, and is likely to be influenced by prevailing national or regional cultures. For example, in some parts of the world it is acceptable for board members to speak directly and bluntly, while in others a more nuanced and diplomatic approach may be needed. So, board cultures will vary, but the fundamental point that a strong and effective culture is needed remains constant across the world.

Spencer Stuart define four types or categories of board culture:

- *Inquisitive boards*, who gather knowledge, explore alternatives and exchange ideas in order to reach the best possible solution.
- *Decisive boards*, who focus on getting the job done. They focus on agendas, outcome-oriented decisions and measurable results.
- *Collaborative boards*, who focus on the greater purpose and on achieving consensus towards that purpose.
- *Disciplined boards*, who advocate strong planning and adherence to rules and protocols, with a strong focus on consistency and managing risk.

These four types of board overlap heavily with the concepts identified by our own research, and we would argue that all these types of board have their weaknesses. Although the inquisitive culture is admirable in many ways, gathering and exchanging information requires an investment of time and can ultimately be insufficient, especially if key voices are missing from the board. There is also a risk of diffusion of responsibility if no one makes key decisions. Decisive boards may 'satisfice' when it comes to knowledge gathering, going with what they know rather than examining every alternative, with a resulting risk of an unquestionable task focus that can lead to groupthink. Collaborative board cultures can also lead to groupthink, especially if the view is that consensus is more important than debate, and these boards can also spend too long achieving consensus when direct action is needed. And without independence and challenge, there is a risk that disciplined boards could slip into a hidebound, rules-based culture, avoiding difficult conversations and refusing to explore different points of view.

The role of the chair and the CEO is an important variable too. The chair plays, or should play, the leading role in setting the tone and culture of the board, but inevitably the character and nature of the CEO has an influence too. The balance between the two plays a big role in shaping the culture of the board. One of the problems of unitary leadership, where the chair and CEO roles are combined in the same person, is that those checks and balances can disappear. It is then up to the rest of the board to try to provide that balance and maintain control of board culture, and as we saw in the case studies, that is often far from easy, particularly if the chair-CEO also has extraordinary voting rights.

There are other ways of classifying cultures too. In his book *Boards, Governance and Value Creation*, Morten Huse similarly divides board cultures into four categories:[5]

- *Barbarian boards* eschew any notion of support or guidance for the executive team and focus instead on monitoring and control. Far from cultivating relationships and bonds of trust with executives, they deliberately keep their distance in order to maintain a neutral and dispassionate stance. They are driven largely by agency theory, seeing themselves as principals and the executives as agents, and unsurprisingly the relationship between the two can be full of friction.
- *Aunt boards* are largely passive. They acquiesce to whatever management propose, not because they trust management but because they lack the initiative or enterprise to do anything else. Huse comments that directors join aunt boards largely because they like to see their name in print. In our own scheme this equates to diffusion of responsibility. Aunt boards lack initiative because no one has taken control or responsibility.

- *Clan boards* are collaborative by nature and also cultivate close relationships with management. They tend to see the company as one big family, in which board and management are involved together, all working towards the same goals. Board members tend to be closely involved with management, working with them but also exercising more direct oversight. They are driven by group dynamics, but we can also see evidence of resource dependence theory; the more resources we have, the more we work together. There is no separation between management and board because the dominant philosophy is about bringing resources to bear to solve problems.
- *Value-creating boards* are also proactive, but they aim to strike more of a balance between collaboration and control. Board members are fully engaged and have good relationships and dialogue with management, but they also maintain their duty of scrutiny and challenge. The value-creating board is also subject to group dynamics but in a positive way; the 'group' in this case embraces not just management and the board itself, but all stakeholders. In this way, value-creating boards largely escape the dysfunctions we have described here.

Huse makes value judgements about different types of board culture and clearly sees the value-creating board as the best option. Clan boards risk getting too close to management and compromising independence; barbarian boards go too far in the other direction and become instruments of domination and control, while aunt boards—again as we saw in some of the case studies—appear to serve no useful function whatever. The value-creating board, on the other hand, would appear to be a balanced combination of all four of the qualities we saw above, inquiry, decisiveness, collaboration and discipline. But how do we get there?

Strategies for Changing Board Culture

To paraphrase the late Warren Bennis, managing culture is like herding cats, but it can be done; there are established strategies for culture management.[6] An article in the *Journal of Applied Psychology* in 2008 describes four different types of culture management strategy, as shown in Fig. 11.1.

Pre-emptive Versus Reactive Strategies. One of the clear themes emerging from our case studies has been that boards, like most collaborative groups, are not very good at taking the time to anticipate problems that might occur, and planning for them *before* they become problems. For example, the chair might perceive issues such as lack of independence on the part of directors, lack of

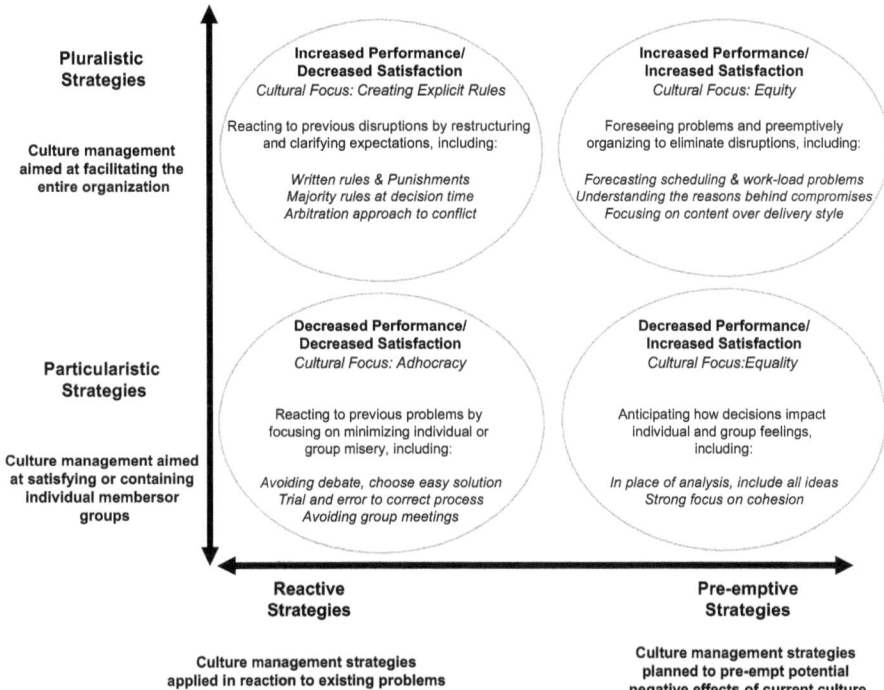

Fig. 11.1 The role of culture management in predicting board outcomes. Source: Figure developed from Kirstin J. Behfar, Randall S. Peterson, Elizabeth A. Mannix and William M.K. Trochim, 'The Critical Role of Conflict Resolution in Teams: A Close Look at the Links Between Conflict Types, Conflict Management Strategies, and Team Outcomes,' *Journal of Applied Psychology* 93, 2008, pp. 170–188

skills or confidence in the part of newly appointed directors, the danger of an overly dominant individual on the board and so on, but not develop strategies to deal with the problem. Other directors then become frustrated and angry and this begins to interfere with board effectiveness, but by then it can be too late because the anger and frustration get in the way of needed change.

Instead, most boards wait for cultural problems to emerge and then react to them once they are in view. An example of a reactive strategy is the board reforms undertaken at Uber in order to reduce the imbalance of power created by extraordinary voting rights and to increase the number of independent directors. Reactive strategies are necessary when things go wrong—the problem is that sometimes, by the time the board reacts, it is already too late and the organization is in terminal decline. Research consistently finds that it is better to anticipate problems than to wait for problems to emerge and be constantly chasing wrongdoers.

However, pre-emptive strategies are not without their problems too. Where organizations often go wrong is trying to do 'culture change' in a vacuum. Too often, they are not clear about what they want to achieve and how change needs to be maintained and embedded in the organizational DNA.

Pluralistic Versus Particularistic Strategies. Pluralistic strategies aim to facilitate the entire group or organization and are intended to create broad, sweeping cultural change that is helpful for the entire group or organization. BP's response to the *Deepwater Horizon* disaster, for example, was to create a sweeping cultural change that encompassed the entire organization, including the board, and made health and safety issues a priority. Pluralistic strategies are easy to describe but hard to do; the entrenched barriers to cultural change can be very severe indeed, and it is estimated that around 70 per cent of large-scale cultural change programmes fail.[7]

The temptation for addressing problems is to go for particularistic strategies, which focus on specific groups or individuals within the organization, the board, the top team, division or function, or location, asking each to be responsible for managing their own culture and maximize it for the benefit of the business. The aim is targeted cultural change in a particular part of the organization, rather like a laser treatment for cancer. This might help solve the problems in that particular group, but it almost always fails for two reasons. First, these targeted changes can also make it harder for different parts of the business to work together if cultural barriers are created and they stand in the way of different parts of the business operating differently. Second, as quickly as you try to change the culture of one part of the business, other parts create pressure to return to old habits. The lesson here is that isolated cultural change is unlikely to be successful. Changing the culture of the board alone, for example, is no guarantee that the culture of the business will follow. It takes concerted efforts to ensure that changes implemented in the boardroom filter through to the rest of the organization.

Figure 11.1 shows how these strategies combined so as to achieve different results, which we classify as *creating explicit rules*, *adhocracy*, *equality* and *equity*.

Equity Culture

> **Examples**
>
> Board and committee working practices are flexible but proactive; board meetings include a balance of critique and support; a lot of attention is given to forecasting and planning for how the organization will react in a crisis; board debate is lively and fluent, with everyone taking part, but some are more influential than others depending on the quality of their arguments. Decisions are reached by consensus in a timely manner, even if this involves compromise.

The best performing boards typically have an equity culture. It is of course necessary to give everyone on the board an equal voice and encourage them to speak their mind, but it is also necessary that the board reaches conclusions and makes decisions, and in a culture of equity, everyone pulls together and focuses on the task at hand and workload is therefore not always evenly distributed. An equity culture would mean, for example, that we have highly diverse board full of talent from many backgrounds and all views are valid, but the reality is in any given action some directors are more central than others. Over time there should be a more equally shared workload, but this is unlikely in the short term.

Unlike cultures of equality where the focus is on making sure each and every individual's needs are met, in cultures of equity there is a pluralistic element meaning that the primary focus is on the effectiveness of the whole board. The board works hard at anticipating issues and, where possible, resolving problems before they arise. The chair has an important role to play in allocating workloads to directors so that the work is shared around fairly, and everyone has a role to play. Board papers are concise and deliver information clearly and are expected to be read beforehand so that time can be devoted to discussion; if executives are delivering lengthy PowerPoint presentations during board meetings, something is going wrong.

Equality Culture

Examples

Making sure every voice is fully heard; a focus on cohesion ('we're all in this together'); decisions delayed until everyone has spoken and full consensus has been reached; diplomacy valued over plain speaking; individuals' rights and feelings take precedence over the needs of the group.

Pre-emptive strategies seek to prevent problems before they occur by ensuring that the board is able to spot problems and make decisions in a timely fashion, while particularistic strategies focus on fixing specific parts of the culture in the hope that these adjustments will improve organization as a whole. A combination of the two is likely to yield a strong equality culture where all members are free to express themselves and where no one's opinion counts for more than the others. Equality is also seen as the best way to create board cohesion, as this will encourage the board to pull together and work as a team.

There can be value to this, especially if the existing board culture has imbalances of power, information asymmetries and dominant factions of the kind we saw in a number of our case studies. This is essentially the formula Uber has used post Kalanick where the board moved to reduce extraordinary voting rights and create a level playing field. Equality and cohesion *are* important and a degree of this needs to be part of every board culture.

But where equality and cohesion become the primary focus of the culture, we then see the emergence of a culture similar to Spencer Stuart's 'collaborative' boards or Huse's 'clan' boards. Collaboration and cohesion become goals in their own right, and equality is a virtue that will always lead to the best decision. Individual sensitivities are prioritized over the decision itself, leading to the use of phrases such as 'we must carry everyone with us' or 'we can make no decision without establishing a consensus.' Everyone's ideas are listened to respectfully, but no deep analysis or critique is made of those ideas in case we disengage someone. We try to make decisions or arrive at solutions that include every point of view, sometimes at time when a sharp and decisive focus is needed. This can slow or even paralyse decision-making. Instead of being pre-emptive, the board ends up delaying its decision, sometimes until it is too late. This is why boards with a strong equality culture are engaging places to inhabit but are too often poor performers.

Explicit Rules Culture

Examples

Promulgating explicit codes of procedure and conduct, with sanctions for failure to comply; insistence on majority-rule decisions rather than consensus and prioritizing agreement over debate; discouragement of 'back channel' communications between directors and insisting communications go through formal, monitored channels.

A combination of pluralistic and reactive strategies is often deployed by boards after a significant disruption to the organization, a financial crisis, for example, or a scandal or breakdown in trust with key stakeholders. In order to fix the problem, the board introduces more explicit rules and regulations to clarify the duties of board members and also to set expectations for others. The exact limits of the board's powers and responsibilities are clearly communicated.

Sometimes, as a result of previous accusations of inaction or delay, the board may also decide that reaching quick decisions is now a priority. Instead of seeking consensus, the board will regularly make decisions that a significant sub-group disagree with through majority-rule voting. Disagreements between directors will be arbitrated by the chair rather than settled through discussion and debate. This is not necessarily a bad thing. As the Spencer Stuart report argued, discipline is important. Creating explicit rules can, up to a point, be very useful for imposing structure where there was none before, breaking down board factions and ensuring that directors put the interests of the board first in front of their own. And, where boards have a poor track record in terms of talking but never making decisions, putting in rules and structures can be effective at ensuring decisions do get made.

Explicit rules cultures generally result in good objective performance, for a while until they become so rule-bound they turn into a bureaucratic board. It starts with directors disengaging because the boardroom has become a miserable place to work. Who wants to have a constant barrage of new rules to follow? Everyone knows that it is too often the few badly behaved ones who spoil it for the rest, and this culture is the living embodiment of that ideal. What this means in practice is that directors value respectful, collaborative relationships that facilitate sharing of information and perspectives and enable them to improve the quality of decisions the board makes. If the group dynamics of the board support this, the directors will be satisfied and more motivated to do their best for the organization. If the dynamics instead push for conformity and squeeze out dissent, levels of satisfaction will decline. This unhappiness in turns means the board will become less effective, in which case the chair may be tempted to impose yet more rules to improve performance and so on and on resulting in a vicious circle and evolution into bureaucracy. Boards need to pay attention to the relationships between directors and ensure those relationships are healthy.

Adhocracy Culture

Examples

Decisions made informally by small groups within the board, through back channels rather than formal group meetings; avoidance of open debate with a preference for settling matters before the meeting begins; lack of formal processes and structures; the same people getting called to serve on committees and form working parties; blurring of the line between executive and non-executive responsibilities.

A combination of particularistic and reactive strategies is what happens after every major board disaster or scandal. The regulators respond with more rules designed to ensure this 'never happens again,' like the Sarbanes-Oxley Act which arrived as a response to the collapses of Enron, WorldCom, Global Crossing and Tyco. Too often those rules are not effective at solving the problem that gave rise to the new rules, and this plus the additional burden of compliance makes directors unhappy. Sometimes boards even inflict this on themselves where the board seldom looks beyond the immediate problem at hand, dealing with each issue as it comes. This is the worst of the four options. Pre-emptive strategies mean directors are more cohesive because they are working to solve problems before they happen, and as noted above, pluralistic strategies will help the whole organization perform better. When you have neither—no cohesion and no common culture—the situation grows dangerous. Systems are ignored, and in extreme cases the board breaks the rules of good governance; a common example is when directors cross the line and become involved in areas of executive responsibility, compromising their independence in the process. Or, the board goes to the other extreme and becomes what Morten Huse referred to as 'aunt' boards, doing virtually nothing and letting the executive have its own way.

When problems arise that must be dealt with, adhocratic boards will also tend to tinker at the margins rather than attacking the heart of the problem, choosing tactical or operational solutions rather than stepping back to look at the bigger picture. They tend to avoid making decisions as a group, preferring back channels to avoid lengthy debate and discussion. They also tend to prioritize the easy solution rather than the best solution, deeming it best to make a decision quickly and move on—or in some cases, avoid or defer the decision until the time has come when it is no longer necessary to decide. They can be 'comfortable' places where no one is unduly stretched or challenged. Paradoxically, this has the effect of decreasing the satisfaction of those directors who actually enjoy stretch and challenge and joined the board for this reason. Instead, they are removed from decision-making and have little to do and their unhappiness increases. Adhocratic boards tend over time to exhibit lower levels of performance and also to reduce the satisfaction of directors.

Effective Boardroom Culture

Given that many of the boardroom disasters are represented in our cases of adhocracy, equality and explicit rules cultures, how those types of boards happen should be relatively clear. What we have not covered in detail at this point is equity-type boardroom cultures, mainly because our focus so far has been on boardroom disasters. From here we shift gears to discuss effective boardrooms. A good example of attributes and practices that drive effective boardroom culture can be seen in the appointment letter of a highly respected FT-100 board chair:

All directors agree to

- uphold the highest ethical standards of integrity and probity, including compliance with the company's Code of Business Conduct and Ethics;
- support executives in their leadership of the business while monitoring their conduct;
- question intelligently, debate constructively, challenge rigorously and decide dispassionately;
- listen sensitively to the views of others, inside and outside the board;
- gain the trust and respect of other board members;
- promote the highest standards of corporate governance;
- devote so much of your time, attention and ability as is reasonably required by the company for the purpose of carrying out your duties and
- not at any time make any untrue or misleading statement relating to the company.

The chair then had a conversation with every director every year about how they live those values and behaviours, including how colleagues would respond to them, what conversations would look like and what other directors would be saying about their interventions.

The result, if implemented well and if frameworks such as board evaluation are put in place to maintain it, is a culture that results in both increased performance and increased cohesion as people are more likely to speak in meetings and to share information. The board functions smoothly and effectively and makes good decisions in a timely manner. Directors feel they are having impact and their own purpose in joining the board is fulfilled. A virtuous circle is created, where highly motivated directors push the board to improve performance still further.

The other side of the coin is the frameworks the board uses to understand the company. Robert Hogan and Robert Kaiser argue that an important part of organizational effectiveness is 'a set of monitoring systems that will allow senior leadership to keep track of the talent level of the staff, the motivational level of the staff, the performance of the management group and the effectiveness of the business strategy.'[8] Properly implemented these will allow the board to keep its finger on the organizational pulse.

Hogan and Kaiser also argue that it is the responsibility of senior leadership to put these systems in place. This brings us back to the issue of the character and personality of those leaders, especially the CEO and the top management team. The latter have a great deal of power and can act as gatekeepers, controlling information that the rest of the board receives (as we saw in the case of Carillion) or even dominating the board and excluding them altogether, as happened at Google, Uber and Royal Bank of Scotland (RBS). The RBS case was particularly instructive. The board was so thoroughly dominated by the CEO that it slipped into groupthink, everyone going along with what they perceived the majority view to be and no one daring to dissent. The systems only work if the people make them work, and once again we see how vitally important it is that there is genuine trust between the CEO and the board.

Spotting Problems Before They Happen

One of the core assumptions of an effective boardroom culture is pre-emptive problem solving. The first line of defence is knowing how to spot the warning signs, the red flags that indicate trouble is brewing within the culture. We offered a few of these in the discussions of the case studies; here are a few more.

(continued)

(continued)

Explicit Rules

- Established procedures from which the board does not deviate; 'this is how we do things.'
- Challenging the orthodoxy is frowned upon, or even sanctioned.
- Debate is squeezed by the rules; when debate does take place, the chair intervenes to make an arbitrary rule.
- Lack of diversity of thought; people think in similar patterns and tend to conform.
- Strong hierarchy within the board, with a high social distance between the chair and other directors.
- Lack of access to information.

Adhocracy

- A few people appear to do all the work, while other board members seem disengaged.
- Decisions are made without due diligence, often using side conversations; board meetings then validate what has already been agreed in those side conversation.
- A blurred line between executive and non-executive responsibilities.
- Weak authority of the chair.
- Lack of access to information.

Equality

- People speak at meetings but are rarely challenged; the atmosphere is excessively polite and there is little or no debate.
- Discussions take a long time and sometimes fail to reach a conclusion.
- Achieving consensus is valued more than reaching a decision.

Managing and Changing Board Culture

The first step to making any changes to board culture, regardless of the strategy, is that the board needs to take ownership of monitoring the culture and holding the CEO to account for the culture of the business. One of the reasons why cultures go bad is that, consciously or unconsciously, boards fail to accept their responsibility for ensuring the culture remains healthy, accepting it as what it is. This goes for board culture as well as that of the wider organization.[9]

The board needs to recognize the role that culture plays in enabling—or constraining—discussion and decision-making. Everything the board does, and indeed much of what the wider organization does, including its values, strategy and business model, are affected by board culture. According to the Financial Reporting Council (FRC), 'For boards, culture starts with their behaviour in the boardroom. Employees need to see that the leadership is held to account and to the same standards as the rest of the organization.'[10] Here are some of things the FRC believes boards need to do in order to manage board culture and create cultural change.

Be Open and Accountable to All Stakeholders. 'Openness and accountability matter at every level,' says the FRC. 'Good governance means a focus on how this takes place throughout the company and those who act on its behalf. It should be demonstrated in the way the company conducts business and engages with and reports to stakeholders. This involves respecting a wide range of stakeholder interests.' It can be difficult for boards to remember this, particularly in cases where a major shareholder sits on the board or has appointed representatives as directors; there may well be pressure to put shareholder interests first, as we saw in many of the case studies above. But investors need to remember that they too are responsible to other stakeholders, and in some cases, it may be necessary to make this point.

Embed and Integrate the Values. This needs to be done across the organization, in human resources, risk, ethics, internal audit and compliance, and many other functions, but that embedding and integrating has to start with the board itself. Values such as transparency, integrity, honesty, respect, safety, teamwork and, above all, trust must be part of the board's systems and procedures, its interactions with each other and with the executive, and its conception of its mission and duty to stakeholders. The board must do more than just talk about the values; it must measure and live them, as well as hold the executive to account for supporting them across the organization.

Questions Boards Need to Ask
- How are we demonstrating behaviour that reflects the behaviour we expect throughout the company? Are we leading by example?
- Have we measured culture and are we discussing culture in sufficient depth at board meetings?
- How are we taking account of culture in our board effectiveness reviews?
- How can we ensure we consider the impact on culture in all the decisions we take?
- Do the committees support the board on culture? For example, if our people are our main asset, do we have a people committee on our board?
- Is there a need for a specific conduct, ethics or culture committee?

(continued)

(continued)

- What behaviours are being driven when setting strategy and financial targets?
- What percentage of board time is spent on financial performance management against targets? And on behavioural performance management? Is the balance right?
- Is company tax policy consistent with stated values?
- How are we challenging groupthink and testing key decisions for cultural alignment?[11]

Assess, Engage and Measure the Culture, and Take Action Where Gaps Occur. Culture is not static; it adapts, evolves and changes, sometimes very quickly, and boards need to be aware of this. Changes in board personnel—especially the chair—are one of the most important causes of cultural change, but changes in the wider organization and its environment can have an impact too. Board members need to be alert to even small changes that can signal broader cultural shifts.

Context is important here too. Size and sector will impact on board culture; the culture in a charity or non-governmental organization will be different from that of a Fortune 500 company, even though they might face many of the same challenges. Geert Hofstede's work on the impact of national culture applies to boards as well as to the organizations they run.[12] Some cultures are more power distant in their approach, and this can mean greater emphasis on deference to authority; other cultures are lower in power distance which might result in greater challenge from lower-level employees of the chief executive, and perhaps even the board. And, of course, every organization has its own unique culture, and this too can affect the culture of the board.

Tools exist which can help boards to better understand their culture and see it in a more reflective light. For example, one of the authors, Randall S. Peterson, has created a measure which does exactly this. The Board Effectiveness Profile™ tool allows directors to compare views of how individual members see the board along seven dimensions:

1. How much power is concentrated in the hands of the chair?
2. How flexible is the board around norms of practice and performance?
3. How cohesive is the board?
4. How much power is concentrated in the hands of the chair versus committees and corporate leadership?
5. Is the board intellectually adaptive?
6. Does the board share a strong sense of collective confidence (belief in its ability to meet current challenges)?
7. What is the board's risk appetite?[13]

Each director describes their perceptions of the board along these dimensions, and their responses are collated using a technique known as Q-Sort to give a collective picture of effectiveness of board decision-making processes. Responses are also correlated with perfect examples of each of our six dysfunctions, as well as a selection of the historical board cultures included in our case studies here. The results can be used to help the board provide collective training and coaching in areas of weakness, create a useful 'companion' dataset in order to compare board evaluation reports, help inform targeted activities that will increase board effectiveness and development of a healthy culture and plan for future needs including board succession. Along with the Board Effectiveness Tool, Professor Peterson has also developed an Organizational Culture Map™ that allows organizations to examine both their own culture and that of the broader organization along dimensions including rate of change, tight-loose rules, norm respecting, teamwork orientation, performance orientation, stakeholder orientation, quality focus, collective energy, and learning and growth.[14] These of course are just a couple of examples; plenty of other techniques have been developed over the years. Culture is measurable and movable, *if* you make the effort and use tools whose structure is informed by evidence-based guidance on measurement and question formulation.

Board Culture and Independent Directors

The principal aim of changing board culture must be first, to foster a culture of independence on the part of the directors themselves, and second, to improve the quality of interaction between board members, and between boards and executives. The culture of the board directly affects how the executive responds and interacts. When boards operate in a clear, evidence-based and transparent fashion, this encourages the executive to collaborate fully with the board and encourages this same culture within the business itself. At the same time, independence of thought and action gives directors the confidence and ability to speak, encourage debate and break the shackles of path dependence and groupthink.

Two things follow from this, both of which have already been mentioned. One is that there needs to be a culture of trust and 'psychological safety' among members, enabling them to speak frankly and freely without fear of retaliation or sanction.[15] The chair plays a key role in establishing and maintaining that culture, and one of our recommendations going forward is that much more attention needs to be paid to the role of the chair: the competencies and skills required for the role, the requisite level of board experience, their own personal knowledge of the organization, the sector and the challenges it faces. The chair should also be responsible for the training and development of board members. Second, boards need to spend more time looking at themselves and their culture, evaluating their competencies and ways of working. They also need to look at how to improve diversity and inclusion, not just of gender, ethnicity and background, but of thought, lived experience and worldview (things which themselves are, of course, influenced by gender, ethnicity and background).

The most effective boards do not rely on feelings or instincts alone to make arguments for change. Instead, they seek evidence to develop and support their views. They are aware that concepts such as culture, conflict and values, which are too often dismissed or talked about as if they are merely a matter of personal opinion, can be systematically assessed and then actively managed based on evidence. And, most importantly, they are not embarrassed to consult organizational culture experts in the same way we all consult experts in finance, technology and cyber security.[16] Only in this way can a board be certain that they remain dynamic and active and do not slip away into the traps in ineffectiveness and complacency that we have outlined in this book.

Making boards more resilient and more effective means creating a cultural space where directors are able to exercise effective scrutiny, raise challenges and hold debates. But it also means recruiting the most effective people onto boards in the first place and getting the right board structure so that independent directors have a voice. We advocate two important principles:

1. There should be a majority of independent directors on the board. It should not be possible for executive directors and directors representing incumbent interests to control the board in the manner we saw in some of the case studies such as Facebook and Uber.
2. The CEO and chair must be accountable. In most jurisdictions this is accomplished by legally separating the two roles so that the same person cannot hold both. Where unitary leadership prevails, it is more important than ever that the CEO/chair be accountable to the board and that their behaviours and actions should be in the best interests of the organization and its stakeholders. Martin Lipton and Jay Lorsch, whom we cited earlier, believed that the role of lead director, or senior independent director, is crucial in this situation. One of the main tasks of the lead director should be to hold the chair/CEO to account by those who are not directly involved in the management of the business.

Getting the Right People with the Right Mindsets Onto Boards

The nominations committee is often the forgotten committee on boards, but its role is absolutely crucial in determining board composition. If the wrong people are recruited onto the board, then the board culture itself will rapidly deteriorate and we will be back to the problem described earlier, a group of people in a room looking after their own interests rather than a cohesive group working in the best interests of the organization and its stakeholders.

In 1992 the Cadbury Report defined the role of independent directors as bringing 'an *independent judgement* to bear on issues of strategy, performance and resources including key appointments and standards of conduct.' The UK's Corporate Governance Code further states that independent directors 'should provide constructive challenge, strategic guidance, offer specialist advice and hold management to account.' To determine whether they are completing these duties, the following questions should be asked.

Do the Independent Directors Demonstrate that They Are the Long-Term Custodians of the Business? This comes back to the point about fiduciary duty and knowing what the role requires. Although steps forward have been made in terms of providing training for independent directors, far too many directors are appointed to their first board with little more than an induction day—often not even that—and are expected to learn on the job. Knowledge of critical issues like strategy, audit, digital skills, remuneration, succession planning and boardroom dynamics is a long-term investment, even for the experienced executive.

Many directors take on the role without fully understanding what it entails or what their responsibilities are. Ideas about what those responsibilities are will vary between countries and cultures; American and Asian boards, for example, are often expected to delegate responsibility for strategy to the executive (in our opinion, this is questionable), while European boards tend to be more hands-on in terms of defining strategy. However, what unites virtually all codes of corporate governance is the notion that the independent directors are the guardians and stewards of the organization. Directors need to learn what this means in practice, what they are responsible for, understand why it is not a simple extension of being an executive, and why maintaining independence is such a vital part of that responsibility.

Do the Independent Directors Ask Questions that Identify Important Issues Which Management Have Overlooked or Not Paid Sufficient Attention? In order to do so, directors need to understand the organization, its business model and its environment, and be familiar with not only its mission and purpose but also how it functions on a day-to-day basis. Of course independent directors do not get involved in everyday management, but in order to govern effectively they need to know how things work. They also need to know the external environment and what challenges the company faces, now and in the future.

Because of this need for knowledge, boards are often tempted to recruit people with prior experience of the sector. This is not to say that industry knowledge is unimportant, quite the opposite. As already noted, none of Carillion's independent directors had prior knowledge of the construction industry, and few on the board of Lehman Brothers had banking industry experience, and in both cases this was a factor in the collapse that followed. Industry knowledge *is* an important characteristic of an independent director, but it is not the only one. An ability to question and analyse is equally vital, if not more so. Without that, prior experience can quickly turn to groupthink or threat rigidity where when someone feels threatened their thinking becomes rigid. And as well as industry knowledge, directors also need functional knowledge too in areas such as marketing, operations, HR, digital, international business and so on. Bringing people into the board with special skillsets is a good way to get a fresh pair of eyes on a problem and spot things managers may have missed, but it will require them to learn about other parts of the business.

Are the Independent Directors Concerned as Much About Value Creation as About Governance? Here we come back again to purpose and mission. Are the directors focused on growing the company and creating value for stakeholders in the form of quality products and services, meaningful employment, a return on capital to shareholders and general benefit to society? There is a tendency on the part of some directors to assume that their only role is ensuring compliance; everything else is the province of the executive. But as the Cadbury Report and many other sources on corporate governance make clear, the provision of support, guidance and advice is also part of the role.

Independent directors are typically described as the stewards of the organization. In this context, stewardship means that the organization engages its mission and fulfils its purpose of service to stakeholders. Ensuring that the books balance and the organization remains a going concern is necessary but insufficient.

Do the Independent Directors Demonstrate Courage and Curiosity? Courage and curiosity are essential qualities of an independent director. Courage is necessary to ask difficult questions, to go out on a limb and be prepared if necessary to be the only dissenting voice in the room. It is particularly important when challenging behaviours such as fraud, corruption or sexual abuse and when the person suspected of these offences is a dominant, charismatic figure in the organization. But courage is also necessary in a wider sense, for example when spotting signs that the board culture may be weakening and bringing these to the attention of the chair and colleagues. This may not always be welcome; not everyone will want to upset the status quo, and peer pressure may be brought to bear. It must be resisted. It takes considerable courage to be the only voice in the room saying, 'things have to change,' but it must be done.

Curiosity leads directors to look beyond the obvious. When confronted with a problem or a dilemma, they will want to know not only what has happened but also how and why. The curious director will seek answers to questions and will not rest until they have found the truth. In essence, then, curiosity helps the independent director learn what questions to ask; courage helps them ask them at the right time, of the right people.

However, asking questions is not enough. Although the individual as solitary advocate of truth sticking fast to what they know is a potent cultural image, research shows that the lone voice never wins. Independent directors need to ask questions, but they also need to gather evidence and build a case for their views, a case strong enough to persuade other directors to join them. We see this time and again in boardroom scandals—someone knew what was happening but could not get others to act. Truth alone does not win, truth supported does. An effective director knows how to build a case and bring others to their point of view.

Assembling a high-functioning board requires directors with these qualities, but it also requires diversity and inclusion of background, experience and mindset. We already have made this point several times and will not labour it again here. But this is a vital point, and one which must be addressed if board culture is to be made more effective. At the very least, we need to be thinking about how we recruit independent directors and where we look for candidates.

That raises an important point: how do we drive this cultural change through? What is needed in order to reform board culture?

Notes

1. Martin Lipton and Jay W. Lorsch, 'A Modest Proposal for Improved Corporate Governance', *The Business Lawyer* 48, 1992.
2. Marc Stigter and Cary Cooper, *Boards That Dare: How to Future-Proof Today's Corporate Boards*, London: Bloomsbury, 2018, p. 142.

3. Jennifer A. Chatman, David F. Caldwell, Charles A. O'Reilly and Bernadette Doerr, 'Parsing Organizational Culture: How the Norm for Adaptability Influences the Relationship Between Culture Consensus and Financial Performance in High-Technology Firms', *Journal of Organizational Behavior* 35(6), 2014; https://www.gsb.stanford.edu/insights/charles-oreilly-finding-corporate-culture-drives-growth.

4. Spencer Stuart, 'In a New Era for Boards, Culture is Key', https://www.spencerstuart.com/research-and-insight/in-a-new-era-for-boards-culture-is-key.

5. Morten Huse, *Boards, Governance and Value Creation: The Human Side of Corporate Governance*, Cambridge: Cambridge University Press, 2007.

6. Warren G. Bennis, *Managing People is Like Herding Cats*, London: Atlantic Books, 1997.

7. https://www.mckinsey.com/featured-insights/leadership/changing-change-management#; https://www.forbes.com/sites/victorlipman/2013/09/04/new-study-explores-why-change-management-fails-and-how-to-perhaps-succeed/?sh=2e9bf9a07137.

8. Hogan and Kaiser, p. 178.

9. Spencer Stuart, 'So What Do Boards Need to Know About Corporate Culture?', https://www.spencerstuart.com/research-and-insight/what-do-boards-need-to-know-about-corporate-culture.

10. Financial Reporting Council, 'Corporate Culture and the Role of Boards: Report of Observations', July 2016.

11. Ibid.

12. Geert Hofstede, *Culture's Consequences: Comparing Values, Behaviors, Institutions and Organizations Across Nations*, London: Sage, 2003.

13. https://www.talentsage.com/our-tools/the-board-effectiveness-profile-tool-for-organizations/; Randall S. Peterson, Pamela D. Owens and Paul V. Martorana. 'The Group Dynamics Q-Sort in Organizational Research: A New Method for Studying Familiar Problems', *Organizational Research Methods* 2 (2), 1999; Randall S. Peterson, 'The Role of Values in Predicting Fairness Judgments and Support of Affirmative Action', *Journal of Social Issues* 50(4), 1999.

14. https://www.talentsage.com/our-tools/the-organizational-culture-map-tool-for-organizations/; Peterson et al.

15. Randall S. Peterson, 'It's Time to Vote Majority Rule Off the Company Board', *Strategy + Business*, 24 October 2018.

16. Randall S. Peterson, 'Boards Need to Get Serious About Managing Organizational Culture', *Forbes*, 3 December 2019.

12

Stakeholder Engagement

One option currently under discussion in many organizations is *stakeholder engagement*. Loosely defined, stakeholder engagement is the involvement of stakeholders in decisions that could affect them. Rather than merely telling stakeholders what will happen, boards identify stakeholders and listen to their points of view through a process of engagement, and then consider and incorporate these views into their decision-making processes. Independent directors play a very important role in ensuring that this happens, acting as links or conduits to stakeholder groups and sometimes serving as their voice on the board.

We argue that stakeholder engagement can play an important role in reducing or preventing the six board dysfunctions. Before looking at how this is done, let us first review what exactly stakeholder engagement is and the current state of the field.

Stakeholder theory has its origins in much older theories about the responsibility of business to society.[1] The term first appeared in the 1960s and the first fully formed versions of stakeholder theory appeared in the 1980s, notably in works such as *Strategic Management: A Stakeholder Approach* by R. Edward Freeman.[2] The concept has since become one of the cornerstones of corporate social responsibility, but it has also been adopted into some mainstream thinking on business strategy and strategic management. 'Stakeholders' has become a very broadly defined term that encompasses employees, customers, suppliers, investors and shareholders, banks and granters of credit, government and regulators, communities and society and even—controversially—'voiceless' stakeholders like the natural environment and unborn future generations, who cannot represent themselves but who

© The Author(s), under exclusive license to Springer Nature Switzerland AG 2022
G. Brown, R. S. Peterson, *Disaster in the Boardroom*,
https://doi.org/10.1007/978-3-030-91658-9_12

nonetheless are likely to be affected by the operations of companies.[3] According to the principles of stakeholder engagement, companies should listen to representatives of some, or even all, of these groups and governance should be informed by the inputs received. In the words of the Harvard Law School Forum on Corporate Governance,

> [t]he fiduciary duty of the board is to promote the value of the corporation. In fulfilling that duty, directors must exercise their business judgment in considering and reconciling the interests of various stakeholders—including shareholders, employees, customers, suppliers, the environment and communities—and the attendant risks and opportunities for the corporation.[4]

Opposed to stakeholder theory is agency theory, which sees governance as a bilateral process between the company and shareholders, the principal-agent relationship. This theory has its origins in the concept of the separation of ownership and control which emerged in the early twentieth century and was refined by Chicago School economists including Milton Friedman in the 1960s and 1970s. According to agency theory, shareholders who have invested capital in the organization should be considered the primary stakeholders, and their interests given priority over other stakeholder groups.

At the heart of the dispute between agency theory and stakeholder theory is a disagreement about whether the primary purpose of a business is to create wealth for shareholders or to generate benefits for wider society. Friedman, of course, famously argued for the former, going so far as to castigate companies for giving money to charity when any surplus rightfully belonged to shareholders.[5] Over the ensuing fifty years there has been a gradual retreat from that position, and many critics of the stakeholder model now focus less on whether it is desirable, and more on whether it will actually work in a way that is fair and equitable to all stakeholders.

For example, in an article entitled 'The Illusory Promise of Stakeholder Governance,' Lucien Bebchuk and Roberto Tallarita accept the good intentions behind stakeholder engagement but have several reservations. 'Stakeholderism,' they believe, arouses illusory hopes about what the company can do for each stakeholder group. Each believes that their interests will be represented, but the competing interests of various stakeholder groups mean that few stakeholders would actually get what they wanted.[6] This raises the problem of stakeholder salience, meaning that the stakeholders with the loudest voices and/or those whose interests are most closely aligned with management will receive the most intention, and others will be squeezed out.

Bebchuk and Tallarita are also concerned that any dilution of shareholder interests in favour of other stakeholder groups will 'insulate' management from shareholder pressure, meaning that management actually becomes less accountable rather than more. Going on from this, it could be argued that clever managers will put stakeholder groups in competition with each other in order to get what they want. Bebchuk and Tallarita conclude that asking companies to engage in stakeholder engagement voluntarily could have unexpected negative outcomes. Only legislation and regulation, they argue, can ensure true and fair stakeholder representation.

Other criticisms of stakeholder approaches include the view that by failing to maximize shareholder wealth, stakeholder engagement is contributing to the long-term instability of the firm; that the definitions of who is a 'stakeholder' are often vague and there are no clear boundaries; and that the stakeholder model provides no objective standards against which corporate agents and performance can be judged.[7] Writing in *Harvard Business Review*, Vijay Govindarajan and Anup Srivastava argue that it will be very difficult to make any sort of progress towards real stakeholder engagement so long as corporate performance metrics—return on capital, payback turnover, asset turnover, margins—remain geared towards the needs of shareholders, and so long as executive remuneration remains tied to those metrics. Like Bebchuk and Tallarita, they are concerned that fine words about stakeholder engagement are often not backed up by real intentions.[8] In an article for *Forbes* magazine, Steve Denning rejects the notion of agency theory with regard to shareholders, but he too believes that general stakeholder theory will lead to a dilution of the interests of the most important group of stakeholders: customers, whom he regards as the 'true north' of the organization.[9]

Preliminary findings from a working group at the Institute of Directors in the UK, which looked across national boundaries and at public sector and third-sector organizations as well as businesses, found a number of practical objections to stakeholder engagement, which can be grouped along the following lines:

1. Stakeholders are believed to lack knowledge. As outsiders, they cannot be expected to understand the complexities of a large and sophisticated business, and the vast majority will have no prior experience of governance.
2. Stakeholders cannot be trusted. Boards discuss many sensitive issues and have access to financial data. What is to stop stakeholders from leaking to one of our rivals?
3. Stakeholders are not interested. Their relationships with the organization are primarily transactional, and so long as they receive the value they

expect—goods and services, wages, return on investment—they are not interested in the workings of the organization.

4. Stakeholder engagement and governance are complex and time-consuming, and would distract the board from more important work.
5. Tradition. We have never involved stakeholders before, why should we do so now?

There is truth to some of these arguments, especially when it comes to direct stakeholder governance. It can be particularly difficult to recruit stakeholders into governance positions—as an example, the difficulty faced by many school governing bodies in recruiting qualified parents as governors—and many stakeholders either do not understand what governance is or do not see what participation would mean for them. In many circumstances, a more arm's-length form of engagement will be both easier and more productive, allowing stakeholders to focus on issues where they have real knowledge and expertise.

However, there is little evidence to suggest that stakeholders are not trustworthy. Reports from Ireland and Sweden suggest that breaches by employees involved in stakeholder engagement are very rare, and one participant in the working group, Janet Williamson, corporate governance lead at the Trades Union Congress in the UK, argues that 'union representatives are frequently entrusted with confidential company information in the course of discussions on pay and collective bargaining and have repeatedly demonstrated their capacity to respect confidentiality requirements, including in very difficult circumstances.'[10]

The arguments are clouded to some extent too that stakeholder engagement as a theory can be put into practice in many different ways. Looking at examples around the world, we see that stakeholder engagement can range across a spectrum from informal consultations, through formal stakeholder bodies that report to boards in a structured way, to stakeholder *governance* where stakeholder representatives sit as directors on the boards of organizations. The latter concept in particular is controversial, and some organizations have found that a board composed of effective independent directors backed by a strong framework for stakeholder engagement is sufficient. On the other hand, companies that do have formal stakeholder directors report that the practice works well. In some European and Asian countries worker representation is required by law.

Stakeholder Engagement and Value

There is no doubt that stakeholder engagement takes time and effort. Stakeholder salience is an issue, and balancing everyone's needs in order to get the best results is tricky, but it can be done. There are parallels here with diversity and inclusion. If stakeholders don't feel included—if they think their views are being disregarded or not taken into account in the final decision—they will become disillusioned and drop away, or even take adversarial positions. However, if they *do* feel included and buy into the values of the company, then evidence suggests they will commit to the company and the interests of all stakeholders, not just their own.

A genuine commitment to stakeholder engagement can have a positive effect on corporate performance. Research over the past decade shows that companies that adopt stakeholder approaches tend to outperform and be more financially sustainable over the long term than those that stick to a strict principal-agent model. In a stakeholder model,

> the role of the board is seen as representing the interests of the corporation itself. The board acts as a 'mediating hierarch' to give all stakeholders the necessary confidence to make company-specific investments that will create a 'pie' larger than the one they can create for themselves and ensure that they are rewarded, at least above what they can otherwise earn.[11]

But this is not just a matter of equity and fairness; stakeholder engagement and governance can also be seen as sensible business. In his book *Grow the Pie: How Great Companies Deliver Both Purpose and Profit*, Alex Edmans argues that by taking care of more of all stakeholders, not just shareholders, companies 'increase the pie' and create more value for shareholders.[12] As stakeholders have a better life and become more prosperous, thanks to the firm's activities, they have more spending power and are more likely to become customers, making the company more profitable and sustainable. Everyone wins.

Edmans also argues that companies should do more than just donate to charity; they need to use their expertise to help stakeholders wherever they can. He uses the example of Coca-Cola, which delivers cool drinks to every part of the planet. In Africa, the Coca-Cola supply chain also carries cool-only medicines such as vaccines. Too often, though, these things do not happen because stakeholder activities are not directly profitable and tracking social benefit back to the company bottom line is extremely hard to do. As a result, companies do not get involved. What gets measured, gets done; everything else is ignored.

Many other studies have found similar results. To give just a few examples, the work of Ioannis Ioannou and his colleagues has found that 'high sustainability companies significantly outperform their counterparts over the long term, both in terms of stock market and accounting performance,' that is the traditional shareholder-oriented metrics that Govindarajan and Srivastava talked about. Ioannou and his colleagues also draw a link between 'high sustainability' and stakeholder engagement, that is the companies that are most engaged in sustainability efforts are also talking to their stakeholders.[13]

Research conducted by the McKinsey Global Institute has also found that 'companies with strong environmental, social and governance norms recorded higher performance and credit ratings through five factors: top-line growth, lower costs, fewer legal and regulatory interventions, higher productivity, and optimized investment and asset utilization.'[14] McKinsey's former managing partner, Dominic Barton, argued in *Harvard Business Review* that responsibility to stakeholders is increasingly becoming an expectation. Similarly, the growing pressure for Environmental Social Governance (ESG) reporting is also creating momentum, especially as companies begin to realize that ESG is about more than just greenwash; social inequality and the environmental crisis are posing existential threats. An article for the Harvard Law School Forum on Corporate Governance noted the following findings:

- Seventy-three per cent of S&P 500 companies in the USA reported weather effects on earnings, and in 90 per cent of those cases the effect was negative.
- Supply chain disruptions caused by climate increased 29 per cent from 2012 to 2019.
- Forty-seven per cent of consumers will refuse to buy a brand that does not align with their beliefs.
- As of May 2019, more than a thousand legal cases relating to climate risk have been filed in American courts.
- Electric vehicles will account for 40 per cent of all global car sales by 2040.
- Eighty-six per cent of millennials said they would take a pay cut to work for a company whose values align with their beliefs.
- Rising population is putting increasing strain on water supplies, and water shortages in some regions could cost up to 6 per cent of GDP.
- Eighty-seven per cent of large global companies have identified deforestation as posing a risk to supply chains, increasing costs and/or causing reputational damage.
- Fifty-five per cent of professional women are less likely to apply for a job with a company where a #MeToo allegation has been made, and 49 per cent are less likely to buy its products and services.

- Companies with more diverse management teams have 19 per cent higher innovation revenue (revenue generated by enhanced or new products and services) and report better overall financial performance.[15]

In the UK at around the same time as the Harvard study, a survey by the Financial Reporting Council (FRC) found that more than half of investors and analysts are now looking specifically at companies' responses to social and environmental issues before making an investment decision.[16] According to the International Risk Governance Center, involving stakeholders in risk assessment can significantly improve the identification and mitigation of risk.[17] And finally, an earlier examination of more than 2200 research studies on the impact of environmental, social and governance (ESG) criteria on corporate financial shows that the vast majority of these—over 2100—conclude that there is a strong positive impact, that is following ESG principles leads to higher performance.[18] Engaging with stakeholders is an important part of ESG.

Adding Value

How does stakeholder engagement add value? Stakeholder engagement forces the board and the executive team to look outside their own world, beyond the confines of the boardroom and the C-suite, across the organization and its external environment, and then to engage with other people and groups. Put simply, the more different, relevant points of view that are represented in the decision-making process, the better the resulting decisions are likely to be. A study by Deborah Ancona and David Caldwell published in *Administrative Science Quarterly* found that the more teams look beyond their own box and engage with the wider world, the higher their performance levels tend to be. For those that deliberately engaged in a planned and comprehensive way, seeking as much information as possible, performance levels are higher still.[19]

There are two interrelated arguments for why stakeholder engagement, whatever form it takes, helps make boards more effective. The first is that it reduces board dysfunction by changing the culture of the board and making it more responsive to the needs of others, rather than an inward-looking organization bent largely on just perpetuating its own existence. Second, because stakeholder boards are more engaged in the outside world, they are likely to see new ideas and technologies earlier than if the focus is internal and local. They are also more aware of risk factors in the environment, factors they might not have been aware of until stakeholders drew them to their attention. Put simply, engaged boards make better decisions. Recognizing this, some shareholders go so far as to proxy their votes to stakeholder relations organizations that act as advocates for stakeholder groups; their presence means the board is forced to hear arguments from other stakeholders.

Moves Towards Stakeholder Engagement

Despite the positive evidence, approaches to stakeholder engagement around the world have been patchy, and with a few exceptions such as Germany and Norway, governments have been reluctant to put their weight behind it. In the UK, for example, public companies are required to make what is known as Section 172 declarations, public statements of how they have listened to and reacted to stakeholder concerns, and it is probable that similar statements will be required of privately owned firms in the future. However, it is left to the companies themselves to determine the nature of their response, and there is little or no monitoring to ensure they follow through on their promises. Whether and how organizations engage with stakeholders is usually down to the personal beliefs of managers and shareholders, and the same is true in most parts of the world.

The McKinsey Global Institute report argues that instead of waiting for government to act, boards themselves need to engage and take primary responsibility for their own board. 'Boards are responsible for the long-term interest of the company,' say the authors. 'It is their role to define its mission and purpose. It's easy for CEOs to make soothing pledges; however, in the absence of support from the board, nothing will change, as it is the board that sets and governs strategy.'[20] The report suggests two complementary approaches to stakeholder engagement. The first is to change corporate governance guidelines to assert the primacy of stakeholder interests, taking in all stakeholder groups including customers, employees and society at large, and not just shareholders. An example is the B-Corp, or benefit corporation, model which emerged in America in 2010 and is slowly gaining traction in other parts of the world. The other approach is to appoint 'new board members with a diversity of experience, skills, and interests who can reflect the concerns and priorities of a wider range of stakeholders, rather than shareholders alone.'[21]

Stakeholder Groups

The stakeholder group most likely to be already directly involved (at least nominally) in governance is shareholders and investors. Nearly every private sector board will have at least one director who represents this group. The problem with investors as stakeholders is that often there is either too much engagement or not enough. On one extreme we have founder-owners like the ones we saw in the case studies, reserving control to themselves and manipulating the board to suit their ends, or activist investors such as hedge funds who demand that boards set strategy to maximize value to them. On the other end of the spectrum we have a large group of investors, probably the majority, who do not have time to pay close attention to their investments and are largely disengaged unless something happens that directly concerns them. Often these investors display a lack of clarity about their investment values and portfolio strategy. Getting the balance of investor engagement right is not easy.

Institutional Ownership

For some institutional investors such as pension funds, insurance companies, investment funds and the like, their policy towards their shareholdings is one of benign neglect. This is partly a matter of belief. Ever since the concept of the separation of ownership and control was advocated by the German politician and industrialist Walther Rathenau in 1919, and popularized in the USA in the 1930s, the belief has been—in the West, at least—that the owners of companies and their share capital should leave the job of management to professional executives.

Sometimes too, this neglect happens by default. Fund managers look after large portfolios of shares and simply do not have the time to devote to close study of the firms in which they invest. They pay attention to one or two key financial metrics, and so long as those hit expected targets, they are satisfied. This is starting to change with more looking at these issues. We noted earlier the Harvard and FRC reports suggesting more investors are now looking at economic and social responsibility, but they are still failing to put sufficient pressure on boards to take action. Another report, this time on reporting by FTSE-100 companies by communications consultancy Black Sun, suggests that many companies are still failing to take stakeholders' views into consideration. For example,

- Only 27 per cent of boards could give examples of how they took stakeholder views into consideration when making decisions.
- Only 35 per cent could show a link between culture and value creation.

- Only 45 per cent of nominations committees could demonstrate a pipeline to achieving greater diversity.
- Only 50 per cent could show who on the board was responsible for risk management.
- Only 60 per cent could demonstrate a long-term strategy.[22]

Clearly, we have some way to go before investor views, and the views of other stakeholders are taken seriously as a matter of routine by every company.

Some institutional investors, including notably some hedge funds, are activist investors who demand that CEOs and boards create value, and hold the board publicly to account if they fail to do so. They might demand that strategies such as share buybacks or divestment of subsidiaries are put into place so as to increase share prices and dividends. But the approach of these activist investors is typically quite narrow; they intend to create value for themselves and seldom think about the needs of other stakeholders.

Private Ownership

Nearly all the scandals and disasters described in this book concern public companies, because the scandals broke in the public domain and the details are a matter of public record. This is not to say that scandals do not happen in private companies; they just tend to happen behind closed doors, with a lot less publicly available evidence.

Especially in Asia, many large companies are still family owned and even if they are listed on the stock market, the family reserves a controlling interest to themselves. In other cases, ownership is concentrated in the hands of private equity funds. Generally speaking, private equity owners are more engaged with the companies they own and will nearly always have direct representation on the board—although there are plenty of examples of private equity funds buying firms and then leaving them to sink or swim, and others who asset strip their acquisitions and then sell the remains.

Private owners still need to preserve the separation of ownership and control, and private equity firms do just that, engaging with the executive on governance and strategy but leaving them to get on with day-to-day operations. But some private equity firms also suffer from the same problems as fund managers; their portfolios are large, and the time they can commit to each investment is limited. Although they exercise more scrutiny than institutional investors, most are still fairly hands-off. Their interest is in long-term value creation, not in governance, and so long as they can see value being created, they tend not to get involved.

Employees

The next group most likely to be engaged is employees. There are differences in practice around the world, with some countries opting for a more consultative model and others involving employees directly in governance. In the UK, the Bullock Report in 1997 recommended mandatory board representation for workers in all companies with more than 2000 employees, but this was never institutionalized. Effective from January 2019, the UK Corporate Governance Code requires that companies instead establish mechanisms for gathering the views of the workforce. The Code does not specify how this should be done, but it also instructs boards to report publicly how it has engaged with the workforce and how the interest of the workers have affected the board's decision-making.[23]

In the USA Scanlon Plans, first introduced in the 1930s, have been used by many companies and public sector organizations as a mechanism for consultation. Studies have shown that workers who are engaged in this way tend to be more committed to the organization, more productive and less likely to leave their jobs.[24]

One of the most developed models of workforce involvement in governance is that of Germany, first established in the 1920s. Employees are represented on corporate supervisory boards and thus have a direct say in how the company is run.[25] Japan, France and many other European countries also have legal requirements for worker representation. In Norway, companies with more than 200 workers must by law have a corporate assembly which appoints members of the board of directors; one-third of assembly members are appointed by the workforce. In China, at least one-third of members of supervisory boards must be workforce representatives, and large-scale infrastructure and public works projects are governed by networks including many different stakeholder groups.[26]

One common form of stakeholder engagement is the cooperative organization, where the organization is owned by its members; usually by workers, but in some cases like the Co-operative Group in the UK, the business is also fully or partly owned by its customers. From its beginnings in the eighteenth century, the cooperative movement has spread around the world and is especially prominent in agriculture with large cooperatives like Land O'Lakes and Sunkist in the USA or ARLA in Europe. There are successful cooperatives in many other sectors too. One of Spain's largest businesses, the Mondragón Corporation, was founded as a set of workers' cooperatives and largely retains its cooperative structure to this day. In the USA credit unions provide banking in communities where the large banks find it less economical to operate. In other cases, companies give shares in the business to workers, which allows worker representation and engagement; the John Lewis Group in the UK is a prominent example.

Other Groups

Customer co-creation is another example of stakeholder engagement which many companies have used successfully. Lego is perhaps the most famous example. Its 'Ideas' platform invites Lego users to submit their own designs and ideas for products, and vote on ideas suggested by others. Customers whose ideas are taken by the company receive 1 per cent of net sales. Co-creation is also common in the automobile industry. BMW's Co-Creation Lab allows customers to not only review future designs but submit designs of their own. While customers can express preference and vote on ideas they like, the final say remains with the company.

The Co-operative Group in the UK has several directors appointed to represent the interests of the members, customers and suppliers of the organization. In China and many other countries, it is common for local government to have a board representative, especially if the enterprise is making a direct contribution to the local economy. Pursuing the need for board diversity and inclusion, many boards will make appointments with a deliberate view of ensuring that there is broad representation in terms of gender, ethnicity, disability and other protected characteristics. And finally, a few progressive boards have designated one or more directors as having special responsibility for the environment and climate change, to ensure there is a voice speaking for these issues.

Public sector and third-sector organizations have also experimented with models of stakeholder engagement and governance. The governing boards of universities in many countries have representatives from staff and student bodies as members, and some also have representation from local communities and companies, for example if a particular company is a large employer in the area and can be expected to employ a large number of graduates. The National Health Service in the UK has established a system of patient representation through Patients' Councils, and school boards often have governors representing teaching staff and the parents of children attending the school.

What Next?

As evidenced by the studies on ESG reporting cited earlier, stakeholders themselves are beginning to put pressure on boards to respond, although change is still very patchy. Rapid increases in executive pay in many parts of the world have finally caught the attention of investors, and there has been a series of shareholder revolts over pay and pension contributions. A report on institutional investors by the OECD concludes that stronger requirements for environmental, social and governance (ESG) reporting may also be having an effect.[27] The OECD report cites examples such as Australia, the Netherlands and Switzerland where pension funds have formed associations to conduct deeper research into companies and advise on proxy voting. In Chile, where there is a high concentration of ownership, public policy has had some impact in compelling investors to be more active, and the OECD recommends that similar policy measures should be adopted in other parts of the world.

In the USA, the Business Roundtable made headlines by formally committing to the principles of stakeholder engagement and governance in 2019, although this commitment was not legally binding. It appears also that some of the CEOs who signed the Roundtable declaration did not consult their own boards, leading observers to question how strong their commitment to stakeholder engagement actually is.[28] In Europe, Australia, Canada and parts of Asia there is increasing acknowledgement that stakeholders need to have some sort of voice in governance.

These are encouraging trends, and there is another force that may ensure that they continue, at least for the foreseeable future: the COVID-19 pandemic. According to an article in *Harvard Business Review* in 2020, 'Covid is re-writing the rules of corporate governance,' even around such apparently straightforward notions as paying dividends.[29] Formerly, corporations paid dividends every quarter—or did not, if they had fallen on hard times—investors banked them and no one thought anything of it. Following the arrival of the pandemic, however, many companies were unable to pay dividends at all while others, faced with uncertainty over the scope and length of the crisis, had to make tough decisions about whether to save money and invest in capacity or pay dividends. This has meant more, longer and deeper discussions with investors, who have their own pandemic-related problems. Investors and companies are being forced to work consciously together. Will this become a habit that lasts?

It is interesting to note that culture and gender can affect perceptions of the efficacy of stakeholder engagement. There is still much opposition to stakeholder engagement in the USA, but European and Asian directors tend to regard the concept more favourably. In the USA, one recent survey also showed that female directors are more likely to prioritize stakeholder governance than male ones. For example, 70 per cent of female directors felt their companies should prioritize human rights issues compared to 58 per cent of their male counterparts, and 62 per cent of women valued having environmental and sustainability expertise on the board while only 47 per cent of men did so.[30] Ironically, it would seem that the best way to achieve greater diversity is to have diversity; in other words, the more diverse the board, the greater the attention is paid to diversity issues.

Stakeholder Engagement and the Six Dysfunctions

From the perspective of this book, do stakeholder engagement and governance make boards more effective? Could scandals like those at BP or Volkswagen have been avoided if stakeholder voices had been heard? As we are unable to turn back the clock, it is impossible to know for certain. Clearly in Volkswagen's case there *were* employee members on the supervisory board, but like the other directors they were unable to make their voices heard in Volkswagen's toxic culture. This reinforces the point that structures alone are not enough. We need cultures that enable people's voices to be heard, and that was sadly lacking at Volkswagen.

The case of BP is more intriguing. We saw earlier how a culture dedicated to profit as the pre-eminent goal led to corner-cutting on health and safety. What might have happened if there had been greater engagement with the workforce, and people were able to speak freely about what was happening on the ground and the risks that were being incurred? Would the board have listened? And if they had, might disasters like *Deepwater Horizon* have been avoided? Similarly, if the boards of Google or Uber had listened to their employees and acted, might scandals of sexual harassment and bullying have been avoided?

It is possible, but it is a counterfactual we can never run so we will never know for certain. Rather than discussing 'what-ifs,' let us instead look at the relationship between stakeholder engagement and the six board dysfunctions, with some examples of companies that have engaged with stakeholders and avoided some of the cultural distortions we identified earlier. An important theme here is the board's ability to think and act independently, to hear what stakeholders are telling them and to act accordingly.

Greater Independence

One of the concerns about stakeholder engagement is that stakeholder groups will focus on narrow self-interest; for example employees will only be interested in workforce matters, or student governors of universities will speak only on issues that directly concern students and let everything else pass them by. Research conducted by a working party for the Institute of Directors in the UK suggests this is sometimes the case; there are stakeholder directors who, in the words of one interviewee, 'become directors simply because they are pleased to be there.' Others, however, are equally as diligent and committed as other independent directors, and sometimes more so. They span a spectrum from the largely passive to the highly active and engaged; in other words, they are typical directors.

On the other side of the coin, boards are often reluctant to admit 'outsiders' onto 'their' patch. There is a lack of understanding of what stakeholders can bring to the table, and there is also a fear of loss of control. Trust lies at the heart of the matter. If there is trust between stakeholders and the board, then there is a good chance engagement will work; if relations are adversarial, then engagement is unlikely to be genuine until relationships can be rebuilt and fences mended.

How engaged stakeholders are tends to depend on the culture of the board and how genuine the commitment to engagement really is. Now, in most countries the requirements for stakeholder engagement—with obvious exceptions like Germany and China—are vaguely phrased and do not require companies to actively commit to any set principles. Regulators themselves seem uncertain about what exactly the purpose of stakeholder engagement should be. Codes of conduct need to focus specifically on this issue, explaining the purpose behind the principle and how it should be enacted to ensure that stakeholder participation is real and has purpose.

In an article for *Corporate Governance* in 2010, Heiko Spitzeck and Erik Hansen argued that stakeholder participation can be measured on two dimensions: stakeholder power and the scope of participation.[31] Stakeholder power refers to the impact stakeholders can have. Is their participation in governance as tokens, or do their voices carry real weight and authority? Is their capacity to give advice only, or do they believe their decisions will be acted upon? Scope of participation refers to how broadly stakeholders can participate in governance. Is their voice only heard on operational and managerial issues, or can they comment and help to decide strategic issues as well? Spitzeck and Hansen argue that the more power and scope of participation stakeholders have, the more they are likely to commit to their role and the organization, the more effective they will be. As we saw, their satisfaction levels will increase because they can see they are having impact, and that will drive them to higher levels of performance.

Providing Missing Voices

Greater stakeholder engagement can also help provide the missing voices that might be lacking, for example, thanks to a lack of diversity and inclusion on the board. The cooperatively owned Rabobank group, based in the Netherlands, has several parallel structures for ensuring employee and customer voices. Ultimate responsibility for governance at Rabobank rests with the elected General Members Council, to which the supervisory boards and the management board report. Beneath the General Members Council are several local members councils, also called client panels in overseas operations.

These councils are in direct touch with local banks and customer groups and gather data on customer views which is then passed back to the General Members Council to inform company strategy. The views of customers are taken seriously and are acted upon. When it became clear that most customers disapproved of Rabobank investing in the arms trade, the bank pulled its investment in a major client and reinvested in what its customers saw as more ethical businesses. Rabobank also has a powerful ethics committee, whose remit extends to virtually every aspect of the business. Employees are encouraged to submit their ethical concerns to the committee, which in turn reports them to the boards and the General Members Council. Rabobank thus has both direct stakeholder representation, the Council, and indirect engagement through the local councils and the ethics committee.[32] Most banks do ethical surveys and respond to customer pressure in some way, but Rabobank has brought ethical considerations into the core of its business model.

Overcoming Cultural Amplification

Stakeholders can often serve as guardians of the organization's values. As employees, as consumers of its goods and services, as engaged investors concerned to see that the company is well run and makes a profit, they see what the company does and how it affects them. Changes to the company's culture will have a direct impact on their interests. Listening to stakeholders can provide a kind of organizational conscience, a voice reminding the board of what its culture needs to be, and this in turn can help prevent that culture from turning in on itself.

The National Health Service in the UK has established a system of patient councils to ensure that stakeholders have a strong voice and are heard. For example, the University of Plymouth Hospital Trust has a patient council with eleven members who attend board meetings to share patient experiences and give feedback. The patient council's stated purpose is to

1. act as the 'Voice of the Patient' ensuring that patient views, perceptions and aspirations are considered;
2. work with the Trust to support the strategic direction for the patient experience strategy with the purpose of achieving the Trust's vision of 'putting patients at the centre of everything we do';
3. agree priorities in response to feedback to enable and influence improvements that deliver an improved patient experience;
4. promote the value of public engagement;
5. actively participate in patient engagement activities and through alignment with clinical areas contribute to improvements in the patient experience at local level ensuring that the patient's views are heard.[33]

The system has had mixed success, but anecdotal evidence suggests that where it operates, NHS Trust boards tend to perform well. The NHS has had its fair share of disasters over the past few decades, but generally these have taken place at trusts where the voice of the patient council was weak, reminding us that board effectiveness is not about ticking the structural box and being compliant, but understanding why the box is there and living the spirit of the idea.

Another organization whose stakeholders reminded it of its purpose and helped to protect its culture is the employee-owned John Lewis Group. In 1999 it was proposed that the group should end employee ownership and be floated on the stock market. The move, which had the support of the company's executives, would have netted each employee about £100,000. However, the central council, composed of employee representatives, voted overwhelmingly against the proposal, arguing that going public would harm the group's values and its culture of service.[34] John Lewis remains employee-owned, and though the group has suffered in recent years thanks to online retail competition, it has still performed better than most of its rivals including House of Fraser and British Home Stores.

Greater Responsibility

Engagement with stakeholders can also be a means of ensuring the board recognizes its wider responsibilities and avoids diffusion. Unilever, which in recent years has taken on greater social and environmental responsibility—for example through its Sustainable Living Plan—operates in many parts of the developing world. Its board is diverse in terms of nationality and ethnicity and also background; several directors have also served with NGOs and charities in the developing world and know at first hand the impact Unilever has on societies and cultures in these regions.

Other organizations have gone further and formalized stakeholder engagement in a way that clearly establishes director responsibility. Anglian Water in the UK has amended its articles of association to restate the company's purpose as 'bringing environmental and social prosperity to the region we serve.' The company's 'Love Every Drop' strategy is designed to ensure water conservation and purity and eliminate waste, and to make sure residents and businesses receive the water they need despite the increasing pressures of climate change. Among other things, Anglian Water has created a Customer Board which, while it has no direct representation on the main board, is in constant dialogue with directors. There is also a customer engagement forum and an online forum, all part of what the company describes as its social contract with customers. The board's duties now include the following:

- adopting a statement of responsible business principles;
- inviting a reputable independent body to scrutinize our policies and performance against these principles; and
- demonstrating in our Annual Integrated Report how we have run the company in accordance with our purpose and the responsible business principles.[35]

Addressing Rule-Bound Culture

Involving stakeholders and giving them more power and authority can also lead to a reduction in central control and a move away from overly controlled cultures. In the nineteenth century the optical instrument maker Carl Zeiss

Jena developed a culture that still sounds modern by today's standards. The chief executive, Ernst Abbé, and his directors allowed employees almost total freedom; they designed their own research projects, set their own budgets and targets, and debated and discussed with each other how to take projects forward and commercialize the results. Carl Zeiss became the world's leading maker of optical lenses and retained that position until it was nationalized in 1945.

The Mondragón Corporation also adopted a decentralized principle of governance, on a much larger scale. It consists of ninety-six cooperative groups and around 81,000 members operating in thirty-seven countries, each with its own board of directors and council of members. All the cooperatives are represented in the General Assembly, which in turn appoints the body primarily responsible for governance, the Governing Council. The actual board of directors is a small executive body, with its chair appointed by the Governing Council. Virtually all responsibility for governance rests with the Council, which in turn reports to the Assembly. Workers thus have a primary role in governance and are the custodians of Mondragón's values. Mondragón has weathered the storms that have beset the Spanish economy better than many publicly owned businesses, and in 2019 had a global income of €11.6 billion.

Overcoming Groupthink

The problem of groupthink on boards has long been recognized. One strategy is to simply make sure that board members are forced to think independently. According to legend, General Motors chairman Alfred P. Sloan once asked his directors if they were in favour of a particular proposal. When all nodded in agreement, Sloan at once removed the proposal from the table and instructed his directors to go away and think of some good reasons to disagree. Only through debate, he reasoned, could the subject be properly considered.

Another option is to include people from outside the senior management team in decision-making. When Sam Palmisano took over as chief executive of IBM he began by devolving partial responsibility for strategy, technology and other key issues to teams formed from diverse parts of the organization. He disbanded the executive committee, which had formerly been the most powerful policy-making unit in the organization and urged these diverse teams to make whatever recommendations they thought were necessary. The board thus had access to creative talent from right across the organization, with a diverse range of voices commenting on key issues around strategy and growth. Under Palmisano's predecessors, IBM had been tightly controlled from the centre; by devolving power in this way, Palmisano also helped supply some missing voices. The result was a period of growth and prosperity for the firm. *Harvard Business Review* declared that he had 'set the standard for the way corporations are run.'[36]

Board Actions Towards Greater Stakeholder Engagement

There is, then, a series of both push and pull factors leading companies and boards towards greater involvement in stakeholder engagement. What can boards do to speed the process? We recommend several actions:

More awareness and discussion at board level: the first step is for boards to understand what stakeholder engagement means, and what level of stakeholder involvement would best suit them in terms of making the board more effective. Whether the board is listening to stakeholder voices and acting based on their views also needs to be part of board assessment and evaluation.

Board succession planning: board evaluations and skills audits should also take account of stakeholder engagement and should have a clear vision of where and how stakeholders can be involved.

Recruitment and training: boards need to look at how and where they recruit new members, especially non-executive directors. Are they casting the net widely enough? Are they making board participation attractive to other stakeholders? Are they explaining the duties and requirements of board membership clearly enough? Is the reputation of the company something that members of stakeholder groups actually want to participate? Also, as noted above, training and induction need to be improved for all directors, not just those representing stakeholders.

Active investors: investors need to be fully and consciously aware of how stakeholder engagement can improve governance, and develop action plans to improve their own effectiveness as investors with a focus on preventing scandals and disasters, spotting problems before they happen and taking pre-emptive action. Independent organizations like ShareAction are actively engaged in monitoring the progress companies are making towards ESG goals and are making information available to shareholders and investors. Engagement with these groups can help investors supplement their own information.

Taken together, these measures should have impact, but only if the culture of the board allows stakeholders to be truly independent and to participate in genuine, authentic discussions. They must be given a share of power, and they must be given sufficient scope of participation to make their work meaningful.

Independent Directors and Stakeholder Engagement

Here we believe the independent directors have a particularly important role to play. While the board as a whole has responsibility for ensuring that stakeholder engagement happens and is meaningful, it is inevitable that executive teams will be focused on short-term results and may not have sufficient time or capacity to engage. Independent board members need to step into the gap, not least because the issues raised by stakeholder engagement are often more long term in nature. Stakeholders will also make the board aware of risks it had not considered before, and risk is an important part of the independent director's responsibilities.

Because of their own unique experience, the range of their contacts and their own involvement with stakeholder groups and with other boards, independent directors will also have a different view of the issues raised by stakeholder groups (and coming back to diversity and inclusion, this is particularly true when directors are members of or have close contact with stakeholder groups themselves). They will also be aware of the wide variations in terms of stakeholder engagement, as evidenced by the Black Sun report we cited earlier. Independent directors can help feed in information from stakeholder groups and guide board thinking, whether they are directly appointed by stakeholder groups or are simply listening and taking on board what stakeholders tell them. This is yet another way in which independent directors can contribute to board effectiveness.

We are sympathetic to the argument that shareholders are the only stakeholder group to actually risk their own money in the form of investment. But other stakeholder groups take risks too, including financial risks. Employees count on businesses to provide jobs; if those jobs are lost, the financial and personal costs to each employee are considerable. Customers require safe products that will not do them harm, and communities have the right to expect that the companies operating in their midst will not damage them. Earlier in this book we saw the costs to all of us when companies fail or make mistakes. Environmental damage, social and psychological harm, losses of income and tax revenue, injury, sickness and death are externalities that we all incur. We are all invested in any listed company by virtue of the services they provide and the taxes they pay, even if we do not hold share certificates. We are the ones who pay the piper, and it seems only fair and just that we should have a say in calling the tune.

Notes

1. R.E. Freeman, R. Phillips and R. Sisodia, 'Tensions in Stakeholder Theory', *Business and Society* 59 (2), 2020.
2. R. Edward Freeman, *Strategic Management: A Stakeholder Approach*, Cambridge: Cambridge University Press, 2010.
3. Pernille Eskerod, 'A Stakeholder Perspective: Origins and Core Concepts', *Oxford Research Encyclopedia of Business and Management*, 2020 https://oxfordre.com/business/view/10.1093/acrefore/9780190224851.001.0001/acrefore-9780190224851-e-3.
4. https://corpgov.law.harvard.edu/2019/08/24/stakeholder-governance-and-the-fiduciary-duties-of-directors/.
5. Milton Friedman, 'The Social Responsibility of a Business is to Increase Its Profits', *New York Times Magazine*, 13 September 1970.
6. Lucien A. Bebchuk and Roberto Tallarita, 'The Illusory Promise of Stakeholder Governance', https://papers.ssrn.com/sol3/papers.cfm?abstract_id=3544978; see also the debate between Bebchuk and Alex Edmans, https://www.london.edu/faculty-and-research/centre-for-corporate-governance/events.
7. Elaine Sternberg, *Corporate Governance: Accountability in the Marketplace*, London: Institute of Economic Affairs, 2004.
8. Vijay Govindarajan and Anup Srivastava, 'We Are Nowhere Near Stakeholder Capitalism', *Harvard Business Review*, 30 January 2020.
9. Steve Denning, 'Why Stakeholder Capitalism Will Fail', *Forbes*, 5 January 2020, https://www.forbes.com/sites/stevedenning/2020/01/05/why-stakeholder-capitalism-will-fail/?sh=6f09fd32785a.
10. Janet Williamson, notes for IOD working party, 2020.
11. Robert G. Eccles, Ioannis Ioannou and George Serafeim, 'The Impact of Corporate Sustainability on Organizational Processes and Performance', *Management Science* 60 (11), 2014, p. 2847.
12. Alex Edmans, *Grow the Pie: How Great Companies Deliver Both Purpose and Profit*, Cambridge: Cambridge University Press, 2020.
13. Eccles, Ioannou and Serafeim; see also Ioannis Ioannou and George Serafeim, 'The Impact of Corporate Social Responsibility on Investment Recommendations: Analysts' Perceptions and Shifting Institutional Logics', *Strategic Management Journal* 36 (7), 2014, and Olga Hawn and Ioannis Ioannou, 'Do Actions Speak Louder Than Words? The Case of Corporate Social Responsibility (CSR), *SSRN Electronic Journal* 2013.

14. Hunt et al., 2020.
15. Veena Ramani and Hannah Saltman, 'Running the Risks: How Corporate Boards Can Oversee Environmental, Social and Governance Issues', *Harvard Law School Forum on Corporate Governance*, 25 November 2019.
16. Dominic Barton, 'Capitalism for the Long Term', *Harvard Business Review*, March 2011; Financial Reporting Council, 'Future of Corporate Reporting: Conclusions from an Online Survey of FRC Stakeholders', 2019.
17. IRGC, 'Involving Stakeholders in the Risk Governance Process', 2020.
18. Gunnar Friede, Timo Busch and Alexander Bassen, 'ESG and Financial Performance: Aggregated Evidence From More Than 2000 Empirical Studies', *Journal of Sustainable Finance and Investment* 4 (4), 2015.
19. Deborah G. Ancona and David F. Caldwell, 'Bridging the Boundary: External Activity and Performance in Organizational Teams', *Administrative Science Quarterly* 37, 1992.
20. Vivian Hunt, Bruce Simpson and Yuito Yamada, 'The Case for Stakeholder Capitalism', McKinsey & Company, 12 November 2020.
21. Ibid.
22. Black Sun, Annual Analysis of FTSE-100 Corporate Reporting, https://www.blacksunplc.com/en/our-thinking/horizon/rewiring-the-ecosystem-for-resilience.html.
23. UK Corporate Governance Code 2019.
24. Eileen Appelbaum, Thomas Bailey, Peter Berg and Arne L. Kalleberg, *Manufacturing Advantage: Why High-Performance Work Systems Pay Off*, New York: ILR Press, 2000.
25. Konstantin Bottenberg, Anja Tuschke and Miram Flickinger, 'Corporate Governance Between Shareholder and Stakeholder Orientation: Lessons From Germany, *Journal of Management Inquiry* 26 (2), 2017.
26. Nicholas Hughes, 'Roles and Responsibilities of the China Legal Representative', *China Briefing*, 2011, https://www.china-briefing.com/news/roles-and-responsibilities-of-the-china-legal-representative/; Ding Ronggui and Liu Fang, 'A Social Network Theory of Stakeholders in China's Project Governance', *iBusiness*, June 2011.
27. FRC, 'The Future of Corporate Reporting'; OECD, 'The Role of Institutional Investors in Promoting Good Corporate Governance', 2011.
28. https://www.wsj.com/articles/stakeholder-capitalism-seems-mostly-for-show-11596755220.
29. Lynn S. Paine, 'Covid is Rewriting the Rules of Corporate Governance', *Harvard Business Review*, 6 October 2020.
30. https://insights.diligent.com/shareholder-engagement/stakeholder-model-corporate-governance/.
31. Heiko Spitzeck and Erik G. Hansen, 'Stakeholder Governance: How Stakeholders Influence Corporate Decision Making', *Corporate Governance* 10 (4), 2010.

32. https://www.rabobank.com/en/about-rabobank/results-and-reports/annual-review/2015/dialogue-with-stakeholders/index.html; https://www.debrauw.com/newsandmatters/rabobank-successfully-implements-new-governance-structure/.
33. https://www.plymouthhospitals.nhs.uk/patient-council.
34. http://news.bbc.co.uk/1/hi/business/451620.stm.
35. https://www.anglianwater.co.uk/about-us/our-purpose/.
36. https://hbr.org/2012/01/how-ibms-sam-palmisano-redefin.html.

13

Improving Board Effectiveness: Practical Steps

Our research has shown that dysfunctional board cultures share a number of common internal and structural problems. These can be briefly summarized as follows:

- Lack of independence: the board *lacks independence from the executive* and fails to hold the executive to account and protect stakeholders, including shareholders from poor or corrupt management.
- Bad or ineffectual board leadership: the chair is unable to establish a strong and functional culture, perhaps because they are unable to orchestrate individual directors and combine their skills and personalities into a cohesive working unit. An ineffective chair poses a particular risk such that the board becomes dominated by the CEO and the rest of the executive. This is a more likely risk when the CEO and chair roles are combined in the same person, giving that person dominance over the rest of the board. It can work with an effective senior independent director. An organization with a *highly amplified culture* may contaminate board culture as a result.
- Lack of competence: this does not mean technical competence; instead, we mean lack of influencing, discussion and listening skills. Most directors are former managers, and in management most influence and persuasion is done one-to-one. But being on a board means knowing how to persuade a group, and far too few executives are actually practised at this. Good non-executive directors will build this skill over time, but these types of influencing skills are seriously underappreciated when appointing new directors. Without the courage and curiosity needed to ask hard questions, *groupthink* and *diffusion of responsibility* begin to creep in.

© The Author(s), under exclusive license to Springer Nature Switzerland AG 2022

G. Brown, R. S. Peterson, *Disaster in the Boardroom*,
https://doi.org/10.1007/978-3-030-91658-9_13

- Lack of board diversity and effective inclusion: too many directors share the same mindset, and there is too much *groupthink* and too many *missing voices*.
- Poorly functioning board structure including a lack of effective committees: the board's work is hampered by lack of clarity about individual roles and responsibilities, or the voting structure may allow certain individuals to dominate, resulting in a *diffusion of responsibility*. Another result can be a bureaucratic and *overly controlled* board where compliance is seen as the only important outcome.
- Lack of effective board evaluation and development: because the board does not question its own culture, it does not realize it is dysfunctional. The chair often chooses who does the evaluation and in some cases the chair might pick someone who will tell them what they want to hear rather than what they need to hear, in effect undermining the purpose of the review. This is turn means the board does not develop and grow.

The best remedies for these problems lie with boards themselves. It is up to boards and directors to take corrective action and not wait for governments and regulators to impose solutions onto them. In fact, it seems clear that regulators have struggled to solve all of the problems—that is why many insiders believe boards have enough regulation already. Compliance with regulations can easily turn into box-ticking exercises that fail to address the deeper cultural problems if directors are determined to obfuscate the rules.

In his book *Why People Obey the Law*, Tom Tyler shows that people seldom obey the law because of fear of punishment. Sanctions are not generally an effective deterrent and in any case are expensive to enforce; if directors want to do something that is explicitly against the law, they are clever people who will find a way of doing so. Compliance is more likely when people feel that the rules are equitable and that all are being treated fairly. For boards, this means that regulatory enforcing of the rules is quite difficult; we have seen that where boards want to cheat, they will do so and there is very little the regulator can do about much of it by way of enforcement. Rather than become entirely punitive, regulators should focus more on how and why the rules protect directors, shareholders and stakeholders more broadly (Fig. 13.1).

Interventions & Non-Obvious Indicators

Distended Boards – Cultural Amplification

Insiders:
- Require an outside assessment of organization.
- Ask open-ended questions about what is good/not-good for culture.
- Engage in culture change.

Outsiders:
- Ask open-ended questions about what really reflects the culture; request examples.
- Require outside board assessment that includes culture analysis.

Non-Obvious Indicators:
- Cultural examples sound mean, uncooperative, overly-competitive, etc.

Bystander Boards – Diffusion of Responsibility

Insiders:
- Require clear terms of reference for all committees.
- Ensure chairs appointed for all committees.
- Ask for committee report at every board meeting.

Outsiders:
- Ask questions re: who is responsible for specific activities (e.g., risk, diversity, org culture, etc.).

Non-Obvious Indicators:
- If "everything" goes through the Chair, there is a problem with how the board enacts roles.

Imbalanced Boards – Missing Key Voices

Insiders:
- Review data re: diversity, turnover. If it's high, ask why.
- Ask Chair/NEDs to focus on belonging & inclusion (diverse people should stay same length of time as others).
- Request skills & diversity audit (current, as well as what the board aspires to have).

Outsiders:
- Review data re: diversity, turnover by group. If it's high, ask why.
- Consider gender pay gap reports.

Non-Obvious Indicators:
- Disparity in turnover data by group.

Conforming Boards – Groupthink

Insiders:
- Focus on Chair – impartial leadership encourages sharing before revealing own position.
- Bring trusted outsiders to challenge thinking.

Outsiders:
- Act as trusted advisor who can challenge the group's thinking.
- Look for – and recommend – additional outsiders to do the same.

Non-Obvious Indicators:
- Failure to consider the real trade-offs when engaging in strategic discussions.

Bureaucratic Boards – Rule Bound Cultures

Insiders:
- Focus on innovation and ideas, not preservation of old ways or cost-cutting as primary way forward.
- Invest the money in where the business needs to go next.

Outsiders:
- Ask about doing things in unexpected ways.
- Business should not stick to a pre-existing "system" to deal with unprecedented events.

Non-Obvious Indicators:
- Dealing with disruption in ways outside the comfort zone is a good sign.
- Sticking to traditional processes may be a red flag.

Subordinated Boards – Lack of Independence

Insiders:
- Focus on board training and selection.
- Encourage use of search firm or outside agency.
- Conduct skills audit to assess existing and needed skills.
- Search for skills, not connections.

Outsiders:
- Look at social connections of board members.
- Be concerned with interlocks with other boards.

Non-Obvious Indicators:
- High social connections among senior managers or execs and NEDs (schools, clubs, etc.)

Fig. 13.1 Interventions and non-obvious indicators

Providing Board Leadership

As a starting point, more emphasis needs to be put on the role and skills of the chair. We have seen numerous examples in this book of how one overly powerful individual, or a small cabal, have dominated a board with disastrous effect. There *must* be independent challenge and scrutiny of the executive, especially the CEO, and, if the latter is acting in matter that is harmful to the interests of stakeholders, be empowered to take steps to remove the CEO from office.

Earlier in the book we discussed the issues that can arise when the role of CEO and chair are combined in the same person. This raises the risk that this individual can dominate the board and that there will be no effective challenge or scrutiny. It is to avoid this risk that most countries require the roles to be kept separate. Once again, though, the problem is not one that can easily be solved by regulation, and we have seen plenty of examples of CEOs dominating their boards, over the top of the chair, oftentimes with serious negative consequences. What matters is that the board is able to challenge and hold the executive and CEO to account. The lead director, or senior independent director, can play a role here, but more importantly all directors need to reflect on this responsibility for scrutiny and challenge and take it seriously. There is no tick-box solution to the problem, no prescription that will give us the 'perfect' formula for the board. What is needed is effective oversight of the executive, allied to the courage and strength of will to make one's voice heard.

What are the qualities of a good chair? Stanislav Shekshnia in *Harvard Business Review* argues that 'the challenge for the board chair is not really about traditional leadership at all. To be sure, the board does have an important leadership function: counselling and supervising the management team. But that responsibility is collective, and the chair's job is to enable the board to fulfil it. To be effective, chairs must recognize that they are not commanders but facilitators.' Eight key principles for good chairs are identified:

1. Be the 'guide on the side,' coaching and counselling without leaping to conclusions.
2. Practise 'teaming,' not team building, bringing people together and helping them find solutions.
3. Be well prepared and set the agenda.
4. Take committees and their composition and membership seriously.
5. Remain impartial.
6. Measure the inputs, not the outputs.

7. Don't be the boss; remember, the board is the collective 'boss.'
8. Represent the company fairly to shareholders without being a 'player.'[1]

The Henley Business School project on independent directors in the public and third sectors also identified several key values and skills that underlie these principles, including high moral standards, humility, listening skills and emotional intelligence. A systematic and evidence-based approach to decision-making and knowledge about the organization and the sector also featured.[2] In the corporate world, sector expertise is what matters and we could also add global business experience to the list. We would especially highlight the personal values of curiosity and openness. Ultimately it is these values that largely determine whether a chair succeeds or fails.

Too many chairs are appointed on the basis of seniority, or their connections and status in the business community, or their track record in a previous role. Just because someone has been a high-functioning executive, a senior civil servant or a senior officer in the armed forces does not automatically make them a good board chair. The skillsets for traditional leadership roles and chairing a board are different. Remember the old adage that 'what got you here, will not get you there.' We give too much weight to past leadership success and not enough time thinking about the skillset required in this different role, with a different situation and different demands. Whether the potential chair met the past challenge is only partially relevant; what matters is whether they are prepared for the next one.

A good chair is in control of their ego and does not impose themselves on the board. The task of the chair is to listen to various divergent points of view—and to encourage people to speak if they remain silent—so that there is a full and informed debate. Listening skills are particularly important; as one executive project put it, 'The good chair listens, the bad chair speaks.' The point about humility is important too; a good chair is the servant of the board, not its master, and their task is to help the board be as effective as possible.

Experience is vital too. Most obviously this includes board experience and knowledge of governance. Expecting someone to be prepared to be chair without much board experience is asking far too much. Chairs need to have enough experience to get a feel for how a board functions and what its culture is. To take just one example, are debates conducted in a forthright manner, or does the culture shun confrontation and lean more towards politeness? Both are acceptable, provided the debate itself is full and complete, but directors can easily be disengaged by a culture they dislike, at which point they will start to withdraw and not participate fully. And finally, a knowledge of the principles of corporate governance and understanding of the different roles of independent directors and the executive are vital.

Chairs also need to have experience of strategy. Strategy is the route by which the organization attempts to enact its mission and fulfil its purpose, and for the board not to have some role in this would be a dereliction of its duty as custodians of the organization. The chair needs to work with the CEO and the rest of the board to set the strategic direction, and thus experience of strategy making is essential. In the modern world, experience of working in a global environment is also vital. Even with rising protectionism and some parts of the world, and the disruption to international trade caused by COVID-19, there are still few sectors that are not touched in some way by the currents of globalization.

Over and over in this book we have seen how misperceptions of risk have led boards and their organizations into disaster. A good chair must have a thorough knowledge of the principles of risk management and experience at assessing risk. A clear-sighted approach to risk, free of as much cognitive bias as possible, can help the chair to guide the rest of the board and ensure issues around risk are fully debated.

Investor relations are a big part of the task of chairs of companies, and chairs of public sector and third-sector organizations will have their own funding bodies who act as stakeholders. Experience at dealing with investors is highly important; without their input of capital, the organization will flounder. Digital skills are increasingly important, and so too are strong personal networks of people the chair can call upon for ideas and insights.

Where are we meant to find these superhumans? People who have all of these qualities in abundance are rare and already chairing boards. However, many of these skills can be honed through training and development. There are a small number of programmes out there for chairs, but not enough of them, and many chairs take their first post with no training at all. We argue very strongly that all chairs should undergo professional training before and during their post, with further continuing professional development expected as normal rather than being considered remedial. This is an area where regulators, legislators and educators could work together to support great board leadership.

Improving the Quality of Independent Directors

Most of the above also applies to other independent directors. They too need skills in areas such as strategy, international business, risk management, digital, influencing and conflict management and they also should have good personal networks, professionals such as executive coaches and critical friends whom they can turn to in order to ask for advice and insight, or even bring in as advisors to the board. They need strong personal characteristics including courage and curiosity, confidence, systemic thinking skills, self-awareness and emotional intelligence, low ego needs and an entrepreneurial mindset.

One of the major imperatives so far as independent directors are concerned is greater clarity about the role. The *Financial Times* once described the role of the independent director as 'task for which no one is qualified':

> The list of attributes required of the non-executive director is so long, precise and contradictory that there cannot be a single board member in the world that fully fits the bill. They need to be supportive, intelligent, interesting, well-rounded and funny, entrepreneurial, objective yet passionate, independent, curious, challenging and fit. They also need to have a financial background and real business experience, a strong moral compass, and be first-class all-rounders with specific industry skills.[3]

The problem is compounded by the fact that many independent directors, especially those starting the post for the first time, go in with little real idea of what is expected of them. Are they meant to ensure that the company is compliant with regulations? Are they there to audit its books? Are they supposed to give advice to the executives and make helpful suggestions? Are they there to run the rule over executive decisions and ensure they are sound? Of course, the answer is yes to all of these things, but that is not always entirely clear.

The dynamics of power can also make it difficult for independent directors, especially inexperienced ones, to mount effective challenges. Powerful executives may attempt to dominate the board and prevent challenge, and as research has shown, the more powerful executives become, the more self-centred and uninhibited their behaviour can become. This is not typically deliberate; most start with the best of intentions, and many fail to see how their own behaviour changes and how power corrodes their understandings of what is ethical and appropriate and what is not. Understanding those boardroom and power dynamics is an important piece of learning for every independent director,[4] in part because it is different from being in a managerial role.

As with chairs, we believe many of these problems can be remedied through more and better training and development. This has been an ongoing issue for many years. The Tyson Report in 2003 argued for more and better training, commenting that 'companies that score high marks on surveys of good corporate governance usually devote considerable time to training their NEDs.'[5] As well as the principles and rules of corporate governance, training needs to concentrate on several areas in particular. The first is interactions between board members and the relationships between directors. Put simply, how do directors work effectively together? This is partly a matter of communications and networking, but there is also the need to work together as a team. Knowing one's place in the team, what one contributes to the team, and what other team members also contribute and how to turn all this into something greater than the sum of its parts, is vital to successful board work. Again, this is often a matter of knowing when to listen, as well as knowing when to speak.

The second area is the more complex relationship between the independent directors and executives. The independent director has sometimes been described as a mixture of coach and referee, advising and supporting the executive while at the same time ensuring the latter play by the rules. But where exactly is the line between executive responsibility and director responsibility? How do directors exercise scrutiny and provide challenge and advice without stepping over the line that separates them from the executive? More effective training would help independent directors to better understand this, and that in turn should give them greater confidence. The directors will know with certainty where they stand and what is expected of them.

One area of growing importance is that of outside advice. No board knows everything, and there are times when it is useful and valuable to bring a third party to bring in specialist knowledge or even just to sense-check and make sure the board is seeing issues clearly. Properly used, consultants and experts with the appropriate experience and skills can be extremely valuable and independent directors should be trained in how to select and use external advisors to best advantage. In saying this, we acknowledge that sometimes consultants are over-used, and sometimes boards bring in consultants to avoid having to make a decision themselves. But there are times when outside advice is genuinely helpful and directors need to understand when and how to employ it.

Finally, independent directors should receive training about the functioning of board committees and how to make them work effectively (see below). Every director should serve on at least one committee and should receive training also in how to chair a committee, with the assumption that it is another important pathway for directors to learn how to be an effective board chair.

Inevitably, too, we must return to the subject of diversity and inclusion. This is an issue to which boards must pay increasing attention. Diversity and inclusion do not happen on their own; they require a proactive effort through evaluation exercises and regular discussion. Boards and chairs must actively manage diversity and inclusion, and failure to do so can easily lead to conflict between diverse and opposing personalities and points of view. The key question as always is: are there missing voices? Are there stakeholder groups struggling to make themselves heard? Does one demographic group constantly turnover compared with the majority? If so, then the board needs to consider whether it needs to take action to better represent the world we live in and the customers served. Particular attention needs to be paid to the role, remit and working practices of nominations committees, who are responsible for board recruitment, and to finding search consultants who can help identify qualified candidates from diverse backgrounds.

A board is a team, and like every good team, a high-functioning board is one where each member has something unique and special to contribute. Demographics are not the only important issue, and token appointments of minorities or people with disabilities will not necessarily lead to an effective board. Gender, disability, age and ethnicity are all important, but so too are things like educational background, socio-economic background, neurodiversity and lived experience.

However, those different backgrounds and lived experiences that we seek are *more likely* to be found among different demographic groups. The point made earlier about the different priorities between male and female directors when looking at human rights, sustainability and so on demonstrates our case. An all-male board might be more likely to dismiss these issues as being of no account, while in a gender-mixed board there is a greater chance of these being given priority, particularly when it is more than one per category. The mix also has to be genuine; appointing one token representative will never be enough. Teams research shows that a single voice is oftentimes ignored. Truth needs to be supported for it to persuade the rest of the board to accept it.

Selection Criteria for Independent Directors

The key to using these criteria for selection and board management is to look for observable behaviours. It is critical to ask and document the answers to simple questions such as what would it look like if someone had 'integrity' or 'judgement' or 'interpersonal sensitivity'? What would they be doing? Saying? What would others be saying about them?

(continued)

(continued)

Personal Characteristics

- Integrity
- Judgement
- Leadership
- Motivation
- Communication skills
- Interpersonal sensitivity
- Listening skills
- Intelligence
- Cultural flexibility
- Sense of responsibility
- Independence

Professional and Managerial Competences

- Strategy
- Technical, for example digital
- Strategic organizational development
- Analytical/problem solving
- Systemic thinking
- Chairing
- Committee membership, for example audit and remuneration

Entrepreneurial Competences

- Vision
- Judgement
- Conviction
- Decisiveness
- Commercial acumen

Improving the Function of the Board

The board needs to know what it is responsible for and then must take control of those key issues. For nearly every board, those key issues will include organizational strategy, audit, succession planning for both the board and the CEO, and remuneration for top executives. Depending on the nature of the business, other issues could include health and safety, safeguarding, property portfolios, investments, ethics, workforce development, fundraising and many others. All of these are issues where the board should be able to exercise its powers of scrutiny and oversight, while at the same time also providing advice and support.

The primary vehicle for this is board committees (or subcommittees, as they are sometimes also known). Each of the key issues the board faces should have a committee dedicated to it so that each can be understood and explored in detail, usually in partnership with the relevant members of the executive team. Committees should have clear remits and be composed of independent directors with relevant skills and experience who can make clear, independent judgements and decisions. They should also make detailed reports to the full board, outlining their conclusions and the reasons behind them. It is okay to make compromises in the interest of getting everyone on board, but the committees must make clear what those compromises are and why they have been made. There are alternatives to a committee system, like the dual assurance system we described earlier, but there must always be some responsibility for more detailed scrutiny of key issues.

The second element of board structure that we have highlighted, with particular reference to Google and Facebook, is vested interests. The boardroom table needs to be a level playing field. Every director should have the same rights to speak and to be heard, and every voice should be taken seriously. If some investors, or some executives, have more power than others, then this is a problem that needs to be addressed. Ensuring this happens is usually the task of the chair, but others can get involved; for example, if the chair is excluding a voice, deliberately or accidentally, other directors should raise the matter with the chair on behalf of the people being ignored.

Improving Board Evaluation

Board evaluation is also vital but is also often overlooked. The Tyson Report in 2003 argued that 'it is both common sense and a documented conclusion of research in behavioural psychology and organizational learning that people and organizations do not learn without data and feedback. Yet most UK companies are not providing these essentials of learning to their boards.'[6] More recently, data from the 2019 Harvey Nash international board survey shows that only about a third of companies complete effective outside board evaluations. Another third go through an evaluation exercise, but usually organize it to get the answers they or the chair want, allowing them to pat themselves on the back rather than undergoing any kind of serious critique. The remaining third do no board evaluation at all.

Internal evaluation exercises, or self-assessment, should be completed annually and involve feedback from every member of the board to every other member of the board. The Financial Reporting Council guidelines suggest that boards should also conduct an external assessment once every three years. This assessment should be run by someone outside of the organization to ensure confidentiality of the data, and the data itself needs to include assessments from each individual director about the culture of the board, especially how included they feel within the board. Feelings of inclusion and belonging are essential to encourage individuals to continue to engage with the board and give their best possible individual input. This is especially important for people who have experienced exclusion based on their personal characteristics. To engage them and get their best, they need to feel a sense of belonging.

Good evaluation should do more than just assess whether the board and directors are compliant and are performing well. Measuring compliance and performance is of course necessary and important, but it is an essentially backward-looking activity. As well as compliance, evaluation should look forward and also be a tool for development. The Chartered Governance Institute defines the purpose of board evaluation as

> first, to provide a robust and objective review of the board's effectiveness to help the board continuously improve its own performance and the performance of the company; and secondly, to demonstrate to shareholders and other stakeholders that the board is committed to performing to a high standard, and that it understands and is addressing any areas of weakness in its effectiveness.[7]

No board is perfect, and it is highly unlikely that it will ever be perfect. Boards should adopt a philosophy of continuous improvement, always looking for opportunities to sharpen their information-gathering, communication and decision-making processes. Evaluation, properly handled, offers the chance to spot windows of opportunity for change and improvement. This, we believe, should be one of the primary purposes of any evaluation exercise.

The following are some of the topics that a good board evaluation, either internal or external, should cover:

- Overall board effectiveness: is the board able to complete duties and meet its responsibilities?
- The effectiveness of the chair: does the chair support the other directors? Is the chair contributing to a strong and independent board culture? Does the chair have a good relationship with the CEO?
- The performance of individual directors: does each director contribute fully at board meetings? Do they engage in debates and offer their own points of view? Are they prepared for meetings and on top of the issues the company faces? Does their engagement style (questioning, listening, advocacy) contribute or erode the functioning of the board? What behaviours would the director need to improve in order to increase their efficacy in the boardroom? Are they behaving and acting in a truly independent manner?
- The performance of committees: do the committees complete their duties? Are they masters of their briefs? Do they conduct the necessary scrutiny of key issues? Are their reports to the board timely and detailed?

- The administration of meetings: do meeting run smoothly and to time? Are the agenda and board papers well prepared? Do directors get all the information they need? Does the meeting allow for full discussion of issues, or are there any constraints?
- Board development: do individual directors undertake continuing professional development? Does the board as a whole undertake development exercises at away-days and so on?
- Communications with other stakeholders: does the board have open lines of communication with investors, employees, customers and the wider community? Are there any missing voices?

As an example, the Board Effectiveness Profile™[8] tool mentioned earlier uses seven scales to describe board members' impressions, observations and experiences and how these interdependent individuals interact and the common perceptions that can arise:

- Intellectual Adaptability
- Collective Confidence
- Chair Directiveness
- Board Cohesion
- Board Norm Flexibility
- Power Concentration
- Risk Appetite

Strengthening Board Culture

The disasters and scandals we have seen throughout this book could have been prevented, if the boards of these companies had been able to avoid the crippling dysfunctions that left them incapable of taking effective action. These dysfunctions compromised board effectiveness, sometimes fatally. But they can be avoided, provided boards and individual directors are sufficiently self-aware, willing and able to act.

1. *Lack of independence*: appoint more independent directors and ensure that selection and training yield people with a truly independent mindset.
2. *Missing key voices*: make stakeholder representation and perspectives a priority. Create broader, better networks for board recruitment and information gathering, to get as many perspectives as possible. Concentrate on

inclusion, so those diverse voices are not hindered from speaking and are taken seriously.

3. *Cultural amplification*: monitor and manage board culture so it stays true to its values. Get outside perspectives to sense-check and be sure the culture is what we think it is. Diversity and inclusion of experience are important here too.

4. *Diffusion of responsibility*: ensure the board has a clear structure and everyone has designated responsibilities, but also, make sure the board culture encourages people to take responsibility rather than sitting on their hands. Again, ensure that the values are understood and lived by everyone on the board, no matter what their background.

5. *Rules-bound culture*: reduce regulations and box-ticking and ensure the board focuses on purpose, not process. Ensure all board members are active to reduce social loafing. Manage conflicts, and do not ignore them. Try to make decisions by consensus rather than majority rule.

6. *Groupthink*: make sure the decision-making process is purposive and rational. All options should be evaluated rigorously to discuss and challenge. Diversity and inclusion important here but also, if necessary, bring in outside experts to provide new perspectives and a different source of challenge.

Strengthening Independence

There are five key dimensions to independence, and all of these require the board's attention. They are *environment, values, attitudes, relationships* and *behaviours*.

Environment

The environment in which the board operates and the external pressures on the board have an impact on the board's ability to be independent. The ownership structure of the board can, as we saw, generate huge pressures against board independence. Over-mighty shareholders or executives—or both—who are determined to get their own way represent a real threat. Their pressure must be resisted, as must the cultural distortions and amplification that result when boards do not pay sufficient attention to their own culture.

More generally there can be other environmental pressures too. Economic forces will influence board behaviour, and times of economic crisis might tempt them to break with their values in the interests of survival. Political trends such as protectionism are also an ever-present threat, with ambitious politicians putting pressure on boards to take actions that conform to short-term political interests. Different sectors will have different pressures too; some like financial services and pharmaceuticals are highly regulated and boards must take care that independence does not compromise legal requirements. The forces that define independence and its limits are constantly shifting and changing.

Values

Independence is an attitude of mind, but it is also a value. It reflects the culture of service that all boards should have. Good independent directors believe in their organization and its mission and purpose so strongly that they are not afraid to criticize it or make recommendations for change. The board's values should encourage and promote this. Courage, humility, service, a belief in truth and a corresponding belief in the ultimate mission of the organization should be among the values that underpin board culture. If these values are present, then the cultural dysfunctions we have discussed in this book can be avoided.

How can these values be promoted and instilled? The chair of course has a vital role to play here and should lead the board by example. Induction programmes are important for setting expectations and ensuring all directors know what is expected of them. Ongoing refresher programmes such as away-days, reminding everyone of the values and purpose of the board, can also be very useful. And finally, the composition of the board itself plays a role too. If the board functions well together, then like any good sports team, its members will constantly remind each other of the values they espouse and may need only light-touch encouragement from the chair.

Attitudes

Closely linked to values are the attitudes board members have to their work. Among the early expectations that need to be set is an understanding of how vital the work of independent directors is. Being an independent director is no longer a sinecure and never should have been. The task requires dedication, responsibility and, as already mentioned, courage.

Again, the chair plays an important role in instilling and reminding directors of their duties. Even before that, however, the board's nominations committee or whatever body is tasked with recruiting new directors should pay close attention to selecting directors who have the 'right stuff.' We have not said much about recruitment in this book, but selecting new directors who have the right attitude plays an important role in strengthening board culture.

Relationships

Relationships between independent directors, and between directors and the executive, often mean the difference between a successful board and a failing one. A board with strong relationships will work as a team and achieve synergy; a board with weak relationships is probably sliding towards diffusion of responsibility, social loafing and groupthink.

The chair needs to take the lead in promoting strong relationships, but individual directors need to play their part as well and be willing to build relationships and networks inside the board and across the organization. Meetings of the board and committees are part of this process, but they are not sufficient. We strongly encourage board members to meet separately. Meetings without the CEO present, and meetings without the chair present, are useful ways to air any problems that may be building and resolve them. One of the by-products of the COVID-19 pandemic has been that most boards have got much better at virtual meetings, which are easy to organize and do not involve travel time. Quick virtual meetings can be a very effective way of building relationships.

Practices and Disciplines

Having an independent mindset is important, but directors need to be sure that their practices reflect their mindset and their values. That means:

- reading board and committee papers and being fully prepared for meetings;
- playing a full part in the work of the board, including joining committees, task-and-finish groups and any other initiatives the board establishes;
- speaking at board meetings, especially to ask questions and register dissenting views;
- making the effort to go on site visits, meet the workforce and customers and hear their views;
- taking the time to get to know fellow directors and executives and understand their points of view and perspective;
- display a willingness to learn at all times.

Here the responsibility lies squarely with the independent directors. No one else can make them do these things willingly; they must take the workload of the director onto their own shoulders. As above, during the selection and recruitment process it is important to identify candidates who do exhibit these behaviours and clearly take their duties seriously. That is as important, if not more so, than experience.

A Role for Both Regulators and Investors

Boards must do more to reform and strengthen their cultures, but there is also a role here for government and regulatory bodies. Firstly, governments and regulators could do more to stimulate training, development and professional qualification, rather than focusing solely on compliance. More and better education for directors, as well as measures to encourage boards and reduce boardroom stigma for directors engaging in educational opportunities, would strengthen boards immeasurably. Thus far, the private sector and educational institutions have offered only sporadic training in some countries—none in others—and there are no generally recognized professional qualifications. Rather than assuming every director appointed is fully qualified from day 1, perhaps it would be worthwhile to create a list of things directors need to know, or even an examination people need to pass to be a listed company director? Governments could certainly take the lead on debating these issues.

Secondly, more robust enforcement of existing rules for companies and directors who are involved in disasters and scandals would make for a stronger sense of justice for stakeholders who view directors and senior executives as getting especially lenient treatment for serious crime. There have been cases, such as Tyco and Enron, where criminal behaviour was involved and here law enforcement agencies have cracked down hard, sending people to prison. But these are almost the exceptions that prove the rule. Being involved in health and safety violations or unsafe working practices rarely invites criminal prosecution of either companies or individuals, even when people are killed. The US regulators have levied fines on organizations that look impressive at first sight, like the $5 billion fine levied against Facebook, but when set against Facebook's global revenues and overall worth, $5 billion is a drop in the ocean. Similarly, the heavy fines levied on banks during the scandals following the 2008 crash have had little impact on either the banks themselves or their shareholders. In most other jurisdictions, including the UK and European Union, fines are much less spectacular.

An Army of Regulators

There are more than four hundred organizations around the world charged with financial and business regulation, including nearly seventy in the USA alone and creating a confusing hodgepodge of regulation. They range in size from the Securities and Exchange Commission in America, which employs more than 4000 people, to the Insurance Authority of the Faroe Islands and the Financial Services Authority of Saint Vincent and the Grenadines. Keeping track of all of them and their separate codes of conduct would be akin to one of the labours of Hercules. Here are a few of the most significant bodies:

USA

Securities and Exchange Commission (SEC)
Financial Crimes Enforcement Network (FinCEN)
Financial Industry Regulatory Authority (FINRA)
Commodity Futures Trading Commission (CFTC)
Federal Deposit Insurance Corporation (FDIC)

UK

Financial Reporting Council (FRC)
Financial Conduct Authority (FCA)
Prudential Regulation Authority (PRA)

European Union

European Securities and Markets Authority (ESMA)
European Banking Authority (EBA)

China

China Securities Regulatory Commission (CSRC)
China Banking and Insurance Regulatory Commission (CBIRC)

India

Securities and Exchange Board of India (SEBI)
Insolvency and Bankruptcy Board of India (IBBI)

Japan

Securities and Exchange Surveillance Commission (SESC)
Financial Services Agency (FSA)

South Africa

Financial Sector Conduct Authority (FSCA)
Prudential Authority (PA)

Brazil

Securities and Exchange Commission (CVM)

Nigeria

Securities and Exchange Commission (SEC)

United Arab Emirates

Securities and Commodities Authority (SCA)
Abu Dhabi Financial Services Regulatory Authority (FSRA)
Dubai Financial Services Authority (DFSA)

Regulators need teeth. We are not advocating for more regulation, far from it. The last thing we need is more box-ticking. But the regulations we have need to be much more strictly enforced with much bigger penalties for those that fail, not directly as an individual deterrent, but penalties that really hurt both the firm and its shareholders. That way even if the executive still does not wish to reform or change, pressure from angry shareholders will create additional pressure for them to do so. Regulators also need powers to intervene before bankruptcy is inevitable, coming into struggling companies or bottom performers, doing board evaluations, replacing board members if necessary, providing training where appropriate and generally acting before the crisis explodes. The same applies with CEOs; regulators should have the power to remove CEOs who are actively damaging companies and destroying value, and to debar them from serving on boards again. This happens already in many other sectors, why not with listed companies?

Regulators should also have the power to publicly identify those companies that do not behave according to codes of governance, issue them with performance improvement notices and even, in serious cases, de-list them from the relevant stock exchanges. In the UK, the Charities Commission has the power to close charities that have breached corporate governance rules. Why do corporate regulators not have the same powers?

Another area where regulators may have a role to play concerns the possible professionalization of the role of the independent director. The role is difficult, and complexity is increasing, but too many independent directors still do not fully recognize the extent of their legal and fiduciary responsibilities. Should organizations still continue to rely on part-timers—who in many small organizations and non-profit organizations are unpaid volunteers—or should professional qualification and certification be made mandatory for anyone wishing to take up the post? There are arguments for both positions.

In the past, in order to ensure that independent directors had the appropriate board experience and understanding of board dynamics, companies have tended to recruit former senior managers, especially CEOs. The problem is that while this does ensure that directors are already familiar with what happens in a boardroom and are able to get their feet under the table fairly quickly, this is very limiting in terms of skills sets and experience. This is indeed one of the causes of the prevailing lack of diversity; many CEOs have very similar profiles and backgrounds, and recruiting them as independent directors narrows boardroom diversity still further.

It is important to recognize that becoming an independent director is not a simple extension of being an executive. The roles and responsibilities are related, but quite different. So too are the relationships, especially the asymmetries of power between independent directors and executives. Management experience is useful, but it is not the only essential set of skills and experiences that boards require. The skills required to be part of a board can be learned, often quite quickly; a lifetime's experience cannot.

The problem is that even though those boardroom skills *can* be learned, very often they are not. Board inductions are rarely thorough enough to provide everything that is needed. There is a strong argument for professional qualifications. These could come through education programmes, or perhaps there could be a certification process whereby those who already have the right experience sit an exam and gain a certificate of competence.

Certification and professional regulation could then open the door for tighter regulation. We have already suggested that boards should be subject to periodic inspection by independent directors from other boards. These reports, if unfavourable, could form the basis for action by regulators. In serious cases, incompetent directors could be disqualified or the entire boards of failing companies dismissed and those companies put into 'special measures,' run by independent experts until they are back on their feet again; similar to the system of administration, but with regulators given the power to intervene *before* the company collapses, rather than waiting until after. If this system could be made to work, it might prevent at least some future collapses and scandals.

On the other hand, it remains to be seen how this system would work. There are questions around how qualifications and certification would be provided and by whom: governments, regulators, business schools? Who would organize and oversee the qualification and inspection processes and what would this cost? Who would pay for the course? If the financial burden of education is placed on the shoulders of would-be independent directors, this could be a disincentive to those from more diverse backgrounds, that is not well-paid former CEOs and other senior executives. This could in turn make the pool of applicants even smaller than it already is, and discourage talented and eager candidates from putting their names forward.

These ideas need further debate and study. We would like to see governments engage with these ideas, and convene working groups to look into the issues further and make recommendations. International coordination would be useful too, so that best practice is shared around the world and we learn from each other.

Whatever happens, the present system, whereby the regulator is forced to wait until the disaster happens and then only sweep the debris, needs a rethink. Early intervention and preventive medicine are vital to prevent crises from erupting in the first place. The same is true of charities, healthcare and many other sectors, not just business. There will of course be strong, short-sighted vested interests who will try to stop this kind of reform, but there is a real opportunity here to make a massive difference to the improvement of board performance and prevent some disasters.

Ideally, investors also need to get more involved. 'Activist investors' are not always the answer since many of them are 'activist' with the one aim of increasing their immediate personal wealth and too many others are focused on particular issues and not interested in general good governance. However, there are investors who are in for the long haul and take a stakeholder point of view and ensure that the businesses in which they own shares are working in the best interests of everyone, not just themselves. As observers like Dominic Barton, the former managing partner of McKinsey, have been saying for years, the best way to maximize shareholder wealth is to create long-term value for other stakeholders. We urge investors to adopt the model of stakeholder engagement, not just for the good of society but to make money for themselves as well.

Collective Responsibility: Directors, Executives, Regulators, Shareholders, Workers, Customers and Taxpayers

The problem of failures of corporate governance is not going away, and it will not go away without purposive action from all of us: investors, customers, employees, taxpayers and citizens. Although scandals and collapses are probably no more numerous than in previous years, because of the size and global reach of modern businesses—and other organizations too—when they do fail, the repercussions are more severe than ever. The costs of these failures and scandals are born by us all. Lost jobs, lost tax revenue, ruined lives and the social and psychological harm that follows, pollution and environmental degradation that destroys ecologies and harms health, and of course, injury and death; these are externalities we pay for wealth creation, the costs of corporate failure that spread through every corner of society.

There is no single solution to the problem. We all need to work together, as citizens, as shareholders, as regulators, to put pressure on boards to improve. Above all, boards themselves need to take charge of the own situation and realize that the entire business sector is being tarnished by a small percentage of irresponsible actors. Is there a role here for helping to police each other?

Given the scale and complexity of the problems we face in the modern world—the looming climate emergency, rampant inequality, economies shattered by the pandemic—we all need business to succeed. The constant stream of collapses and failures cannot continue. We need more and better education and training for directors (hence this book). We need more and better stakeholder engagement. We need more independence of thought and action, to ensure directors have the power to make real change. Above all else, we need a new sense of responsibility, an understanding of what being an independent director and board member means and how board decisions affect the lives of all of us. Incredible wealth creation happens through these businesses. We need them to do better.

Notes

1. Stanislav Shekshnia, 'How to Be a Good Board Chair', *Harvard Business Review* March–April 2018.
2. Brown et al., 2020.
3. Ibid.
4. Cameron Anderson and Jennifer L. Berdahl, 'The Experience of Power: Examining the Effects of Power on Approach and Inhibition Tendencies', *Journal of Personality and Social Psychology* 83 (6), 2002; Dacher Keltner, Deborah H. Gruenfeld and Cameron Anderson, 'Power, Approach and Inhibition', *Psychological Review* 110 (2), 2003.
5. The Tyson Report, p. 16.
6. The Tyson Report, p. 17.
7. ICSA, 'Review of the Effectiveness of Independent Board Evaluation in the UK Listed Sector: Summary of Responses to the Public Consultation', London: The Chartered Governance Institute, 2021.
8. TalentSage LLC.

Appendix A: Corporate Scandals and Disasters

Corporate scandals and failures take place on a spectrum, with incompetence and blundering on one end and deliberate corruption at the other. More often than not, a combination of the two is involved. 'Corruption' does not necessarily imply law-breaking. It can also include unethical or immoral behaviour. Tax reduction, for example, is not necessarily illegal, and in some tax havens it is actively encouraged. Nevertheless, as the Mossack Fonseca affair and more recently the leakage of FinCEN files have clearly shown, there are strong moral and ethical implications. Corruption is any deliberate action undertaken for gain or deception; incompetence merely means doing the wrong things or, more often, doing nothing at all.

To recite the entire history of business scandals and disasters would be both tedious and depressing. Our purpose in this book is to identify what went wrong and, in particular, to answer that vital question: where was the board? To this end, we will now look at a number of different types of failure, and try to put a finger on what the board was doing—or not doing—and why. In some cases it is difficult to know for certain; in others, silence about what the board was doing can itself be eloquent. Table A.1 shows some of the examples that have occurred in recent times, while Fig. 4.1 shows how they relate to our six board dysfunctions. We then go on to discuss a few of these examples in more detail. These too are part of the tip of the iceberg; the visible faces of corruption and incompetence that we can all see and read about.

© The Author(s), under exclusive license to Springer Nature Switzerland AG 2022   **229**
G. Brown, R. S. Peterson, *Disaster in the Boardroom*,
https://doi.org/10.1007/978-3-030-91658-9

Table A.1 A taxonomy of scandals and disasters

Problem	What happened
Theft, fraud and bribery	• Rio Tinto: paid bribes in Guinea to secure a licence for an iron ore mine
	• Compass: bribed a UN official in order to secure lucrative contracts
	• Shell: accused of paying bribes to secure oil licences in Nigeria
	• Rolls Royce: admitted paying numerous bribes overseas, £671 million in fines
	• GlaxoSmithKline: fined $490 million for bribing doctors and hospitals in China
	• Petrobras Brazil: officials took bribes in exchange for awarding contracts to other firms: two former presidents jailed, court cases settled for $853 million
	• Samsung: paid bribes to close associate of President Park of South Korea, who was impeached and imprisoned
	• Kobe Steel: manipulated data about product quality
	• HBOS: manager jailed after fraud cost bank and its customers £245 million
	• Danske Bank: charged with laundering more than €200 billion of money coming from suspicious sources, mostly Russia and Estonia
	• Takata: fined $1 billion for falsifying data about airbag safety
	• Health South: CEO sold $75 million in stock shortly before company announced a large loss
	• Clone Systems: sold shares in advance of publication of data rejecting drug trial
	• WorldCom: CEO inflated earnings in order to maintain share price, accounting irregularities of $3.8 billion
	• Tyco: CEO and CFO defrauded the company of more than $150 million
	• Deutsche Bank: paid $205 million in fines in the USA for its part in foreign exchange scandal
	• Turing: bought rights to drugs and raised prices by up to 5000 per cent
	• Valeant: increased prices of some life-saving drugs by up to 500 per cent
Privacy and data violations	• Equifax: lax security allowed massive data hack, settled for $700 million
	• Facebook: allowed Cambridge Analytica to harvest user data without their knowledge

(continued)

Table A.1 (continued)

Problem	What happened
Sexual discrimination and harassment	• Google: accusations of sexual harassment made by women against several senior male employees, who were protected by the company • Weinstein Corporation: numerous accusations of harassment and rape led to the company's collapse • Fox News: accusations of sexual harassment, lawsuits including one still in progress • Uber: developed a culture in which sexual harassment by senior executives went unpunished
Tax evasion and avoidance	• HSBC: fined $192 million for helping thousands of customers evade taxes • Facebook: under scrutiny for its offshore tax arrangements • Apple: forced to pay €13 billion after Ireland broke state aid rules • McDonald's: investigated by EU for avoiding €1 billion in taxes by use of Luxembourg subsidiary
Accounting irregularities	• Tesco: overstated profits by $326 million; share price declined sharply, senior executives forced to resign • Satyam: falsified accounts by $1.5 billion; auditors PwC failed to notice • Carillion: collapsed with debts of £7 billion after directors concealed true financial position • Toshiba: overstated profits by $1.9 billion over seven years; a subsequent overstatement has also come to light • Freddie Mac: paid $50 million to settle accounting fraud charges • BT: accounting fraud in Italian subsidiary leads to losses of £530 million • Xerox: fined $10 million for accounting fraud • Accounting firms: a series of audit failings by the Big Four and other firms have led to hundreds of millions in losses and several corporate collapses, including those noted above
Mis-selling and price-fixing	• Payment Protection Insurance (PPI): mis-sold PPI has cost UK banks more than £38 billion • Goldman Sachs: knowingly misled customers about mortgage-backed securities, fined $5.1 billion • Wells Fargo: opening false bank accounts cost £3 billion in settlements and fines • Madoff Investment Securities: operated Ponzi scheme, defrauded investors of around $65 billion, although some of the money was later recovered • Pfizer: fined £84 million by UK regulator for charging excessive and unfair prices for drugs • European truck makers: formed cartel to fix prices, fined over £2.5 billion by regulators
Abuse of market power	• Google: fined nearly €7 billion by the European Commission for unfair competition

(*continued*)

Table A.1 (continued)

Problem	What happened
Health and safety failures	• BHP Billiton: collapse of Mariana dam killed nineteen people, court cases still ongoing
	• Union Carbide: toxic gas leak killed over 16,000 people and injured thousands more
Labour abuses	• Nike: allegations of use of child labour by suppliers
	• Sports Direct: workers 'treated without dignity or respect'
	• Marks & Spencer: accused of stocking garments made by maltreated workers in Turkey
Environmental and social failures	• Volkswagen: defeat device falsified emissions, $25 billion in fines
	• Glencore: funded campaign of disinformation about green energy
	• BP: pipeline spill in Alaska, Texas City, refinery explosion, *Deepwater Horizon* disaster
	• Mitsubishi Motors: falsified fuel consumption figures, scandal caused losses of $1.4 billion
	• Southern Water: fined £120 million for polluting UK rivers with sewage
	• Rio Tinto: blew up the 46,000-year-old caves in Western Australia's Pilbara region in 2020 to extract $188 million worth of high-grade iron ore, devastating the Puutu Kunti Kurrama and Pinikura (PKKP) people
Collapses and bankruptcies	• Lehman Brothers: collapsed in 2008, precipitating global financial crisis
	• Royal Bank of Scotland: bailed out by UK government for £46 billion in 2009
	• AIG: rescued by US government with $180 billion investment to keep it afloat
	• Northern Rock: taken into public ownership after first run on a UK bank in 150 years
	• Bear Sterns: sold to JP Morgan Chase after share price fell from $133 to $10
	• Anglo-Irish Bank: taken into public ownership in 2009 after risky loan left the bank in financial trouble
	• London Capital and Finance: 12,000 investors lost £237 million when finance house collapsed in 2019
	• British Home Stores: closed in 2016 with debts of £1.3 billion
Executive pay abuses	• £14 million salary award to BP CEO Bob Dudley in 2016, despite the firm making losses
	• Shareholder revolt in 2018 when AstraZeneca fails to cut CEO's pension contribution
	• 33 per cent pension contribution of Lloyds CEO in 2019 referred to as 'naked greed'
	• Only 36 per cent of FT-100 companies cut executive pay during the 2020 pandemic

Theft, Fraud and Bribery

When we think of corruption the first examples that come to mind are often cases of bribery, collusion, theft and fraud. When these cases occur, the reaction of the board is usually to blame a 'rogue executive' who is summarily dismissed, and establish an inquiry to uncover what went wrong. The inquiry should start with the board itself, of course, but it rarely ever does.

Theft: Tyco

In the years leading up to 2002 Dennis Kozlowski and Mark Schwartz, CEO and CFO respectively, of international security company Tyco defrauded the company of more than $150 million dollars, much of which they spent on their own lavish lifestyle. After the scandal broke, Kozlowski and Schwartz maintained that the board had authorized payments to them. The board denied this, but it is interesting to note that in the same year, 2002, another director of the firm pleaded guilty to charges of securities fraud after he received a $20 million payment for helping to broker an acquisition.[1]

After Koslowski and Schwartz were sent to prison, a new chairman, Edward Breen, and a new lead director, John Krol, were appointed. Their view of what had happened was simple. As Breen said, 'The fall of Tyco was brought about by a lack of governance and accountability.' Board culture had become corrupt and dysfunctional, and board members were overly deferential to the dynamic CEO. The audit committee in particular seems to have been culpable in not noticing the large sums which had been pilfered. Breen and Krol asked the entire board of directors to resign. Some went willingly; others resisted, but Breen got his way and appointed a completely new board and start rebuilding the board culture. 'The board has to live by its values and principles,' he said. 'It starts with the board.'[2]

Fraud: Takata

From 2000 through 2015, Tokyo-based auto components maker Takata Corporation defrauded customers and auto manufacturers, providing falsified airbag inflator test data to make its airbag inflators' performance look better than it actually was. Despite the fact that the inflators repeatedly had serious problems—including ruptures causing injuries and deaths—Takata executives 'continued to withhold the true and accurate inflator test information and data from their customers.'[3] At least 16 deaths and over 180 injuries were caused by the defective airbag inflators, leading to the biggest manufacturer recall in US history involving nearly 70 million defective parts and affecting 42 million vehicles. The global recall of unsafe inflators topped 100 million.

The inflators were designed to open airbags in a crash by using a small explosion phase-stabilized ammonium nitrate (PSAN), a chemical that, if exposed to prolonged high temperatures and humidity, can deteriorate and burn too fast. Under those circumstances, the 'small' explosion designed to inflate an airbag became sufficient to blow apart a metal canister, 'hurling shrapnel into drivers and passengers.'[4] The company was aware of this defect for years, but intentionally hid evidence demonstrating the airbag inflators could explode with excessive force, in part because it could consistently undercut its competition on inflator pricing. As early as the 1990s, rival Autoliv had engineers examine the Takata airbags based on a request by General Motors to match Takata's price. Autoliv advised that it could not and would not replicate the PSAN airbags because the chemical was too volatile, and therefore too dangerous, for airbag use. 'In fact, the dangers of PSAN were common knowledge in the industry—enumerated in patents by airbags makers, including Takata—and in the scientific literature.'[5]

In the USA, Acting Assistant Attorney General Kenneth A. Blanco observed that Takata had abused the trust of customers and the public alike: 'For over a decade, Takata lied to its customers about the safety and reliability of its ammonium nitrate-based airbag inflators [and allowed] airbag inflators to be put in vehicles knowing that the inflators did not meet the required specifications.'[6] In February 2017, Takata pled guilty to a single count of wire fraud and agreed to pay criminal penalties of $1 billion.

The US also sought to extradite three Takata executives, Shinichi Tanaka, Hideo Nakajima and Tsuneo Chikaraishi, from Japan to face criminal charges, with prosecutors arguing that the executives spent as many as fifteen years manipulating crucial safety data when they were well aware that the airbags' metal inflators could explode, causing injury or death. As one of the executives explained to the others in a 2005 email, they had no choice but to manipulate the safety data, and they must 'cross that bridge together.' '[The executives] falsified and manipulated data because they wanted to make profits on their airbags, knowing they were creating risk for the end-users, who are soccer moms like me,' said US Attorney Barbara L. McQuade.[7]

At the time the indictments and the guilty plea came down, every member of Takata's board was a Japanese male. This lack of diversity may have led to what one observer referred to as the avoidance of 'risky communication'; directors did not talk to each other about hard issues because they were unwilling to confront them directly. The board and the executives may as well have been operating in different worlds.[8]

Fraud: Kobe Steel

Kobe Steel, Japan's third largest steelmaker, admitted in October 2017 that it had falsified data about the strength and durability of its aluminium and copper products, which were supplied to over 500 customers, including auto manufacturers Toyota, Honda and Subaru.[9] The metals were then used in the manufacture of trains, airplanes and automobiles.

In March 2018, the company issued an investigative report that confirmed 688 cases of 'misconduct,' that employees had changed or faked data on the quality of products and that the organization had 'deep-seated issues' relating to corporate culture and compliance. The scandal led the resignation of CEO Hiroya Kawasaki, changes in senior management, an indictment under Japanese competition law and legal action in both the USA and Canada.[10]

The report highlighted 'a management style that overemphasized profitability and had inadequate corporate governance' in a systemic scheme that spanned five decades and crossed multiple factories and locations. The widespread data manipulation was conducted with the knowledge and involvement of many employees, including those in management. The report notes a lack of transparency in the corporation's culture, which 'prioritized winning purchase orders and meeting delivery deadlines, over ensuring quality.'[11] As a retired Kobe employee explained, 'The corporate culture was to look the other way even while you saw what was going on.'[12]

This was not the company's first misadventure in data fabrication; in 2006, Kobe Steel had admitted falsifying soot-emissions records at its Kobe Works and Kakogawa Works plants. The fabrication of strength and durability information followed 'exactly the same set-up,' said Shoichi Tarumoto, the then-mayor of Kakogawa, adding that 'it looks like nothing has changed at Kobe Steel.'[13] The company tried to rebound from the records falsification scandal and put preventive measures in place, but its efforts were met with scepticism; there were doubts as to whether such a deeply entrenched cultural pattern of behaviour would readily shift.

Bribery: Rio Tinto

In 2016 the Anglo-Australian mining company Rio Tinto found itself embroiled in scandal when news broke that one of its senior executives had authorized a payment of $10.5 million to a close friend of the president of Guinea in order to secure the licence for a valuable iron ore deposit at Simandou. Leaked emails suggested that both the current CEO, Sam Walsh, and the previous one, Tom Albanese, were aware of the deal.[14] Both the Serious Fraud Office (SFO) in London and the Securities and Exchange Commission (SEC) in the USA launched investigations.

The board did what boards often do, expressed its shock and indignation and fired the executive who had paid the bribe. The company's legal counsel also took early retirement. An independent investigation was launched by the board, which maintained it was unaware of what was happening. That myth was exploded in 2017 when the senior independent director was charged with conspiracy to commit fraud by the SFO. The SEC brought charges against Albanese and another executive that same year.[15]

Was the board deceived? The charges against the senior independent director (a former chief executive of Barclays Bank) suggested that the SFO, at least, thought not. But even if we give the remaining directors the benefit of the doubt and accept that they were ignorant of the bribe in Germany, a different and equally damning question remains: why didn't they know what was going on? This was not the first time Rio Tinto had been involved in dubious practices. Several senior figures in its Chinese division had been jailed for bribery and espionage in 2010, and Albanese, the former CEO, had been forced to resign after the bungled purchase of a loss-making mine in Mozambique. In 2017 the SEC brought charges against him and Rio Tinto's former CFO, alleging that they mis-represented the financial health of the mine.[16]

The board should have ensured that the company had a strong anti-corruption policy and that this policy was effectively enforced. Its failure to do so suggests that there was a culture of lack of responsibility. No one was prepared to confront the status quo, not even the chairman, whose response to the SFO charges against the senior independent director was to defend that director as a man of integrity.

Bribery: Compass

In October 2005, an international investigation relating to corruption in the United Nations procurement process uncovered extensive evidence of bribery and collusion in connection with the awarding of UN contracts.[17] The wide-ranging investigation implicated Compass Group PLC (Compass)—the world's largest catering company—which had been awarded contracts to supply food to peacekeepers in Sudan, East Timor, Liberia, Burundi, Eritrea, Lebanon, Cyprus and Syria. In that same month, Compass announced the suspension of Peter Harris, CEO of its subsidiary Eurest Support Services (ESS) and a member of Compass's executive committee. Harris had previously been considered a potential successor to the company's departing CEO, Michael Bailey. The company also launched an internal investigation led by the law firm Eversheds and an accounting team from Ernst & Young. The investigation was overseen at board level by Steve Lucas (an independent director of Compass Group PLC and chair of the board's audit committee).[18] Three months and £5 million later, the company revealed that the inquiry had identified 'serious irregularities.' ESS was suspended as a UN-registered vendor.

The concerns highlighted in the investigation eventually were incorporated into a series of lawsuits brought by ESS competitors Es-Ko International and Supreme Foodservice, alleging that the organization had illegally conspired to rig UN contract awards and circumvent a legitimate bidding process by, among other things, paying bribes and impermissibly obtaining and relying on confidential documents. The cases were based on accusations that five senior executives at ESS had paid bribes in order to win contracts for the supply of food supplies to UN peacekeepers. In particular, CEO Peter Harris was alleged to have secured the contracts by paying Alexander Yakovlev, a Russian UN official, hundreds of thousands of dollars by routing the bribes through a New York-based company called IHC. Among other actions, Yakovlev was said to have provided ESS executives with confidential UN documents relating to a bid on a $62 million contract that was then awarded to Compass. Yakovlev subsequently pled guilty to having taken $1 million in corporate bribes after a separate UN investigation led to criminal charges.

In October 2006, Compass announced the settlement of two US-based lawsuits. Admitting no liability, the company agreed to pay up to £40 million to its rivals, with CEO Richard Cousins, the chief executive of Compass, stating that the settlement was 'in the best interests of the business and shareholders' and noting that his focus 'on the future and this settlement is a major step in putting the matter behind us.'[19]

Ironically, the board's oversight of UN contracts sat with Peter Harris, as ESS CEO and member of Compass's executive committee, and he was ultimately fired for paying bribes.[20] There appears to have been no board scrutiny of Harris's activities by the board.

Privacy and Data Violations

Like bribery, fraud and theft, privacy and data violations can be classed as corrupt behaviour, even if they do not always violate the law; this is an area where the law is sometimes behind morality. Boards have struggled to exercise effective governance in this area, largely because technology is now so complex that few boards fully understand it. They are not alone, of course; regulators have also been behind the curve in understanding the potential for the abuse of mobile phones and social media technology. Unscrupulous organizations and people exploit this ignorance for their advantage.

Equifax

In March 2017, using an online customer complaint site that had known security vulnerabilities, hackers gained access to extensive personal data held by credit reporting giant Equifax.[21] By May, the attackers had located extensive data, including millions of user names and passwords. By leveraging Equifax's out-of-date security tools, the attackers invisibly extracted the data. Equifax became aware of the breach in July. The personal information of over 147 million Americans, many of whom were not even Equifax customers, was compromised.[22]

When the scandal broke the finger-pointing began, including accusations of inexcusable data security flaws, the company's failure to disclose the breach and its failure to respond effectively (including directing customers to a new, insecure domain and erroneously sending customers to an 'assistance' site not even owned by Equifax). The sale of stock by executives gave rise to insider trading claims, resulting in at least one criminal charge. Within three weeks of disclosing the breach, CEO Rick Smith had stepped down. A new chief security officer was also hired.

By January 2020, Equifax had agreed to a $700 million global settlement that resolved proceedings brought by the Federal Trade Commission, the Consumer Financial Protection Bureau, and the US states and territories.[23] As part of that settlement, Equifax agreed to implement a comprehensive information security programme, the creation and execution of which would undoubtedly involve the board. Key aspects included the following:

- Designating an employee to oversee the programme;
- Conducting annual assessments of internal and external security risks and implementing safeguards to address potential risks;
- Obtaining annual certifications from the Equifax board of directors or relevant subcommittee attesting that the company has complied with the order, including its information security requirements;
- Testing and monitoring the effectiveness of the security safeguards;
- Ensuring service providers with access to personal information stored by Equifax, also implementing adequate safeguards to protect the information.[24]

The company also had to provide the board with both the programme itself and any material evaluations thereof (but only once every twelve months). Equifax was also required to provide a quarterly update to the board of any 'covered incidents' that arose.

In February 2020, in an extraordinary move that emphasized the seriousness of the attack, the US Department of Justice brought criminal charges against four members of the Chinese military. There is so far no evidence that the stolen data has been used for any criminal purposes, but nonetheless, it is still out there.

Sexual Discrimination and Harassment

Most nations have banned sexual discrimination and harassment, but they persist nonetheless, and in many organizations they are an entrenched part of the culture. Boards have a legal responsibility to ensure that women—and despite isolated examples to the contrary, it is nearly always women who are the victims—are not discriminated against and are not subject to harassment. All too many boards fail to discharge this responsibility, or even recognize that it exists.

Discrimination often takes subtle forms. Much has been written about the glass ceiling, whereby women can only rise to a certain level in a hierarchy; as we saw in Chap. 1, some progress is being made, but not enough. Boards of directors—especially boards dominated by men—can be hostile places for female CEOs, as evidenced by the brief tenures of Patricia Russo as CEO of Lucent in 2002 and Ellen Pao at Reddit in 2015. At Hewlett-Packard, Carly Fiorina was often undermined by her own board of directors, who forced her resignation in 2003 after a confidential restructuring plan was leaked, claiming that she was difficult to work with. Other reports described the male-dominated board as 'dysfunctional' and Fiorina's replacement was a male executive whom she had earlier fired.[25] Had the board been more diverse, and more independent of a few dominant investors, might Fiorina have received by more support? Or was the lack of support due to the fact that she was perceived as an outsider in a male-dominated industry?

Fox News

Sometimes—too often—discrimination leads to outright sexual harassment. In 2016, Fox News anchor Gretchen Carlson sued her own boss, head of news Roger Ailes, on grounds of sexual harassment. The suit also included Fox News's board of directors. The board's response was to sacrifice some of the executives who were in the eye of the storm, but otherwise admit nothing and retract the drawbridges. Ailes was fired, and Fox eventually settled with Carlson out of court for an estimated $90 million.[26] Part of the settlement included the establishment of a panel to improve workplace culture at Fox and eliminate sexual harassment. Once again, the stable door had been bolted after the horse had fled.

Or had it even been bolted? In 2017 Fox News undertook a review of its human resources policies including mandatory training on issues such as sexual discrimination and harassment. 'We encourage any employee who has a sexual harassment, discrimination or misconduct complaint of any form to report it immediately,' said CEO Suzanne Scott and media president Jay Wallace in a joint statement.[27] But in June 2020, allegations of sexual harassment and rape were made by a former employee against news anchor Ed Henry. This time the executives moved swiftly to fire Henry, but another court case followed quickly.

Weinstein Company

Perhaps the most notorious example in recent times was the scandal at the Weinstein Company in October 2017, when the American media reported allegations of sexual misconduct by more than a dozen women against media mogul Harvey Weinstein. More accusers quickly came forward, and within weeks more than eighty complaints had been lodged with the authorities. The company faced what one director referred to as 'an immediate and intense backlash' as producers and investors refused to do business with the company. Belatedly, the board of directors—which included Weinstein's brother—fired him, but it was too late. In 2018 the company filed for bankruptcy, and its assets were later sold for a bargain price.[28]

Where was the board while Weinstein was bullying and abusing his victims, causing them harm? It is an excellent question. The all-male board of the Weinstein Company claims to have either been ignorant of what was happening or perhaps turned a blind eye. The company was highly successful—277 films, 28 Academy Awards, over $2 billion in revenue—so why would anyone want to rock the boat? The other directors rebelled against Weinstein only when it became aware that his toxic reputation was killing the company. In the aftermath of Weinstein's dismissal, three more directors resigned their posts, but if there were discussions about Weinstein's conduct, they were not made public. And although Weinstein did eventually issue a public apology, the board has made no apology to Weinstein's victims. Missing those key voices, especially of women, who might have been prepared to publicly challenge Weinstein's behaviour, the board fell into the trap of lack of independence and failed.

Tax Evasion

In many organizations, taxation is seen as something like the pandemic; they either erect protective barriers to protect themselves or put as much distance between it and themselves as possible. Legitimate tax avoidance is often justified with reference to the principle, established by Milton Friedman and the Chicago School and enshrined in law in some jurisdictions, that the principal duty of the board is to ensure returns to shareholders and to maximize shareholder wealth. This argument has been endlessly debated, but even Friedman believed that companies should pay their fair share of tax.[29]

Tax avoidance is legal and countries such as Ireland and Singapore have deliberately reduced taxes in order to attract inward investment. Other countries have offered themselves as tax havens simply because they want the revenue. Companies such as Amazon have famously taken advantage of this by domiciling themselves in countries with low-tax regimes. Amazon has done nothing illegal, but society takes an increasingly dim view of tax avoidance and Amazon has suffered a certain amount of reputational damage as a result.[30] A Friedmanite would argue that this has not impacted on Amazon's profits; the counter-argument, from a stakeholder point of view, would be to question whether Amazon is really fulfilling its duty to the societies and countries where it operates.

Tax evasion, on the other hand, is another matter. Even where it is flagrantly illegal and can be severely punished, executives still push the boundaries, and sometimes break them. Boards, and particularly the audit committees that every board is required to have, are supposed to stop this from happening. They do not always succeed.

HSBC

In 2007, an ex-HSBC employee leaked data on over 100,000 HSBC clients in 203 countries.[31] It was the largest banking leak in history up to that time, covering over 30,000 accounts and £78 billion in assets. It also became the basis for an international investigative reporting project between *Le Monde*, the *Guardian*, BBC Panorama and the International Consortium of Investigative Journalists, and led to an ongoing series of government investigations and, ultimately, massive penalties for the bank's role in assisting customers in evading tax.[32] The bank affirmatively assisted its customers in disguising and hiding assets across the globe, enabling the violation of a host of tax laws.

In 2008, the Swiss private banking sector was shaken by a US Department of Justice (DOJ) criminal investigation into UBS for tax evasion. As that inquiry proceeded, HSBC Switzerland adjusted its own internal practices in an attempt to halt tax-evading practices. In early 2009, HSBC contacted the DOJ, confessed its involvement and actively cooperated with the government in the prosecution of US taxpayers. The bank ultimately entered into a deferred prosecution agreement with the DOJ, admitting that its Swiss operations had conspired for a decade with HSBC employees, subsidiaries, fiduciaries and US customers to enable its customers to conceal offshore assets and income for the purpose of avoiding legally owed US taxes. The bank's activities included assisting taxpayers in filing false returns, identifying clients by numbers or code words rather than legal names, discouraging clients from receiving correspondence from the bank while in the US, and advising and assisting in the creation of shell companies to conceal taxpayer accounts and sidestep the bank's own obligations to report client holdings to the US government. The final fine, imposed in 2019, exceeded $192 million.[33]

Despite coming clean in the US in 2009, HSBC seems not to have examined the wider implications of its Swiss practices in supporting tax evasion.[34] The threads continued to unspool. In 2014, French authorities commenced an investigation that established that the bank's Swiss operations had assisted clients in evading tax on $1.6 billion in assets. The investigation ultimately led to the imposition of a €300 million penalty in 2017.[35] In 2015, the Swiss government fined the bank £28 million (40m CHF) for money-laundering.[36] In 2019, HSBC incurred a €294 million fine in Belgium for tax offences including 'serious and organized tax fraud, forgery and falsification of records, money-laundering and illegal use of financial intermediaries.'[37] In early 2020, the bank was still resisting attempts by the Argentine government to recoup over $3.5 billion in claimed evaded taxes.

Curiously, in the UK HM Revenue and Customs (HMRC) had access to the leaked data from 2010 and determined that over 1000 British HSBC clients had failed to pay taxes. By 2015, only one tax evader had been prosecuted, and the UK government determined in 2016 that no charges would be brought against the bank. HMRC had, however, collected an additional £135 million in taxes owed. Stephen Green, who led HSBC at the time of the tax evasions, was made a Conservative peer in 2010 and served as minister of trade and investment until 2013.

HSBC's tax evasion problems did prompt some scrutiny of the board, particularly of board compensation and the potential waning of the actual independence of the independent directors. By spring of 2015, calls were being made for HSBC to keep a prior promise to appoint the next board chair from outside the organization, which it had already committed to doing pre-scandal. Questions were raised about the independence of long-standing, highly compensated outside directors, including Rona Fairchild (annual salary £500,000) and Sir Simon Robertson, both of whom had been on the board for at least nine years. The bank responded stating that the non-executive directors in question were 'independent in character and judgment' despite their long tenures and high compensation.

Accounting Irregularities

Audit committees are also implicated in cases of accounting irregularities where companies deliberately falsify their accounts, either to disguise financial losses and hide these from shareholders and the market or perhaps for more corrupt purposes. Often there is more than a hint of desperation about these attempts to 'cook the books.'

Tesco

In 2014 accountants at supermarket chain Tesco, under pressure in its home market and still counting the losses after its disastrous attempt to enter the American market, overstated the group's profits by £326 million. Inevitably, the share price fell; the market value of the company declined by about £2 billion, and the Serious Fraud Office launched an investigation. The chairman and CEO were forced to resign, eight other executives were suspended and three directors were ultimately charged with criminal offences, though all three were eventually acquitted.[38]

The checks and balances on company accounts should have ensured that this did not happen, but those checks and balances did not function adequately. The SFO rightly investigated the company's auditors, PwC, who failed to spot the irregularity, but primary responsibility rests with the board and the audit committee which clearly failed in their duty. The independent directors, who had already been criticized for lacking retail experience, failed to take responsibility. As the *Financial Times* commented, 'At Tesco, everyone is at fault and no one is to blame.'[39]

Satyam

PwC was also implicated in the Satyam scandal in 2009 when the Byrraju Ramalinga Raju, executive chair of Satyam Computer Services, admitted to falsifying the company's accounts to the extent of $1.5 billion. In this case the government's Central Bureau of Investigation moved quickly, dismissing the entire board and pressing criminal charges against the chair and a number of other executives. PwC was fined heavily and banned from auditing companies in India for two years. The punitive action taken against the board was in part because the directors had failed to challenge Raju, the founder of the company and a dominant figure who had strong links with local politicians.

What is striking about the Satyam affair is how long it had been going on underneath the noses of the directors. Raju later admitted that the original accounting fraud had been relatively small; when the results from one reporting period did not look good, he altered the figures to make them look slightly better. When the next set of figures were also poor, he altered them again and so on and on until he was trapped in a downward spiral with no way back. Eventually he lost his nerve and confessed. The entire board was taken completely by surprise; no one had seen this coming. Lack of independence and failure to demand information and hold the chair to account cost the directors and the company very dearly.[40]

Toshiba

As with Satyam, the accounting fraud at Toshiba was long-lasting and occurred without the board ever apparently suspecting a thing. Over the course of seven years from 2008, executives falsified accounts and overstated profits by an estimated ¥225 billion, or $1.9 billion. A subsequent investigation found that the fraud happened right across the organization, with accounting irregularities in every major department. The investigation also concluded that this was not a series of accounting errors; the fraud was deliberate and intentional and came with instructions from the top of the company. A fine of $60 million dollars was levied against the company, and the CEO was forced to resign.

The investigation laid the blame at the door of senior executives, commenting that there 'existed a corporate culture at Toshiba where it was impossible to go against the boss' will.'[41] That deep-seated culture also precluded any kind of whistleblowing, and with the CEO controlling the flow of information to the board, independent directors were left in the dark. Nor, it seems, was this problem fixable simply by changing the people at the top. In 2020 the *Japan Times* reported that a Toshiba subsidiary had recorded fictitious sales totalling ¥43.5 billion, or around $360 million, between 2015 and 2019. In other words, this subsidiary had begun recording fraudulent sales even while the investigation into the previous fraud was still happening. Toshiba maintained that its subsidiary was the victim of fraud by an external agency, but admitted it had failed to investigate the problem.[42] The story continues.

Mis-selling and Price-Fixing

Selling products which are known to not work, or at least not work for everyone, is one of the oldest kinds of fraud. Greedy, unscrupulous managers, or those who are under excessive pressure, continue to bend the rules and even break them. It seldom ends well; sooner or later, consumers realize they have been sold worthless goods or services and the affair explodes into a scandal.

Payment Protection Insurance

One of the largest mis-selling scandals of all time is the case of payment protection insurance in the UK, where banks sold an insurance package designed to protect borrowers, mortgage and credit card holders in case they fell into financial hardship. However, there were significant holes in the scheme and many of the people who took out PPI were not actually covered. In some cases, consumers were also sold products which included PPI premiums in the price without their knowledge or were told that they were more likely to have an application approved if they agreed to pay for PPI. The Financial Conduct Authority ordered that mis-sold PPI premiums should be repaid in full, with interest. As of May 2020 this had cost the UK banking industry £38.3 billion in repayments and millions more in fines.[43]

Here is a case of governance failure affecting not just one firm but an entire industry. Managers saw an opportunity for profit and took it, and no one seems to have thought to query whether this product was legitimate or effective. Staff were incentivized to sell PPI and were paid bonuses based on the value of policies sold.[44] There is no evidence that boards ever considered whether PPI was being mis-sold; and when the first court cases began, the banking sector defended its position and insisted that PPI was a good policy. Only when the Financial Conduct Authority intervened did the banks finally capitulate, and they are still counting the cost.

Wells Fargo

Wells Fargo had a long-standing reputation for sound management, having emerged successfully from the 2008 financial crisis and lauded by *American Banker* as 'the big bank least tarnished by the scandals and reputational crises.'[45] But in February 2020, the US Justice Department announced a $3 billion settlement of criminal and civil claims against Wells Fargo based on fourteen years of mistreatment of its retail banking customers. Employees sought to meet impossible sales goals by fraudulently opening millions of accounts in customers' names, going so far as to forge signatures, create fake personal identification numbers and illicitly transfer customer funds.[46] As Wells Fargo executives faced multiple criminal charges, the Office of the Comptroller of the Currency imposed millions of dollars in fines, including a $17.5 million fine against CEO John G. Stumpf (named *American Banker's* 2013 'Banker of the Year') and a $25 million fine against former head of retail banking, Carrie L. Tolstedt (the erstwhile 'Most Powerful Woman in Banking').[47]

Senior executives created an intensely pressured environment by consistently raising sales targets, despite evidence that they were unrealistic and unachievable. The bank set daily sales goals, including branch manager quotas for number and types of products sold; unmet targets were simply added to the next day's branch goals. Disputing that these practices put too much pressure on employees, CFO Tim Sloan stated that he was 'not aware of any overbearing sales culture.'[48] The bank did have controls abuse-prevention policies in place: splitting customer deposits to open multiple accounts was a 'sales integrity violation'; there was an ethics programme in place; aspects of bonuses were tied to instilling company values, minimizing risk; hedging and/or pledging of equity awards were banned; and provisions were in place to claw back bonuses that were earned inappropriately.

Despite these measures, the multi-year, systemic fraudulent practices were deeply entrenched. During the last five years of the ongoing fraud, the bank responded to ongoing customer complaints by firing thousands of employees and disciplining tens of thousands more, and took affirmative steps to hide the problem from investors. Tolstedt repeatedly ignored alarms raised by other executives about the company's 'cross-selling' practices, lying to both regulators and the Wells Fargo board.

In 2016, things began to unravel as the bank announced a $185 million settlement of claims brought by Los Angeles regulators based on the unauthorized opening of as many as two million customer accounts. The Consumer Financial Protection Bureau observed that by allowing thousands of employees to inflate their sales figures, 'Wells Fargo built and sustained a cross-selling programme where the bank and many of its employees served themselves instead, violating the basic ethics of a banking institution including the key norm of trust.' Additional historical patterns of defrauding customers were revealed, and even though the bank insisted the fraudulent accounts were trivial in number, the reputational damage was enormous.

The board of directors hired external counsel to conduct an independent investigation that ultimately 'sharply criticized the bank's leadership, sales culture, performance systems, and organizational structure as root causes of the cross-selling scandal.' The report specifically highlighted the use of unattainable sales goals, tolerance for 'low-quality accounts' (products that customers did not want or that were cancelled or never used), and management's failure to see the clear correlation between increased goals and increased misconduct. Leadership failures were also key, with Stumpf and Tolstedt both creating a culture in which negative news was not welcome and airing of contrary views was deeply discouraged. Lastly, the report concluded that the board of directors had 'regularly engaged' on the issue of the problematic practices—but that

> Tolstedt effectively challenged and resisted scrutiny from both within and outside the community bank. She and her group risk officer not only failed to escalate issues outside the community bank, but also worked to impede such escalation. … Tolstedt never voluntarily escalated sales practice issues, and when called upon specifically to do so, she and the community bank provided reports that were generalized, incomplete, and viewed by many as misleading.

As the scandal unfolded and claims by regulators increased, the board insisted that they were 'misinformed' and that Tolstedt had 'minimized and understated' the real scope of the problem. By allowing a few overly powerful executives to act as gatekeepers of information, and by failing to verify the information they received, the board removed itself from the rest of the organization and failed to understand the problem or even that the problem existed in the first place.

Abuse of Market Power

Around 80 per cent of mobile phones in Europe use Google's Android operating system, and Google, it seems, could not resist the opportunities this offered. In 2017, an investigation by the European Commission found that Google had given an illegal advantage to another of its products, an online comparison-shopping service. 'What Google has done is illegal under EU antitrust rules,' said EU commissioner Margrethe Vestager. 'It has denied other companies the chance to compete on their merits and to innovate, and most importantly it has denied European consumers the benefits of competition, genuine choice and innovation.'[49]

Google maintained that it was merely offering customers more flexibility and ease of use, but the Commission disagreed and levied a fine of €2.42 billion. That, however, was only the beginning. The Commission had also been investigating an even more serious matter, namely that Google was using its market position to require mobile phone manufacturers to pre-install other Google software including Chrome and Google Search. According to the Commission, this was a restriction of consumer choice and an abuse of market power. In 2018 another fine was levied, nearly double the size of the first at €4.3 billion.[50] The board of Google lacked the power to challenge the executive. Unless and until the culture changes, we can expect to see further scandals and disasters.

Health and Safety Failures

As noted in Chap. 1, corporate disasters are not consequence-free and sometimes lives are lost. In Chap. 6 we looked more closely at the *Deepwater Horizon* disaster in the Gulf of Mexico, but another case which has parallels with it is the Mariana dam disaster in which the Australian mining company BHP Billiton was involved.

BHP Billiton

In 2015, a dam at Samarco's iron ore mine at Mariana in the Brazilian province of Minas Gerais in 2015. Two nearby villages were flooded, and nineteen people lost their lives. The collapse also released toxic mud which entered the downstream water system and ultimately reached the Atlantic Ocean.[51] Multi-billion-dollar court cases are still in progress and the Brazilian authorities pressed criminal charges against all three companies.

Immediate responsibility rested with Samarco, the mine's owner, but Samarco was jointly owned by the Brazilian company Vale and the Australian mining giant BHP Billiton. According to *Forbes* magazine, in 2012 Vale had been named the worst company in the world for a range of environmental and human rights abuses.[52] (Later, in 2019, another dam collapse at a Vale-owned mine at Brumadinho in Minas Gerais killed 270 people.) It also emerged that a report in 2013 indicates there were structural weaknesses in the Mariana dam, but the report had been suppressed. The governance question for BHP Billiton is, given Vale's record and given the existing problems at Mariana, why was the board willing to partner with the Brazilian firm? We do not know what discussions took place at the BHP Billiton board, but they should have included an adequate discussion of the risks of getting involved with Vale, including the latter's prior environmental record.

Union Carbide

The Bhopal disaster is one of the most infamous health and safety disasters in the modern era, partly for its scope and scale and partly for the sheer horror of what happened. In late October 1984, a mechanical failure at Union Carbide's plant at Bhopal meant that a tank containing 42 tons of liquid methyl isocyanate could not be removed. Several attempts to rectify the problem failed. Subsequent investigations found that most of the safety systems designed to contain the methyl isocyanate were not working. Late in the evening of 2 December 1984, water found its way into the tank, triggering a reaction which began converting the liquid into a gas. This gas in turn began to leak into the surrounding atmosphere.

Nearby workers detected the leak and reported the matter to their supervisor at 11.45 p.m. The supervisor postponed making a decision for nearly an hour, during which time the gas began to escape from the tank with alarming speed. Workers were forced to evacuate the factory. A siren was sounded to warn people living nearby, but was quickly turned off again, apparently in line with a company policy which stated that the siren should not be used in order to avoid alarming people. The alarm was fully sounded finally at 2.15 a.m., by which time the gas cloud had enveloped the surrounding communities. Some people who woke coughing and choking attempted to flee from the gas, but running meant that they inhaled the gas more quickly. Children also suffered more heavily as the gas, which was heavier than air, began to concentrate at lower levels.

More than half a million people were exposed to the gas, of whom 170,000 required medical treatment. Eight thousand died in the immediate aftermath, many within a few hours, and at least 8000 more died over the subsequent weeks and months. The gas particularly affected pregnant women and the number of stillbirths more than doubled. Two thousand head of livestock, essential to the local economy, also died, and the gas also tainted water supplies and led to water shortages.

The Indian government initially claimed damages of $3.3 billion, eventually settling for $470 million. In 1991 magistrates in Bhopal charged former Union Carbide chairman and CEO Warren Anderson with manslaughter and declared him a fugitive from justice when he failed to appear in court. The case foundered when the US courts refused an extradition request from India. The board of Union Carbide maintained consistently that it had no liability, and claimed that an employee had sabotaged the plant.[53] While the failure of safety systems at the plant may not have been the fault of the board, they did have a responsibility to take ownership of the disaster and deal with its consequences.

Labour Abuses

Like fiddling the books, squeezing work from underpaid employees is an ancient practice, and one which continues to survive despite a wealth of evidence showing that well-paid, well-treated workers are far more productive than ones who are treated badly. But temptation to sweat the workforce remains.

Sports Direct

In 2016, UK retailer Sports Direct made unwanted headlines when it emerged that workers at the company's warehouses had to endure appalling conditions and were sometimes working for less than the minimum wage. A subsequent parliamentary inquiry commented that Sports Direct's 'size and success is founded on a business model that enables the majority of workers ... to be treated without dignity or respect.'[54]

That was by no means the end of the company's troubles. In 2016 two major investors in Sports Direct, Legal & General Asset Management and Aberdeen Asset Management, openly criticized the board, voted against the reappointment of the chair and all the independent directors, and backed a trades union-sponsored resolution for an independent review of labour practices in the company.[55] In 2017 it was alleged that the company's computer system had been hacked and the personal details of staff taken, but the company had not yet told the staff about the problem. In 2019 it was in trouble again, this time for concealing information from its auditors, Grant Thornton, who threatened to quit.[56] One observer described Sports Direct as 'an embarrassment to UK corporate governance. Years of ineffective chairing seem to have taken their toll, and the company veers from one mistake to the next.'[57]

The CEO, Mike Ashley, founded the company in 1982 and took it public in 2007, and remains the dominant figure on the board. There also seems to be a high turnover at board level. A study of the board in July 2020 shows that no independent director has been with the board for more than four years and many for considerably less. Although they are experienced professionals—and there is now a staff representative on the board—they have not had time to cohere as a group. No director apart from Ashley himself remains from the time of the 2016 scandal.[58]

Nike

Did the over-mighty chair play a role in the sweatshop scandal that engulfed Nike in 1996? Phil Knight, one of the founders of the company in 1964, served as CEO until 2004 and chaired the board until 2015. As is common practice in the USA and some other jurisdictions, he served as both chairman and CEO, and was easily the most powerful person in the company.

In 1996, a photograph of a fourteen-year-old boy in Pakistan sewing pieces of a Nike football together was published and widely distributed around the world. It emerged that the boy was not only underage, but he was also paid roughly $0.60 per day. Nike defended itself, claiming this was an isolated lapse of its labour policies. But rumours of Nike products made by sweatshop labour had already been circulating for several years, and it took two more years—including a leaked report from the company's own auditors showing unethical labour practices in one of its supplier factories in Vietnam—for Knight to finally make an apology and vow to tighten scrutiny of its suppliers.[59]

The company's reversal of tack included a full and frank apology for what had happened—'we blew it,' one Nike public report on the scandal concluded—and by 2010 *Corporate Governance Magazine* hailed Nike as one of the world's most responsible companies[60] (an image that has been called into question by Nike's subsequent links with the athletics coach Alberto Salazar, who has been investigated for possible drug use by the athletes he trains). But it took time to rebuild the company's battered reputation, and even today the hint of scandal lingers; where matters such as child labour is concerned, society has a long memory.

There were plenty of chances to avoid this scandal. From the very beginning, the board should have demanded close audits of Nike's suppliers and insisted on seeing those audits. Once the rumours of sweatshop labour began flying in 1994, they should have demanded more information and remedial action. Did they do so? If so, it is not visible as no action seems to have been taken. There is no evidence that the board put pressure on Knight, the all-powerful CEO and chair, or took independent action in any way to reform the company's labour practices.

Pollution

Economists sometimes refer to externalities, that is the cost of production or consumption of a product that is born by third parties, not the original producer and consumer. A classic example is passive smoking. Cigarette smokers pay the cost of the product, but an additional cost of consumption is born by non-smokers who breathe the same air as smokers, inhaling fumes and suffering consequent health damage.

Air pollution caused by automobiles is another important case of externalities. The driver of the car pays for it and the fuel they put into it, but the exhaust fumes and brake dust the car emits affect the health of all. Air pollution caused by cars has been shown to weaken both the lungs and the immune system, both of which were affected by COVID-19. Studies have shown how higher rates of COVID-19 deaths correlated with areas of high air pollution. Even before the pandemic, the impacts of pollution on public health were well known.[61]

Volkswagen

That did not appear to bother some people at Volkswagen, starting with the former CEO, Martin Winterkorn, who lobbied the European Union 'not to overburden the automotive industry with excessive emissions targets,' despite the fact that air pollution was already becoming a significant public health problem in many parts of Europe.[62] In 2015 reports emerged that Volkswagen engineers had developed a 'defeat device' that gave false readings of emissions from Volkswagen diesel cars, showing that the engines complied with environmental standards whereas in fact the real level of emissions was far higher.

The scandal was a severe blow to Volkswagen, which suffered a significant dip in sales, especially in the USA. By 2019 more than $25 billion in fines had been levied against the company and Winterkorn was facing criminal charges in the USA. And, of course, the share price declined sharply, hitting shareholder wealth. There were no winners in this story; everyone lost, not least people living in built-up areas with high levels of air pollution. We will probably never know how many deaths and significant illnesses occurred as a result of this particular piece of cheating.

The German newspaper *Bild Zeitung* alleged that Winterkorn knew about the defeat device before the scandal broke.[63] Another report suggests that the chair of the VW supervisory board, Ferdinand Piëch, was also aware as early as March 2015 and asked Winterkorn what he planned to do. The report suggested the two men were 'at a distance' on the matter. Piëch was a former automotive engineer and designer with a reputation as an autocratic hard man. He had previously served as head of the management board, where a fellow automotive executive, GM's vice-president Bob Lutz, described his style as 'a reign of terror and a culture where performance was driven by fear and intimidation,' and believes that Piëch was responsible for the culture at Volkswagen that drove engineers to develop the defeat device.

> I imagine that at some point, the VW engineering team said to Piëch, 'We don't know how to pass the emissions test with the hardware we have.' The reply, in that culture, most likely was, 'You will pass! I demand it! Or I'll find someone who can do it!'[64]

In April 2015, Piëch was forced to resign after losing a power struggle with Winterkorn, his presumed successor, but Winterkorn himself was forced out of the business a few months later when news of the scandal broke. And while these two big beasts were locking horns, where was the rest of the board? Presumably they were keeping their heads down and avoiding the developing disaster. Excessive power concentrated in a few hands and lack of independence of the board had once again caused scandal and financial loss, and potential harm to people exposed to diesel fumes.

Glencore

Concern for the environment was also remarkably absent at mining company Glencore which, between 2017 and 2019, funded a campaign of disinformation about green energy in an attempt to protect its coal interests, especially in Australia. The operation, known within the company as Project Caesar, saw up to £7 million a year was paid to a lobby group. Some of the money was spent on 'fake news' projects, websites and social media campaigns designed to denigrate clean energy. Data was also gathered—legally—on environmental organizations such as Greenpeace, and it was further alleged that Glencore spied on its own employees to make sure they were not leaking information through social media.[65] Although Glencore had broken no laws, when the scandal was made public the reputational damage was considerable. Australian Prime Minister Kevin Rudd referred to Glencore's activities as a 'national disgrace.'

This was not the first time Glencore's reputation had been exposed. 'Glencore's history reads like a spy novel,' said financial journalist and former Glencore investor Andreas Weitzer.

> During my years as a commodity trader in Russia I could witness Glencore's operational style at close quarters. It is a company always sailing close to the wind, currying favour with politicians and executives without ever being found guilty of embargo busting or bribery. It was accused of child labour, tax evasion, environmental damage and violence against indigenous peoples by governments and NGOs on many occasions. They always had to back down because of a lack of hard evidence. Fine-line-walking is part of the genetic makeup of the company.[66]

Project Caesar was no isolated case, but a part of Glencore's operating model. Why did the board allow this to happen? Unlike some other boards, at the time of Project Caesar the Glencore board was full of experienced, seasoned non-executive directors, including several former mining executives and a former advisor to the African National Congress. The chair of the board was Tony Hayward, who had been CEO of BP at the time of the Deepwater Horizon crisis and was therefore no stranger to issues around reputational damage.[67]

We may never know what discussions went on at Glencore's boards, but the lack of action to reign in Project Caesar is puzzling, to say the least. Did the board genuinely not know what was going on? But the campaign of disinformation was no secret; it would hardly have been effective if it was. Did no one think to ask whether Glencore, given its history, had clean hands in this matter?

Bankruptcies

Sometimes, even though there is no corruption, malfeasance or deliberately immoral behaviour, executives drive companies over the edge of a cliff. That appears to be pretty much what happened at Lehman Brothers in 2008.

Lehman Brothers

From the late 1960s, when the Lehman family ended their involvement with the bank, the culture of the organization changed from one of service to the community to one of growth and competition. The competition was not just with other banks; executives and traders competed with each other for bonuses and power. In the 1980s the company became involved in several notorious scandals including insider trading at the investment bank Drexel Burnham Lambert and the corrupt British financier Robert Maxwell; one of its vice-presidents was convicted and imprisoned for his part in the Drexel affair.

But the culture did not change. The man who perhaps epitomized that culture more than any other, Richard Fuld, became executive chairman and CEO in 1994. Fuld centralized power in his own hands, demoting or firing rivals for power. His policy of aggressive expansion through the boom years of the mid-2000s won him many plaudits, and in March 2008 *Barron's Magazine* named him one of the thirty best CEOs in America. Six months later his bank collapsed, and *Time* magazine named him one of the twenty-five people to blame for the financial crisis.[68]

The story is a familiar one. Fuld's centralization of power in himself led to the board becoming weak and unable to exercise scrutiny or oversight. Few of the independent directors had any banking experience, and several were long retired with little recent business experience of any kind. They lacked the knowledge, experience and confidence to argue against the dominant figure of Fuld. Many of the cultural dysfunctions we identified earlier—lack of independence from the executive, missing voices, lack of taking responsibility, groupthink—can be identified here. Fuld led Lehman Brothers into destruction and, by and large, the board sat and watched him do so. One of the most powerful American banks collapsed, taking many other institutions and large parts of the global economy with it.

Executive Pay Abuses

Complaints about excessive levels of executive pay and pension contributions have been building for decades. In 1965, the average American CEO-to-worker compensation ratio was 20–1, that is CEOs earned on average twenty times the average wage of their workers. Since then, CEO compensation has risen by nearly 1000 per cent, and the average compensation ratio is 70–1. Some CEOs are earning more than 400 times as much money as their employees.[69]

Elsewhere the average is even higher; according to one study, Canadian CEOs made 227 times more than the average worker, while in Australia the figure is 221–1.[70] In the UK, the Equalities Trust has calculated that more than two-thirds of FT-100 CEO are earning more than 100 times the average UK salary.[71] Other international comparisons are hard to make as relatively few companies publish comparative data, but it is worth noting that Japanese

CEOs earn about one-tenth the money of their US counterparts, meaning the ratio is likely to be much lower.[72]

Executive pay is one of the issues that has aroused public indignation and criticism. More importantly, it is also a matter of increasing concern to shareholders, who are questioning why money is being diverted into executive pockets especially when the company is losing money. There was a series of shareholder revolts over executive compensation in 2012, and the issue emerged again in 2016 when BP announced a £14 million salary award to CEO Bob Dudley in 2016, despite the firm making record losses and cutting a number of jobs, triggering another revolt. Stefan Stern, director of the UK's High Pay Centre, forecast that the trend would continue. 'We are reaching a point where the largest CEO packages represent a material issue for shareholders that is big enough to require serious consideration,' he said. 'We could be reaching a point where more shareholders will argue that it is too damaging to businesses' own interests to allow top pay to rise this high.'[73]

Stern was right that shareholders would continue to express concern, but this does not seem to have curbed executive demands for higher and higher pay. To take just a few examples, in 2018 there was another revolt when AstraZeneca failed to cut its CEO's pension contribution from 30 per cent to 10 per cent, while in 2019 the 33 per cent contribution to the pension fund of Lloyds Banking Group's CEO—at a time when the company was still paying record compensation over the PPI scandal—was described as 'boundless greed.'[74] Shareholders and the public alike have been incensed by the failure of nearly two-thirds of FT-100 companies to cut executive pay during the pandemic, despite many of them receiving government assistance through the jobs furlough scheme.

Notes

1. https://hbr.org/2003/12/how-were-fixing-up-tyco; https://www.sfgate.com/business/article/Former-director-of-Tyco-fined-Board-member-2745039.php.
2. Ibid.
3. Takata Corporation Pleads Guilty, Sentenced to Pay $1 Billion in Criminal Penalties for Airbag Scheme. *U.S. Department of Justice* (27 February 2017).
4. Airbag manufacturer Takata Corp. Pleads Guilty to Fraud, to Pay $1 Billion Penalty. *The Star* (27 February 2017).
5. Who Are the Victims of Takata's Fraud? *Safety Research & Strategies, Inc.* (18 January 2017).

6. Takata Corporation Pleads Guilty, Sentenced to Pay $1 Billion in Criminal Penalties for Airbag Scheme. *U.S. Department of Justice* (27 February 2017).
7. 3 Takata Executives Face Criminal Charges Over Exploding Airbags. *The New York Times* (13 January 2017).
8. Could Board Diversity Have Prevented the Takata Scandal? *AutoNews* (4 February 2017).
9. Kobe Steel Admits Data Fraud Went on Nearly Five Decades, CEO to Quit, *Reuters* (5 March 2018).
10. Japan's Kobe Steel Indicted over Quality Scandal, *BBC* (20 July 2018).
11. Japan's Kobe Steel Indicted over Quality Scandal, *BBC* (20 July 2018).
12. Scandal-hit Kobe Steel has a 'Look the Other Way' Culture, They Say in Hometown, *Reuters* (5 November 2017).
13. Ibid.
14. https://www.dailytelegraph.com.au/business/rio-tinto-bribery-scandal-two-former-chief-executives-embroiled-in-email-trail/news-story/fe4216a2852d6a25fa150e6acbd257f4.
15. https://www.smh.com.au/business/companies/rio-tintos-governance-a-fiasco-as-director-charged-with-fraud-20170621-gwvk04.html.
16. https://www.mining-technology.com/features/mining-scandals-four-incidents-that-shook-the-industry/.
17. UN Oil for Food Scandal Spreads to Compass Arm. *The Telegraph* (19 October 2005).
18. Ten Questions and Answers: Compass.' *The Telegraph* (28 October 2005).
19. Compass Settles Claims of Bribery in UN Contracts. *The Guardian* (17 October 2006).
20. Ten Questions and Answers: Compass.. *The Telegraph* (28 October 2005).
21. Equifax Data Breach FAQ: What Happened, Who Was Affected, What Was the Impact?, *CSO Online* (12 February 2020).
22. How the Equifax Hack Happened, and What Still Needs to be Done, *CNET* (7 September 2018).
23. Equifax Breach Affected 147 Million, but Most Sit Out Settlement. *The New York Times* (22 January 2020).
24. The Governance Implications of the Equifax and Facebook Settlements. *Harvard Law School Forum on Corporate Governance* (14 August 2019).
25. https://money.cnn.com/2005/02/09/technology/hp_fiorina/index.htm; Carly Fiorina, *Tough Choices: A Memoir*, New York: Portfolio, 2006.
26. https://www.reuters.com/article/us-fox-settlement-idUSKBN1DK2NI; https://corpgov.law.harvard.edu/2017/12/19/settlement-of-workplace-harassment-suit-at-21st-century-fox/.
27. https://www.foxnews.com/media/fox-news-terminates-ed-henry-after-outside-probe-into-sexual-misconduct-claim.

28. https://www.bloomberg.com/news/articles/2018-03-20/weinstein-co-files-for-chapter-11-bankruptcy-in-delaware-court; https://money.cnn.com/2017/10/17/media/harvey-weinstein-weinstein-co-board/index.html.

29. Milton Friedman, *Capitalism and Freedom*, Chicago: University of Chicago Press, 1962.

30. https://www.bbc.co.uk/news/magazine-20560359.

31. HSBC Bank 'Helped Clients Dodge Millions in Tax.' *BBC* (10 February 2015).

32. HSBC Aided Tax Avoidance. MoneyExpert (10 Feb 2015).

33. HSBC Swiss Unit to Pay $192 Million in Latest U.S. Tax Evasion Deal. *Reuters* (7 August 2019).

34. Taxing Times at HSBC. *RiskScreen* (8 January 2020).

35. HSBC to Pay €300 million to Settle Tax Investigation. *BBC* (15 November 2017).

36. HSBC Pays Out £28m over Money-Laundering Claims. *The Guardian* (4 June 2015).

37. HSBC Agrees to 300mln Euro Settlement of Belgian Tax Fraud Case. *Reuters* (6 August 2019).

38. https://www.telegraph.co.uk/business/2019/01/23/former-tesco-executive-carl-rogberg-cleared-fraud-charges/; https://www.bmmagazine.co.uk/in-business/how-did-the-tesco-accounting-scandal-unfold/.

39. https://www.ft.com/content/71118e80-4a20-11e4-bc07-00144feab7de; https://www.marketscreener.com/TESCO-PLC-4000540/news/Tesco-Strengthens-Board-After-Accounting-Error-19145515/.

40. https://timesofindia.indiatimes.com/business/india-business/Satyams-chairman-Ramalinga-Raju-resigns-admits-fraud/articleshow/3946088.cms; https://economictimes.indiatimes.com/articleshow/62452514.cms.

41. https://www.fraud-magazine.com/article.aspx?id=4294990480.

42. https://www.japantimes.co.jp/news/2020/02/15/business/corporate-business/toshibas-latest-scandal-subsidiary-found-booked-%C2%A543-5-billion-fictitious-sales/.

43. https://www.fca.org.uk/data/monthly-ppi-refunds-and-compensation#header.

44. https://www.which.co.uk/news/2019/07/ppi-mis-selling-scandal-an-insider-view/.

45. The Wells Fargo Cross-Selling Scandal. *Harvard Law School Forum on Corporate Governance* (6 February 2019).

46. The Price of Wells Fargo's Fake Account Scandal Grows by $3 Billion. *The New York Times* (21 February 2020).

47. The Wells Fargo Cross-Selling Scandal. *Harvard Law School Forum on Corporate Governance* (6 February 2019).

48. The Wells Fargo Cross-Selling Scandal. *Harvard Law School Forum on Corporate Governance* (6 February 2019).

49. https://europeanbusinessmagazine.com/business/google-hit-with-record-fine-for-abusing-market-power/.

50. https://www.afr.com/technology/googles-abuse-of-power-reveals-the-modern-disease-of-oligopolies-20180723-h130d8.

51. https://www.bloomberg.com/news/articles/2015-11-05/samarco-says-dam-in-brazil-burst-teams-are-working-on-site.

52. https://www.forbes.com/sites/kenrapoza/2012/01/30/worst-company-in-the-world-award-goes-to/#1d2512ed6a0a.

53. Dan Kurzman, *A Killing Wind: Inside Union Carbide and the Bhopal Catastrophe*, New York: McGraw-Hill, 1988; Ingrid Eckerman, *The Bhopal Saga: Causes and Consequences of the World's Largest Industrial Disaster*, New Delhi: Universities Press, 2005.

54. https://www.theregister.com/2017/02/08/sports_direct_fails_to_inform_staff_over_hack_and_data_breach/.

55. https://www.theguardian.com/business/2016/aug/25/sports-direct-corporate-governance-criticised-investor-forum.

56. https://www.ft.com/content/74d96c4c-bdeb-11e9-b350-db00d509634e.

57. https://www.theguardian.com/business/2019/jul/29/sports-direct-shares-results-mike-ashley-house-of-fraser.

58. https://www.sportsdirectplc.com/about-us/leadership.aspx.

59. https://www.commondreams.org/headlines01/1020-01.htm; https://www.forbes.com/sites/csr/2010/06/08/the-parents-of-csr-nike-and-kathie-lee-gifford/#5baf44a1f416.

60. https://www.forbes.com/sites/csr/2010/06/08/the-parents-of-csr-nike-and-kathie-lee-gifford/#5baf44a1f416.

61. For example, https://www.hsph.harvard.edu/news/hsph-in-the-news/air-pollution-linked-with-higher-covid-19-death-rates/; https://www.cdc.gov/air/air_health.htm.

62. https://www.forbes.com/profile/martin-winterkorn/#4231ee6a432a.

63. https://www.forbes.com/sites/bertelschmitt/2016/09/25/winterkorn-behind-dieselgate-coverup-new-docs-suggest/#7cf6b1d1477d.

64. https://www.roadandtrack.com/car-culture/a27197/bob-lutz-vw-diesel-fiasco/.

65. https://www.mining-technology.com/features/mining-scandals-four-incidents-that-shook-the-industry/; https://www.cmcmarkets.com/en-gb/opto/can-glencores-glen-share-price-withstand-project-caesar-scandal; https://www.theguardian.com/business/2019/mar/07/revealed-glencore-bankrolled-covert-campaign-to-prop-up-coal.

66. https://timesofmalta.com/articles/view/My-rollercoaster-ride-with-Glencore.679510; see also https://www.swissinfo.ch/eng/politics/paradise-papers-fallout_swiss-justice-minister-calls-for-commodities-crack-down/43669572.

67. https://www.glencore.com/who-we-are/our-leadership/.

68. https://abcnews.go.com/Business/Economy/story?id=5951669&page=1.
69. https://www.payscale.com/data-packages/ceo-pay.
70. https://phys.org/news/2020-01-canadian-ceos-average-worker.html; https://www.epi.org/publication/ceo-compensation-2018/.
71. https://www.equalitytrust.org.uk/taxonomy/term/136.
72. https://www.japantimes.co.jp/news/2016/01/06/business/japans-ceos-underpaid-underwhelming/.
73. https://www.theguardian.com/business/2016/apr/14/bp-pledge-shareholder-anger-ceo-bob-dudleypay-deal.
74. https://uk.finance.yahoo.com/news/shareholder-rebellions-over-executive-pay-surged-at-uk-companies-in-2019-000118682.html.

Appendix B: Directors' Checklist

The following questions are ones that directors need to ask themselves, not just once in their careers but repeatedly as they go forward. For would-be directors, this checklist offers insight into the responsibilities of board members. The first six sections relate to our six cultural dysfunctions and the 'red flags' that might signal their appearance, as discussed in Chap. 4. The remaining sections deal with general board, chair and director responsibilities.

Lack of Independence

1. Do you ever seek advice from outside of the executive team, either within the organization or externally?
2. When facing crises or major problems, do you distinguish between the executive and the independent directors?
3. Are the latter seen as an important resource in helping to make difficult decisions, or are they expected to rubber stamp whatever the executive puts before them?

© The Author(s), under exclusive license to Springer Nature Switzerland AG 2022
G. Brown, R. S. Peterson, *Disaster in the Boardroom*,
https://doi.org/10.1007/978-3-030-91658-9

Missing Key Voices

4. Is your organization the subject of a social media campaign or protests?
5. If so, are these protests being discussed in the boardroom, or are they being pushed aside?
6. If the latter, it may be that there is no one to represent the dissenters on the board. Or, have you looked at turnover of employees by diversity categories?
7. When it is uneven, that is a strong signal that your workplace, and likely your board, is missing key voices?

Cultural Amplification

8. Would you tell your 'war stories' about what goes on in your organization to your friends and family? Or would you keep silent because they 'would not understand'?
9. Do you have to explain your organization's culture to other people, in order for them to understand what is happening to you?

Rules-Bound Culture

10. When a crisis hits, do you focus first on process or on content?
11. How difficult is it to challenge or change the process? Are there generalized customs concerning who needs to sign onto what, or are there specified processes/formulas?

Groupthink

12. Do you feel under pressure to agree constantly with the rest of the board? Do you hold back from speaking your mind?

13. Do you go along with the majority in public, while secretly wishing you were able to visibly disagree? Or do you feel that if everyone else has taken a position, it is your duty to go along with them and not make waves?
14. Are you challenging people at the right time?

Diffusion of Responsibility

15. Is the board monitoring how things happen in addition to what happens? How is at least as important as what.
16. Do you feel uncomfortable when someone else on the board says or does something embarrassing?
17. If not, are you taking enough responsibility? Remember, boards need to speak to the world with a unified voice, so if someone says something that turns out to be incorrect, it reflects poorly on you.
18. Do you pretty much always require a formal vote on key issues?

Board Culture

19. How are we demonstrating behaviour that reflects the behaviour we expect throughout the company? Are we leading by example?
20. Have we measured culture and are we discussing culture in sufficient depth at board meetings?
21. How are we taking account of culture in our board effectiveness reviews?
22. How can we ensure we consider the impact on culture in all the decisions we take?
23. Do the committees support the board on culture? For example if our people are our main asset, do we have a people committee on our board?
24. Is there a need for a specific conduct, ethics or culture committee?
25. What behaviours are being driven when setting strategy and financial targets?
26. What percentage of board time is spent on financial performance management against targets? And on behavioural performance management? Is the balance right?

27. Is company tax policy consistent with stated values?
28. How are we challenging groupthink and testing key decisions for cultural alignment?

Board Effectiveness

29. How much power is concentrated in the hands of the chair?
30. How flexible is the board around norms of practice and performance?
31. How cohesive is the board?
32. How much power is concentrated in the hands of corporate leadership?
33. Is the board intellectually adaptive?
34. Does the board share a strong sense of collective efficacy (belief in its ability to meet current challenges)?
35. What is the board's risk appetite?

Independent Directors

36. Do the independent directors demonstrate that they are the long-term custodians of the business?
37. Are the independent directors concerned as much about value creation as about governance?
38. Are the directors focused on growing the company and creating value for stakeholders in the form of quality products and services, meaningful employment, a return on capital to shareholders and general benefit to society?
39. Do the independent directors demonstrate courage and curiosity?

Stakeholder Engagement

40. Is it clear who the main stakeholders are?
41. Does the board understand what stakeholder engagement means? What level of stakeholder involvement would best suit the board in terms of making the board more effective?

42. Does the board listen to stakeholder voices?
43. Is action based on stakeholder views part of board assessment and evaluation?
44. Are investors fully and consciously aware of how stakeholder engagement can improve governance?

Board Evaluation

45. The effectiveness of the chair: does the chair support the other directors?
46. Is the chair contributing to a strong and independent board culture?
47. Does the chair have a good relationship with the CEO?
48. The performance of individual directors: does each director contribute fully at board meetings?
49. Do they engage in debates and offer their own points of view? Are they prepared for meetings and on top of the issues the company faces?
50. Are they behaving and acting in a truly independent manner?
51. The performance of committees: do the committees complete their duties?
52. Are they masters of their briefs?
53. Do they conduct the necessary scrutiny of key issues?
54. Are their reports to the board timely and detailed?
55. The administration of meetings: do meeting run smoothly and to time?
56. Are the agenda and board papers well prepared?
57. Do directors get all the information they need?
58. Does the meeting allow for full discussion of issues, or are there any constraints?
59. Board development: do individual directors undertake continuing professional development?
60. Does the board as a whole undertake development exercises at away-days and so on?
61. Communications with other stakeholders: does the board have open lines of communication with investors, employees, customers and the wider community?
62. Are there any missing voices?

Select Bibliography

Ancona, D.G., and D.F. Caldwell. 1992. Bridging the Boundary: External Activity and Performance in Organizational Teams. *Administrative Science Quarterly* 37, 634–665.

Anderson, C., and J.L. Berdahl. 2002. The Experience of Power: Examining the Effects of Power on Approach and Inhibition Tendencies. *Journal of Personality and Social Psychology* 83 (6), 1362–1377.

Appelbaum, E., T. Bailey, P. Berg, and A.L. Kalleberg. 2000. *Manufacturing Advantage: Why High-Performance Work Systems Pay Off*. New York: ILR Press.

Axelrod, N.R. 2007. *Culture of Inquiry: Healthy Debate in the Boardroom*. Washington, DC: BoardSource.

Barton, D. 2011. Capitalism for the Long Term. *Harvard Business Review*, March.

Bates, J.L. 1963. *The Origins of Teapot Dome: Progressives, Parties and Petroleum, 1909–1921*. Urbana: University of Illinois Press.

Behfar, K.J., R.S. Peterson, E.A. Mannix, and W.M.K. Trochim. 2008. The Critical Role of Conflict Resolution in Teams: A Close Look at the Links Between Conflict Types, Conflict Management Strategies, and Team Outcomes. *Journal of Applied Psychology* 93, 170–188.

Bennis, W.G. 1997. *Managing People Is Like Herding Cats*. London: Atlantic Books.

Boivie, S., M.K. Bednar, R.V. Aguilera, and J.L. Andrus. 2016. Are Boards Designed to Fail? The Implausibility of Effective Board Monitoring. *Academy of Management Annals* 10 (1), 319–407.

Bottenberg, K., A. Tuschke, and M. Flickinger. 2017. Corporate Governance Between Shareholder and Stakeholder Orientation: Lessons From Germany. *Journal of Management Inquiry* 26 (2), 165–180.

Brand, J.E. 2015. The Far-Reaching Impact of Job Loss and Unemployment. *Annual Review of Sociology* 41, 359–375.

© The Author(s), under exclusive license to Springer Nature Switzerland AG 2022
G. Brown, R. S. Peterson, *Disaster in the Boardroom*,
https://doi.org/10.1007/978-3-030-91658-9

Brown, G. 2015. *The Independent Director: The Non-Executive Director's Guide to Effective Board Presence*. Basingstoke: Palgrave Macmillan.

Brown, G., A. Kakabadse, and F. Morais. 2020. *The Independent Director in Society*. Basingstoke: Palgrave Macmillan.

Burnham, J. 1941. *The Managerial Revolution*. London: Putnam.

Casson, M. 2009. *The World's First Railway System: Enterprise, Competition and Regulation on the Railway Network in Victorian Britain*. Oxford: Oxford University Press.

Chang, E. 2018. *Brotopia: Breaking Up the Boys' Club of Silicon Valley*. New York: Portfolio.

Chapman, P. 2008. *The Last of the Imperious Rich: Lehman Brothers, 1844–2008*. New York: Portfolio.

Chatman, J., and F. Gino. 2020. Don't Let the Pandemic Sink Your Culture. *Harvard Business Review*, 17 August.

Chatman, J.A., D.F. Caldwell, C.A. O'Reilly, and B. Doerr. 2014. Parsing Organizational Culture. *Journal of Organizational Behavior* 35 (6), 785–808.

Cheffins, B.R., ed. 2011. *The History of Modern US Corporate Governance*. Cheltenham: Edward Elgar.

Daily, C.M., R. Dalton, and A.A. Cannella Jr. 2003. Corporate Governance: Decades of Dialogue and Data. Introduction to Special Topic Forum. *Academy of Management Review* 28, 371–382.

Dennehy, E. 2012. Corporate Governance: A Stakeholder Model. *International Journal of Business, Governance and Ethics* 7 (2), 83–95.

Dixon, N. 1976. *On the Psychology of Military Incompetence*. London: Cape.

Eccles, R.G., I. Ioannou, and G. Serafeim. 2014. The Impact of Corporate Sustainability on Organizational Processes and Performance. *Management Science* 60 (11), 2835–2857.

Eckerman, I. 2005. *The Bhopal Saga: Causes and Consequences of the World's Largest Industrial Disaster*. New Delhi: Universities Press.

Edmans, A. 2020. *Grow the Pie: How Great Companies Deliver Both Purpose and Profit*. Cambridge: Cambridge University Press.

Elliott, G. 2007. *The Mystery of Overend & Gurney: A Financial Scandal in Victorian London*. London: Methuen.

Eskerod, P. 2020. A Stakeholder Perspective: Origins and Core Concepts. *Oxford Research Encyclopedia of Business and Management*. https://doi.org/10.1093/acrefore/9780190224851.013.3.

Farris, P.W., N.T. Bendle, P.E. Pfeifer, and D.J. Reibstein. 2010. *Marketing Metrics*. Upper Saddle River: Pearson.

Financial Reporting Council. 2016. Corporate Culture and the Role of Boards: Report of Observations, July.

———. 2019. Future of Corporate Reporting: Conclusions from an Online Survey of FRC Stakeholders.

Fiorina, C. 2006. *Tough Choices: A Memoir*. New York: Portfolio.

Forsyth, D.R. 2009. *Group Dynamics*. New York: Wadsworth.

Freeman, R.E. 2010. *Strategic Management: A Stakeholder Approach*. Cambridge: Cambridge University Press.

Freeman, R.E., R. Phillips, and R. Sisodia. 2020. Tensions in Stakeholder Theory. *Business and Society* 59 (2), 213–231.

Friede, G., T. Busch, and A. Bassen. 2015. ESG and Financial Performance: Aggregated Evidence from More Than 2000 Empirical Studies. *Journal of Sustainable Finance and Investment* 4 (4), 210–233.

Friedman, M. 1962. *Capitalism and Freedom*. Chicago: University of Chicago Press.

———. 1970. The Social Responsibility of a Business Is to Increase Its Profits. *New York Times Magazine*, 13 September.

Gardner, H.K., and R.S. Peterson. 2019. Back Channels in the Boardroom: How to Prevent Side Conversations Between Directors From Blocking Progress. *Harvard Business Review*, September–October.

———. 2020. Executives and Boards, Avoid These Missteps in a Crisis. *Harvard Business Review*, 24 April.

Govindarajan, V., and A. Srivastava. 2020. We Are Nowhere Near Stakeholder Capitalism. *Harvard Business Review*, 30 January.

Hambrick, D.C., and P.A. Mason. 1984. Upper Echelons: The Organization as a Reflection of Its Top Managers. *Academy of Management Review* 9, 193–206.

Hawn, O., and I. Ioannou. 2013. Do Actions Speak Louder Than Words? The Case of Corporate Social Responsibility (CSR). *SSRN Electronic Journal*.

Hofstede, G. 2003. *Culture's Consequences: Comparing Values, Behaviors, Institutions and Organizations Across Nations*. London: Sage.

Hogan, R., and R.B. Kaiser. 2005. What We Know About Leadership. *Review of General Psychology* 9 (2), 169–180.

Hunt, V., B. Simpson, and Y. Yamada. 12 November 2020. *The Case for Stakeholder Capitalism*. McKinsey & Company.

Huse, M. 2007. *Boards, Governance and Value Creation: The Human Side of Corporate Governance*. Cambridge: Cambridge University Press.

ICSA. 2021. *Review of the Effectiveness of Independent Board Evaluation in the UK Listed Sector: Summary of Responses to the Public Consultation*. London: The Chartered Governance Institute.

Ioannou, I., and G. Serafeim. 2014. The Impact of Corporate Social Responsibility on Investment Recommendations: Analysts' Perceptions and Shifting Institutional Logics. *Strategic Management Journal* 36 (7), 1053–1081.

Janis, I.L. 1982. *Victims of Groupthink*. Boston: Houghton Mifflin.

Jennings, M. 2006. *The Seven Signs of Ethical Collapse*. New York: St Martin's.

Johnson, M.K., and C.R. Raye. 1981. Reality Monitoring. *Psychological Review* 88 (1), 67–85.

Jung, C.G. 2006. *The Undiscovered Self: The Dilemma of the Individual in Modern Society*. New York: Berkley.

Keltner, D., D.H. Gruenfeld, and C. Anderson. 2003. Power, Approach and Inhibition. *Psychological Review* 110 (2), 265–284.

Kurzman, D. 1988. *A Killing Wind: Inside Union Carbide and the Bhopal Catastrophe.* New York: McGraw-Hill.

Latané, B. 1981. The Psychology of Social Impact. *American Psychologist* 36 (4), 343–356.

Latané, B., and J.M. Darley. 1970. *The Unresponsive Bystander: Why Doesn't He Help?* New York: Appleton-Century-Croft.

Laudicina, P.A. 2004. *World Out of Balance: Navigating Global Risks to Seize Competitive Advantage.* New York: McGraw-Hill.

LeShan, L., and H. Margenau. 1982. *Einstein's Space and Van Gogh's Sky.* New York: Macmillan.

Lewis, M. 1989. *Liar's Poker.* New York: W.W. Norton.

Lipton, M., and J.W. Lorsch. 1992. A Modest Proposal for Improved Corporate Governance. *The Business Lawyer* 48, 59–77.

Mackay, C. 1852. *Extraordinary Popular Delusions and the Madness of Crowds.* London: Bentley.

Magrath, C.P. 1967. *Yazoo: Law and Politics in the New Republic.* New York: W.W. Norton.

Mandis, S.G. 2013. *What Happened to Goldman Sachs: An Insider's Story of Organizational Drift and Its Unintended Consequences.* Boston: Harvard Business Review Press.

Mannix, E., and M.A. Neale. 2006. Diversity at Work. *Scientific American,* August–September.

McLean, B., and P. Elkind. 2003. *The Smartest Guys in the Room: The Amazing Rise and Scandalous Fall of Enron.* New York: Portfolio.

Merton, R.K. 1996. *On Social Structure and Science.* Chicago: University of Chicago Press.

Milgram, S. 2009. *Obedience to Authority: An Experimental View.* New York: HarperCollins.

OECD. 2011. *The Role of Institutional Investors in Promoting Good Corporate Governance.* OECD Publishing.

Paine, L.S. 2020. Covid Is Rewriting the Rules of Corporate Governance. *Harvard Business Review,* 6 October.

Paul, H. 2013. *The South Sea Bubble: An Economic History of Its Origins and Consequences.* London: Routledge.

Peterson, R.S. 1999. The Role of Values in Predicting Fairness Judgments and Support of Affirmative Action. *Journal of Social Issues* 50 (4), 95–115.

Peterson, R.S., P.D. Owens, and P.V. Martorana. 1999. The Group Dynamics Q-Sort in Organizational Research: A New Method for Studying Familiar Problems. *Organizational Research Methods* 2 (2), 107–139.

Peterson, R.S., D.B. Smith, P.V. Martorana, and P.D. Owens. 2003. The Impact of Chief Executive Officer Personality on Top Management Team Dynamics: One Mechanism by Which Leadership Affects Organizational Performance. *Journal of Applied Psychology* 88 (3), 795–808.

Post, C., and K. Byron. 2015. Women on Boards and Firm Financial Performance: A Meta-Analysis. *Academy of Management Journal* 58 (5), 1546–1571.

Salancik, G.R., and J. Pfeffer. 1978. *The External Control of Organizations: A Resource Dependence Perspective*. New York: Harper and Row.

Shekshnia, S. 2018. How to Be a Good Board Chair. *Harvard Business Review*, March–April.

Sims, R.R. 1992. Linking Groupthink to Unethical Behavior in Organizations. *Journal of Business Ethics* 11, 651–662.

Smith, G. 2014. *Why I Left Goldman Sachs*. New York: Hachette.

Spitzeck, H., and E.G. Hansen. 2010. Stakeholder Governance: How Stakeholders Influence Corporate Decision Making. *Corporate Governance* 10 (4), 378–391.

Staw, B.M., L.E. Sandelands, and J.E. Dutton. 1981. Threat Rigidity Effects in Organizational Behavior: A Multilevel Analysis. *Administrative Science Quarterly* 26 (4), 501–524.

Sternberg, E. 2004. *Corporate Governance: Accountability in the Marketplace*. London: Institute of Economic Affairs.

Stigter, M., and C. Cooper. 2018. *Boards That Dare: How to Future-Proof Today's Corporate Boards*. London: Bloomsbury.

Swinson, C. 2019. *Share Trading, Fraud and the Crash of 1929: A Biography of Clarence Hatry*. London: Routledge.

Teger, A.I., and D.G. Pruitt. 1967. Components of Group Risk-Taking. *Journal of Experimental Social Psychology* 3 (2), 189–205.

Thiam, M.E.B., J. Liu, and J. Aston. 2018. Ignoring Personal Moral Compass: Factors Shaping Bankers' Decisions. *Journal of Financial Regulation and Compliance* 27 (3), 357–379.

Tyler, T.R. 1990. *Why People Obey the Law*. New Haven: Yale University Press.

Tyson, L. 2003. *The Tyson Report on the Recruitment and Development of Non-Executive Directors*. London Business School/Department of Trade and Industry.

U-Din, S., and D. Tripe. 2018. The Impact of Global Financial Crisis on Shareholder Value and Operational Efficiency of Banks. *SSRN Electronic Journal*, January.

van Staveren, I. 2020. The Misdirection of Bankers' Moral Compass in the Organizational Field of Banking. *Cambridge Journal of Economics* 44 (3), 507–526.

Weick, K.E. 1995. *Sensemaking in Organizations*. Thousand Oaks: Sage Publications.

Westphal, J.D. 1999. Collaboration in the Boardroom: The Consequences of Social Ties in the CEO/Board Relationship. *Academy of Management Journal* 42, 7–24.

White, R. 2012. *Railroaded: The Transcontinentals and the Making of Modern America*. New York: W.W. Norton.

Wilkinson, A., J. Donaghey, T. Dundon, and R.B. Freeman, eds. 2020. *Handbook of Research on Employee Voice*. Cheltenham: Edward Elgar.

Zander, A. 1993. *Making Boards Effective*. San Francisco: Jossey Bass.

Index[1]

---

[1] Note: Page numbers followed by 'n' refer to notes.

www.ingramcontent.com/pod-product-compliance
Ingram Content Group UK Ltd.
Pitfield, Milton Keynes, MK11 3LW, UK
UKHW021827240725

461171UK00004B/46